ENGLAND

A PORTRAIT

By the same Author

WESTERN POLITICAL THOUGHT
HOBBES AND HIS CRITICS
POLITICS AND OPINION IN THE NINETEENTH CENTURY
VISCOUNT SAMUEL, A BIOGRAPHY
A NEW OUTLINE OF WORLD HISTORY
HENRY VIII, A BIOGRAPHY

ENGLAND
A PORTRAIT

By

JOHN BOWLE

READERS UNION · ERNEST BENN
LONDON 1968

This RU edition was produced in 1968 for sale to its members only by Readers Union Ltd at Aldine House, 10–13 Bedford Street, London and at Letchworth Garden City, Herts. Full details of membership may be obtained from our London address. The book is set in 11 point Baskerville type and was printed by Western Printing Services Ltd, Avonmouth, Bristol. It was first published by Ernest Benn Ltd.

To
E. B. B.

Preface

WHEN I was asked to write this book, there seemed two ways to set about it; either it would be a panorama of modern Britain with a commentary on current affairs, or an historical portrait. As an historian, I have chosen the second course; to trace the characteristics that have come through and observe how they are re-interpreted, creating the portrait by cumulative examples, so that the reader can see it emerge and reflect upon it.

A book of medium size on so vast and well documented a theme is bound to be subjective and selective; writers, like artists, if they are to create anything, must have their own vision. My own range, I know, is limited; I am not an economist, a statistician, or an expert in sociology. But I do have one qualification: I am English. All my forebears on both sides have come from Wessex since the mid-seventeenth century; we may not have been very enterprising, but we have been autochthonous. This background, I realise, may give a certain bias of mind: I have travelled a good deal on both sides of the Atlantic, but my roots are in England, and in Southern England. The reader has been warned.

I would like to thank the Trustees of the Rockefeller Foundation at whose Villa Serbelloni at Bellagio part of this book was written; Mr. John Quentin Davies for his help in planning and revising the book; my publishers for their singular helpfulness over the production, and Mrs. Barbara Phillips for typing the script.

JOHN BOWLE

Oxford
November, 1965

Acknowledgments

ACKNOWLEDGMENTS are gratefully made to the following publishers and owners of copyright material for permitting quotations from the works named in brackets: Mrs. George Bambridge, Methuen and Co., Ltd., Macmillan and Co., Ltd., and Doubleday and Company, Inc. (*L'Envoi, The 'Eathen*, etc., by Rudyard Kipling); B. T. Batsford Ltd. (*The English Reformation*, by A. G. Dickens); Jonathan Cape Ltd. (*The Men Who Ruled India*, by Philip Woodruff); Cassell and Co., Ltd. and Houghton Mifflin Company (*The Second World War*, by Sir Winston Churchill); The Clarendon Press, Oxford (*The Crisis of the Aristocracy*, by Lawrence Stone; *From Domesday Book to Magna Carta*, by A. Lane Poole; *The Fourteenth Century*, by May McKisack; *The Ocean in English History*, by J. A. Williamson; *The Age of Reform*, by E. L. Woodward; *The War of the Second Coalition*, by A. B. Rodger); William Collins Sons and Co., Ltd. (*The Struggle for Europe*, by Chester Wilmot); Faber and Faber Ltd. (*Collected Shorter Poems*, by W. H. Auden); The Trustees of the Hardy Estate, Macmillan and Co., Ltd. and Macmillan Company, New York (*Far From the Madding Crowd, Collected Poems*, by Thomas Hardy); Macmillan and Co. and the Macmillan Company of New York (*The England of Elizabeth*, by A. L. Rowse); John Murray Ltd. (*Collected Poems*, by John Betjeman); Captain Siegfried Sassoon, C.B.E. (*The Heart's Journey*); Martin Secker and Warburg Ltd. and Harcourt, Brace and World Inc. (*Collected Essays*, by George Orwell; published in the U.S.A. under the title *Such, Such Were the Joys*).

Contents

BOOK ONE

BOOK TWO

BOOK ONE

Chapter 1

Origins

THIS book, like Dean Inge's before it, is about England; not about Britain, even mainly about Great Britain. It evokes the spirit of a civilisation which belongs both to Europe and to the English-speaking world and which grew up, like that of Hellas and Renaissance Italy, on a very small scale. Important Welsh and Scottish contributions have blended into this culture; but it derives mainly from Southern England, and Welsh and Scots society have been described in separate volumes.

Having lost, or handed over, the greatest empire in world history – for in sheer size the empire at its climax surpassed those of Iran, China, Rome or even of the Mongols – England remains the origin and springboard of the English-speaking culture, and still a creative influence. Today the English interest the world mainly for the quality of their achievement. Political and social tensions loom large in modern Britain, but they no more fascinate most outsiders than the internal controversies of other nations; it is the original creative impulse, rooted in a long past, which has made this civilisation so important, and which, in spite of current distractions and changes, is still there, emerging in new forms. That is what now particularly concerns the rest of mankind.

The development of England falls naturally into two phases. It was first a rural and mercantile country; self-sufficient, though already maritime: then, after the Industrial and Technical revolutions, it became a massive megalopolitan power with oceanic and global interests; top-heavy with a vast population exporting to live, the weight of wealth and settlement concentrated around London and the midland and northern industrial towns.

The first England was made by the Anglo-Saxons and Anglo-Danes, superimposed on Romano-Celtic and prehistoric peoples; and it was later ruled by a Norman-French speaking aristocracy,

3

culminating in the society described by Chaucer. Out of a century of plague and war and bastard feudalism, this Catholic, medieval, country developed into the compact go-getting Tudor realm, when a relatively parvenu monarchy and a more insular establishment nationalised the Church, adapted an improved administration to new purposes, and began, by Elizabeth's time, to look, not to the Continent, but across the oceans.

This new oligarchy along with those of the old nobility who had survived in affluence – and more of them did than some historians suggest – prevented the consolidation of an absolute Kingship in the continental fashion, and within a still aristocratic structure created a Protestant business commonwealth more akin to that of another northern maritime people, the Dutch, but with much greater landed resources behind it. The Tudor and Stuart English are already recognisably like their eighteenth- and nineteenth-century descendants; confident, forthright in speech, with an eye to the main chance; a hard, but intermittently imaginative people, with a touch of kindness and wry humour. They made the world of Shakespeare; then of John Aubrey and Dryden and Swift; then, in the eighteenth century, came the world of Reynolds and Gainsborough, Dr. Johnson and Gibbon – of the coffee houses and the garrets of a London transformed by Wren after the Great Fire; of country houses and parks and lively, yet unpretentious, country towns, still the cultural focus of their counties. Although the Anglican Church remained the official establishment, strong traditions of Nonconformity survived, particularly in London and the seaport towns. And underneath this varied minority culture were the yeomen and peasants of a still mainly rural society.

Then, gradually, England changed. Coal and iron industries had developed in Tudor and Stuart times; now a pall of industrial smoke began to drift over larger areas of the Midlands and the North and over the growing sprawl of the metropolis, which today has a population larger than that of any Scandinavian state. There grew up a huge city, the capital of a world-wide Empire and Commonwealth; Greater London, the thunder of traffic in its name. For this altered England was the pioneer of that strange, gradual, often terrible experience, still best described as the Industrial Revolution. Swifter and successive technical revolutions followed, again shifting populations and industry, the new light industries moving south-east. And England now included not only Scots, Welsh and Irish, but people of continental, Jewish and Commonwealth descent. If the basic Englishry still persists, it faces a challenge common to all the old West European countries, confronted with an Atlantic civilisation which technologically and financially knows no boundaries, and in which a new, more cosmopolitan way of life is on the move.

Before that more mechanised, more uniform civilisation comes in – and we are only in its early dawn – it is well to look at the essential qualities of the old English culture and polity; to recall their setting in the landscape and architecture which still means much to those born to it and which can still tell the visitor a great deal. To discern, in particular, those elements in the old England which have come through and form part of a living present. Only these living aspects will be touched upon, for this book is not simply another short history of England, but a portrait and an assessment.

Much of the old culture, in fact, survives into modern mass civilisation: in law and government and the City; in the Churches, the universities and schools; in the minds of the people, still very insular, particularly in the still rural areas.

II

The southern part of a small island in the north-eastern Atlantic, washed by the Gulf Stream and sloping from the western mountains and moors down to the Midland and East Anglian plains; then up to the chalk downs of Wiltshire, Dorset and Hampshire and on to Sussex and Kent, had already been settled by successive peoples since prehistoric times; Neolithic long heads, Bronze Age Beaker folk, Iron Age Celts. Before the island came into the orbit of the Mediterranean culture of Rome, a basic population was already blended and established.

The relics of these early peoples are spread about Southern England, in particular on the chalk downs. The earliest and largest Neolithic monument is at Avebury, in north Wiltshire, where the great Sarsen stones are arranged in a circle large enough to contain the entire modern village and approached by a long avenue, now in part restored. To see these megaliths, especially in the dusk or the rain, spaced out along their grassy rampart, is to sense at once that they are part of an Atlantic culture of immense antiquity that extended from the Mediterranean round the Iberian and Breton peninsulas. Stonehenge, in south Wiltshire, is rather different; 'that celebrated piece of Antiquity,' as Defoe would call it, 'the wonderful Stonehenge'. Though it originated in Neolithic times, its main structure dates from the Bronze Age and its affinities are with Mycenae and Tiryns in the Peloponnese; it is part of that Bronze Age culture which had already spread trade routes across the Alps and through Bohemia to the Baltic, down the Rhine and Meuse to the Low Countries; which practised a Sun cult that found its most elaborate northern expression in Denmark, and which is apparent in the earlier rock drawings in the Val Camonica north-east of Lake Como.

But the Iron Age Celts left the most massive memorial: Maiden Castle in Dorset, south-west of Dorchester, is the most elaborate and well constructed of the great fortress towns from which new conquerors out of Western Gaul dominated the native farmers and peasantry, whose considerable wealth they were able to exploit. Close to Chesil Beach, that strange pebble bank which sweeps from Portland Bill to beyond Bridport and which provided ammunition for their slingers, they had easy access to a good harbour near the area now Weymouth. These people were among the most formidable of the pre-Roman conquerors: the Romans called them the Durotriges, and it took the future emperor Vespasian himself, in the mid-first century A.D., to storm their stronghold. So Avebury, Stonehenge and Maiden Castle remain in the country that became Wessex; recalling in their actual presence the prehistoric culture of this decisive part of the island, already well populated before the Romans arrived.

But the richest centres of prehistoric culture were in East Anglia and Kent, and here the inhabitants are first clearly described. For it was there, in 54 B.C., that Rome first struck: Julius Caesar advanced as far as what would be Hertfordshire and obtained the submission of Cassivellaunus, the king of an Iron Age Belgic tribe which had come in from Northern France. Nearly a century later, the legions of Claudius, the stepfather of Nero, more systematically invaded the island; the Romans captured Caractacus and put down Boudicca, the queen of the Norfolk Iceni, after her savage rising against their alien power.

III

The Roman settlement of the island lasted for about three and a half centuries; nearly the time-span between the attempt of Guy Fawkes in 1605 to blow up the entire Jacobean establishment and the present. The romanised chiefs imposed a Mediterranean veneer; they settled, like cats, in the sunniest places, and installed central heating against the damp. They imported the standardised patterns of Roman mosaics, most of them rather vulgar, a few attractive. Some of these romanised pavements have survived: in the villa at Chedworth in the high Cotswolds towards Gloucester, from under several feet of earth, a miniature suite of baths has been excavated, one pavement with a pattern like a good Persian rug; and the floor of the dining-room is decorated with figures of the Seasons – a man hooded against the Cotswold cold bringing in a hare; a winged sunburnt boy with a garland. At Cirencester the pavements are larger, but more standardised; at Chichester they decorate a big villa which must have faced right onto the sea. The patterns at Verulamium are equally elaborate, and at Bath remain the well-preserved pools and colonnades of a sophisticated spa.

In London, already a considerable port, a temple of Mithras, whose cult was popular in the armies, has been unearthed; and away in the north, across the Northumbrian and Westmorland moors, is the long line of the great Emperor Hadrian's wall, running beneath the cloud shadows from sea to sea. There were garrison towns, strategically placed on the borders of what would be North and South Wales, and the square-cut machicolations and red brick at Colchester in Essex recall the walls of Rome itself. High above Dover, after all the centuries, the big Roman beacon overlooking the Straits still stands intact; westward, now landlocked, are the Roman naval ports at Pevensey and Portchester.

The Celts, well established before the Romans came, live most strikingly in their art which also revived when standardised Roman influence waned; a magnificent embossed and enamelled shield dredged out of the Thames near Battersea; a Celtic sun-god with writhing convoluted tresses, from Bath; a fine pre-Roman mirror in bronze from Desborough.

These are only the more familiar romanised and Celtic relics, things that one can touch and see; and the old walls and pavements are still as the tribesmen must have seen them; megaliths and hill forts, too, are still set in structurally the same landscape.

Such relics are almost our only contact with these centuries, going back out of the Roman daylight into the prehistoric dawn: for these people can hardly speak to us in writing. A few Latin inscriptions to local worthies or local gods: sub-Roman lettering on an effigy or tomb; some plaintive dog Latin from Welsh clergy after all was a memory and they had taken refuge from the heathen in the hills. Legends of Arthur, a sub-Roman war leader, were romanticised in the Middle Ages and used for Tudor propaganda.

Only in one aspect this long and decisive past is less obliterated than historians used to think. At the Pitt-Rivers museum at Farnham, for example, near Blandford in Dorset appropriately in the heart of the ancient Wessex culture of barrows and hill forts, the anatomical evidence is plain. The Neolithic people were small, with long, low heads, and narrow foreheads; light-boned, doubtless wiry and quick. Their descendants are still recognisable. The Bronze Age Beaker folk skulls are far more massive, with high foreheads and strong jaws; the teeth, in general, far superior to those of the modern population, unless, as often, smashed in battle or sacrifice. Solid people, the builders of Stonehenge, they must have been well built and formidable. The Belgic and Gallic strain, too, brought a stronger physique, and the pre-Roman population living out on the chalk downs may have compared well with many of their medieval and urbanised, post-industrial, nineteenth-century descendants.

For these people are ancestral to the later English: the old legend that the Anglo-Saxons exterminated them is long discredited and must go the way of the woad-painted savages burnt in wicker cages by Druids at Stonehenge, for the Druid cult came in quite late with the Iron Age Celts, well over a thousand years after the main Bronze Age sun temple of Stonehenge was set up.

So, before ever Caesar came, saw and decided not to conquer, and before the legions of Claudius and Vespasian subdued the island, the basic strata of population had been laid down; and anyone who looks at the country people of Wessex, or indeed at the population of the great towns, will observe that the Victorian legend of the English as mainly fair-haired Teutons makes no anthropological sense. This prehistoric background here, as on the Continent, was decisive long before the Romans laid a veneer of southern urban civilisation on the island. There was already wealth in wheat and barley, mead and ale, fruit and game and fish, or the Romans would not have settled; and their flimsy but well-planned towns and often well-found villas became, for ten generations or more, the setting of peaceful lives; of civility and comfort for a minority; of hunting and entertaining and the routine of well-conducted, albeit slave, households, not to be paralleled in the island for over a thousand years, if the peasantry remained poor and barbarous.

IV

Biologically important, the influence of this romanised Celtic background is culturally very indirect: through a flair, perhaps, for line and decoration and through Celtic Christianity, far more important in Ireland: indeed, it came back that way into heathen England. When they did not speak demotic Latin, these people spoke a language ancestral to Welsh.

English literature came first out of Germania – the huge pre-historic world of Teutonic migration and settlement which had long been established in what is today Germany, along the Baltic shores, in Denmark, the Low Countries and Northern France; and which had spilled over, intermittently, by infiltration and attack, into the Roman empire. One of these tides of migration – and not the most massive – seeped into the romanised island, bringing a way of life, debased, barbarous and bloody: their enemies noticed how these people stank. But it had a code of honour and a literature of its own, deriving from folk memories of enormous conflicts and migration on a continental scale. This is the world behind *Beowulf*, the most complete of all the Teutonic epics that survive and written in a language ancestral to English.

Through the dark fifth and sixth centuries – and they were

dark – 'ignorant armies clashed by night'. Up and down a demoralised and debased countryside the invaders looted and raped and killed; they called the romanised Celts *Welsche*, the normal German word for foreigners (Luther would apply it to the Italians): and sometimes as mercenaries, sometimes as pirates, mainly as peasant farmers, they slowly mastered the land. The conquest and settlement took a long time, and in the West country it was still incomplete by the days of King Ine in the late seventh century. It proceeded out of the estuaries of Kent and Essex and Suffolk; up the Thames valley to Reading and along the Kennet; by Wallingford and west under Uffington Camp (already marked by its Iron Age Celtic horse cut in the chalk and similar to the designs on tribal coins), and perhaps to Barbury Camp north of Marlborough. They also came up from Southampton Water along the Test valley, and from the mouth of the Avon at what would be Christchurch; through Fordingbridge and Breamore to Britford and so by Old Sarum, already an Iron Age fort, along the upper Avon and out on to Salisbury Plain; and so, perhaps, by Stanton St. Bernard and Milk hill on to the Marlborough downs and into Berkshire. In Suffolk and East Anglia, in Lincolnshire up the Welland and in Yorkshire up the Humber, they settled; the most civilised tribe had got into Kent, probably from the Rhineland.

But most of them came from what is now Denmark; from heathy Jutland and the flat lands of Schleswig-Holstein south of the present frontier at Flensburg; from the coast of Lower Saxony between Hamburg and Bremen, from the sandy fog-bound coasts of Gröningen and Friesland, and from the West Frisian islands. They came out of a world of polders and marshes and heaths, of enormous cloudscapes and slow, swampy rivers and the cold of the grey North Sea. Where Homer's seas are wine-dark, in *Beowulf*, set originally in the Baltic in East Denmark and South Sweden, the sea is a grey devourer of men. Here was a world in contrast with the Celtic West, the Cornish cliffs and Welsh mountains and the green and blue rollers of the Atlantic: it produced different people, for many of whom the famous description is probably correct, that their 'lips met like the two halves of a muffin'.

Their weapons were very primitive: only the leaders had splendid ornaments and helmets sometimes adorned with boars'

teeth, and wore mail shining 'like ice'. Most of them were un-
armoured; they are depicted, without helmets, staring in stupid
bewilderment at a Roman city, leaning on round-bossed shields
and long spears; they also had the *scramasax*, a peculiarly nasty
knife. Their craft were horrible; long, narrow, unseaworthy, hard
to row – inferior to the fine Viking ships; and from their rural
slums on the Continent they settled, by Roman standards ob-
scenely, with their women and bawling children, in the ill-
guarded sub-Roman land.

They were prehistoric heathen, and it was not until A.D. 597,
well over a century after the invasions had begun – five or six
generations – that Pope Gregory the Great sent St. Augustine to
Kent, and brought the island again into the orbit of Rome. Even
then the conversion was very gradual; nor was it helped by the
defeated refugee Celtic Church driven into Wales. If the Celtic
missionaries from Iona had decisive influence in the North,
naturally the Roman rule and Calendar soon predominated. The
gulf between the Celtic and Anglo-Saxon peoples would remain
for centuries – the Irish chronicles still refer to Henry VII, the
first Tudor sovereign, as the 'King of the Saxons in London'.

But of course the Germanic settlers interbred with the sub-
Roman population. They preferred to live outside the few and
dilapidated cities and to make their own burial places with their
own rites; they also, though the fact has been too much stressed
at the expense of Romano-Belgic agriculture, began to open up
the richer valley soils with the ox-drawn German wheeled
plough, which would also develop vast areas of the north German
plain eastward in the great colonisation of the early Middle Ages.
Coming from the Low Countries, the Anglo-Saxons understood
irrigation, and as the generations passed, they cleared some of the
forest and began to transform the landscape. They tended to live
in villages, where the Romano-Celtic peoples had lived in separate farms and hamlets; but this development was much determined by the country concerned.

The place names of Wiltshire, for example, the heart of
Wessex, are predominantly Anglo-Saxon; Bemerton, 'trumpeter's
(bymere) farm'; Charlton, 'ceorl's farm'; Enford, 'duckford';
Fugglestone or Foulston, 'Fugol's farm' ('bird' as personal
name); Grovely Wood; 'Grafan lea', Grafan's copse; Idmiston,
'Idmear's farm'. But there are Romano-Celtic survivors as well

– Andover from *dubro*, water; Durrington; the Avon itself; the Nadder; Bedwyn; Cricklade in Hampshire; Meon and Liss. 'Hills stand, rivers flow, for ever. The Thames was the Thames and Arden was Arden, long before any man of Germanic speech had set foot on this island.' [1]

Both the place names and the anatomical evidence – as well as common sense – suggest that the invaders enslaved, interbred, but did not utterly root out or massacre; their descendants retained a strong strain of pre-Saxon as of pre-Romano-Celtic blood. The conquered, normally, tend thus to win out.

Unlike the Romano-Celtic peoples, the Anglo-Saxons or Old English can speak directly to us: their literature, heathen and Christian, already expressed recognisable traits of the English character. They grumble; they endure; they are dogged to the point of heroism in battle; when Christian, they are often kindly. There is also a hard aristocratic code of honour, of the warrior's loyalty to his lord; in the heathen poems, a deep underlying pessimism; an interest, too, in clumsy riddles which shows how thick, intellectually, many of these farmers must have been. There is already, also, casualness an insularity. The heathen epic *Beowulf* is pervaded with a weird sense of doom and cold and the grim sea, for it reflects Baltic folk memories; and the English '*Deor*' the poem of 'cold exile', with its refrain '*that evil was got over, so my be this*', means, in effect, 'dogged as does it'. The brooding lament over the ruins of Bath – 'wondrous is this wall stone; broken by fate, the castles have decayed, the work of giants is crumbling', even perhaps already foreshadows a characteristic romanticism, for the English would invent the romantic movement in a quiet way.

And the most famous battle piece of the Old English describes a celebrated defeat – like Corunna or Dunkirk.

> *Here lies our lord, all hewn down*
> *Her lith ure ealdor eall forheawen,* [2]

runs the song of Maldron, written at the close of the tenth century in the time of Æthelred the Redeless – the Ill-Advised. It des-

---

[1] G. M. Young, ' Place Name Studies ', in *Today and Yesterday*, Hart-Davis, 1948, pp. 204 ff.

[2] For the convenience of readers unlearned in Anglo-Saxon the 'th' letters have been modernised, here and below.

cribes the defeat of Byrhtnoth, Ealdorman of Essex, by the Danes; and undaunted, it concludes with the hackneyed yet still splendid lines:

> *Thought the harder, heart the keener,*
> *Mood (Courage) the more, as our might lessens.*
>
> *Hige sceal the heardra, heorte the cenre*
> *Mod sceal the mare, the ure maegen lytlath.*

And Christianity early released a slightly rollicking lyric note in Caedmon's

> *Now let us praise the Guardian of Heaven's Realm.*
> *Nu sculon herigean heofonrices Weard.*

Chapter 2

The Old English

THE fame of the Norman Conquest has long obscured the achievements of this Old English civilisation. 'Here was a mist of ignorance', wrote Aubrey, the seventeenth-century antiquary, 'for six hundred years. They were so far from knowing the Arts that they could not build with stone. The church at Glaston was thatched ... and their very kings were a sort of farmers ...'[1] 'They were descended', wrote his contemporary, the first Sir Winston Churchill, 'from Gambrinius (the first inventor of good Ale and Beer, which they have loved too well ever since) and knew no way to outvie each other but ... by a kind of greasy riot.'[2] The misleading tradition would live on.

In fact, the culture of Anglo-Saxon England was greatly superior to anything Norman: 'In the eighth century indeed', Churchill's most famous descendant would write, 'England had claims to stand in the van of western culture';[3] and by 1066 'a country with a sufficiency of boroughs and markets for a lively national and international trade, with a well-organised currency of good silver pennies, lay at the Conqueror's feet ...'.[4]

The causes of this superiority are worth examination; far back though they be, the Old English are direct ancestors to most of the present population, some of whose qualities are apparent in them. The Conquest only imposed a foreign influence; there was no break in continuity simply because the native culture was out of fashion, driven underground for a few generations.

[1] *Brief Lives and other Selected Writings*, by John Aubrey, ed. Anthony Powell, Cresset Press, 1949, p. 2.
[2] *Divi Britannici*. Being a remark upon the Lives of All the Kings of this Isle. London, 1675.
[3] Winston S. Churchill, *A History of the English Speaking Peoples*, Cassell, 1956—, Vol. I, p. 68.
[4] D. M. Stenton, *English Society in the Early Middle Ages*, Penguin, 1952, p. 161.

II

Like all the Teutonic peoples, the Anglo-Saxons were warriors, and amid the squalor and barbarism of the fifth and sixth centuries, their war-lords had a barbaric splendour. The ship burial at Sutton Hoo in East Anglia can compare with the richest relics of other German chieftains; the inlaid brooches, cloisonné enamels, the quasi-Homeric helmet, the panoply of war-gear and feasting buried in a ship eighty feet long, show the wealth of even a minor royalty. And the vendettas of the Old English are no worse than the crimes of the contemporary Goths in Italy or of the Merovingian Franks in Gaul: through the darkness gleam ideals of honour, endurance and military panache.

With the coming of Christianity, a contrasting aspect of the Old English character is also discernible. St. Augustine's mission to Kent and London, and Paulinus' Northumbrian mission, and the reconciliation of the Celtic Church, led up to the Archiepiscopate of Theodore of Tarsus of Canterbury, which first made all England part of Roman Christendom: it marked a second, more lasting, Mediterranean conquest.

Amid a barbaric but vigorous people the Northumbrian culture quickly produced remarkable men: Benedict Biscop, who got together a rudimentary library; Bede, far the best historian in Western Europe of his time, whose anecdotes of the conversion and of amiable saints are still vivid. And some of the women, their status high as in other Germanic societies, show similar distinction: Abbess Hilda of Tadcaster, for example, converted by Paulinus, was reputed 'so wise that not only ordinary folk but kings and princes used to come and ask her advice in their difficulties.'

St. Wilfrid, Bishop of York, who lived part of his life near Oundle, was widely beloved: shipwrecked on the Frisian coast, he soon turned the local heathen into 'God's own people', if not for long: he was apparently 'of blameless faith and honest mind.' Even if one discounts much hagiography, it is clear that the Old English, like their nineteenth-century descendants, had a real missionary concern: St. Chad, who 'always preferred to undertake his preaching mission on foot rather than on horseback', helped convert the Midland heathen and became the first bishop of

Utrecht; in the eighth century St. Boniface of Crediton in Devon became the Apostle of the Germans and Archbishop of Mainz; and the Scandinavian countries were mainly converted by English missionaries.

Indeed piety could disrupt government, as when a king of the East Saxons, 'a very handsome and lovable young man, whom the entire nation greatly hoped would inherit and uphold the sceptre of the Kingdom', left wife, family, lands and country to become a monk in Rome.[5] In the south, in Kent, the Laws of Æthelberht in the early seventh century already firmly support the Church; and payment of 'Rome Scot', afterwards termed 'Peter's Pence', was early and willingly accorded by the most faithful of the northern nations. The endowments made over the years by the rulers and magnates were immense; nearly one-third of England, as Henry VIII found when he nationalised them in a very different world.

The élite of the Old English were often good warriors and churchmen; the people were in the main good farmers who set about colonising the land: 'There can be no doubt that the succeeding two centuries (c. 650–850) ... saw an intensification of these processes of colonisation and settlement. The Anglo-Saxons with greater or lesser admixture of Celtic blood, strengthened the hold of man upon nature in England.'[6]

There grew up a civilisation able to sustain a rich minority culture, linked by religion and trade with the Continent, and dynamic enough to influence the German and Baltic world from which it had itself emerged.

III

By the ninth century this promising people suffered an atrocious setback, if the long-term result was advantageous. Out of still prehistoric reservoirs of heathendom, the Scandinavian Vikings swarmed into the island: the first attack was held, but the second made England briefly part of a Danish empire. In face of the first onslaught, the southern English fought back hard: Alfred

[5] Bede, *A History of the English people*, trans. L. Sherley-Price, Penguin Books, p. 300.

[6] H. R. Loyn, *Anglo-Saxon England and the Norman Conquest*, Longmans, 1962, p. 44; q.v. for an admirable account.

(871–901), a redoubtable warrior, drove the invaders from Wessex, and his descendants came to dominate all England. Athelstan and Edgar had European prestige, famous contemporaries of the Saxon dynasty in the Germanies and the Macedonian dynasty in Byzantium. The assassination of Edward the 'Martyr' at seventeen, when 'greedily draining the cup' after hunting at Corfe in Dorset in 978, led to the reign of that guilt-ridden neurotic, Æthelred the Redeless;[7] and the murder of young Edmund Ironside with an iron hook when necessarily off guard led to a short-lived Danish dynasty; but the Old English civilisation was never wrecked. An Anglo-Danish ruling class emerged and the Scandinavian settlers were assimilated. Ghastly as the earlier onslaughts had been – for the invaders had overrun the North and most of the Midlands, Cambridgeshire and East Anglia and terrorised the South – by the eleventh century Canute was Christian. Originally a fierce Viking who would mutilate hostages (*magnae nobilitatis et elegantiae pueros*), he went on pilgrimage to Rome; for having heard of the power of St. Peter to bind and loose, 'he deemed it useful in no ordinary degree to gain his patronage before God', in particular as he was preparing to attack St. Olav of Norway.[8]

Nor did he represent barbarism: these heathen Danes and Norwegians came of a vigorous and wealthy culture going back to the Bronze Age. With their well-keeled, ocean-going, intricately carved ships; their accumulated loot and treasure from piracy and trade; their rich armour, bright cloaks and terrible axes; their fierce tradition of military and naval glory famed in the Sagas; their onslaughts were part of a far-flung movement which had brought Rurik to Novgorod in the time of Alfred, the convert Vladimir of Kiev to dominate the Russian waterways by the time of Canute, and Rollo, the Scandinavian pirate, to found the Norman state. The Vikings certainly added a harder, more independent, more acquisitive strain to the Old English. For their settlement was very extensive: Danes in most of Yorkshire and the East Midlands, Derby, Leicester, Stamford; in Norfolk and Suffolk; Norwegians in the Lake District and in the coastal part

---

[7] He apparently had a lifelong aversion to candles, with which he had been 'beaten' in childhood, when there was nothing else to hand.

[8] R. W. Southern, *The Making of the Middle Ages*, Hutchinson, 1953, p. 136, quoting Florence of Worcester.

of Lancashire. Their descendants were to be different, as they are still, from the southern English: more dour, more close, more pertinacious, more self-sufficient. The Scandinavians also reinforced the English flair for rudimentary self-government. Elicited and developed by strong kings, it would become England's great political contribution to the world. Tocqueville, writing in the 1830's, would call the institutions of American New England a 'beacon set upon a hill'; he would admire the tradition of local self-government, the 'rotation of banal offices', willingly performed; the combined independence and responsibility. That tradition was originally Old English and Anglo-Dane.

The Germanic tribesmen had brought with them a sense of community centering on tribal kings, and a habit of settling local affairs in 'folk moots' convened by the king's reeve; often in the open by some landmark or boundary, as at Modbury in Dorset, or the Moot at Downton in Wiltshire. Gradually these procedures came to supersede tribal blood feuds and vendettas of kinship: there grew up a customary *law of the land*. Law ceased to be a personal attribute and became public, deep-rooted in a way of life.

For the King's power, though sketchy and intermittent, came to link up with these public assemblies. By the tenth century under Edgar – not before – folk moots had been organised into monthly hundred and half-yearly shire courts, and supplementary private manor courts had grown up. Land meant jurisdiction, since for protection and control every man must have a lord. The contrast is already striking with the clan feuds of the Irish and the Highland Scots, the latter carried on into the eighteenth century.

Of course, the customary law had at first been unwritten, remembered by old men 'time out of mind'. Then, as the Church's influence increased, law came to be written down: formal oaths and counter-oaths had always been important and 'oath helpers' would swear, if not to the facts, to a reputation. There were whole tariffs of fines, graded by the social standing of the injured party.[9] And if, in graver cases, the charge were not cleared by the 'oath helpers', the Church provided the 'ordeal', another substitute for taking the law into one's own hands. The case, too difficult for human judgment, was thus put to God; if the accused

[9] See the author's *Western Political Thought*, Methuen Paperbacks, 1961, pp. 160-1.

floated, he was guilty; if he sank, he was quickly fished out, for had not the water 'received' him? There were ordeals, too, by red-hot iron, boiling water, and by the 'morsel', an ounce of bread or cheese which choked the guilty. This was presumably the most popular, except among the highly strung.

But major theft, murder and treachery were 'botless', not to be compounded for, demanding the gallows – though the humane Athelstan raised the age of execution from twelve to fifteen. Since the Norman custom of blinding or castration (thought more merciful) had not yet come in, the main punishments for other crimes were fines.

These crude methods of justice were at least rooted in local life and responsible people helped to carry them out; they also tried to see that hedges and fences were kept in repair; that cattle did not stray, that rents in kind were honestly paid.

The initiative, of course, came from King and magnates, though the habit of deciding local affairs locally was widespread. England has always been intensely class conscious, and anyone who approaches the Old English society 'in the hope of discovering a primitive democracy is fated to receive a rude shock.'[10] The distinction between 'gentle' and 'simple' is primordial: as among other Teutonic peoples, the warrior came first, and beneath the grades of Eorl Gesith and Ceorl, each with their steeply graded blood price, came the labouring peasants and the slaves.

The English monarchy is still the best established in the world and the cult of Kingship is early; Christianity added a more consecrated prestige to the original war-leader, mascot, and symbol of the folk. The gruelling Anglo-Danish wars enhanced the standing of King, of the great Ealdormen and of the King's fighting thegns, and already, when a merchant 'throve' and made three voyages at his own expense, he was of 'thegn right worthy'. The English class system, so tenacious, was already adaptable.

By the ninth century, many magnates were rich; though much of the land was still waste and famine haunted the people after the devastations of war, the country was naturally productive and merchants were already exporting textiles and wool.[11]

[10] Loyn, op. cit., p. 199.

[11] Capable, too, of sharp practice; Charlemagne complained that the new kind of English cloaks were too short; no 'good in bed or for riding', and 'when sitting down for the calls of nature', he complained, 'I suffer from cold in the thighs'. (Quoted by Loyn, op. cit., p. 86 n.)

Slaves and hunting dogs had been exported since Celtic and Romano-Celtic times, and the trade went on. In the early eleventh century English merchants were slave-trading to Italy, exporting woollen and linen textiles, spears, shields and silver to Pavia. There was trouble at the customs, where the English had 'grown violent', and Canute, when in Lombardy, arranged a flat-rate payment in kind of ten per cent, which included 'two fine greyhounds with enamelled collars'. This trade, though hardly extensive, was already 'not negligible'.[12] Some unlucky slaves were exported not to Italy, but to newly colonised Iceland, where there were already important fishing grounds.

The Danish invasions not only occasioned the rise of fortified boroughs; they also increased trade with the Danish-occupied parts of Ireland, with Friesland and the Baltic. Butter, cheese, salt and even local wine went over the North Sea. Since Roman times London had been economically predominant, as it was always to remain. When in 886 Alfred recaptured it, the exploit secured him the submission of all England outside the Danish areas. It now had a 'folk moot on the hill by Paul's' and it was swarming with Anglo-Saxon, Flemish, Frisian and Scandinavian merchants. The Danes had their own cemetery, to which at least the head of Canute's son Harold was committed, after it had been thrown into the Thames by the order of his half-brother, Hardicanute, and retrieved by a fisherman. Canute was sometimes known in Scandinavia as 'the King of London': already Frisian and Flemish cogs plied between the Port of London and the Scheldt, where the great Viking stronghold on Walcheren commanding its mouth held merchants as well as pirates.

Both external and internal trade thus already gave rise to guilds for rudimentary insurance and mutual aid. At Bedwyn in north Wiltshire, for example, if a guildsman's house was burnt, the others contributed to rebuild it, and at Abbotsbury, in 1040, 'a Dorset thegn of Scandinavian origin made a magnificent gift of a guildhall and site';[13] some compensation after two centuries for his heathen forebears' devastation of neighbouring Charmouth.

The Old English coinage, too, was particularly good; for Athelstan insisted, on pain of mutilation and even death, that

[12] R. W. Southern, op. cit., pp. 42–3.
[13] Loyn, op. cit., p. 141.

there 'should be one currency throughout the realm'. The English penny takes its name from the heathen King Penda of the Midlands in the seventh century; it was a silver coin, worth at least thirty shillings in our money, and by the time of Alfred there were generally twelve pence to a shilling and two hundred and forty to the pound – then a very large sum. If the advantages of a decimal coinage were early disregarded, the coins were often technically superior and their value more stable than those current at the time in France or Germany.

IV

This prosperity and relative order had been secured by the epic fight of Alfred and his descendants against the first big Danish attack and by the expansion of the West Saxon Kingdom; under Edgar it was so well established that the second major Danish invasion under Sweyn and Canute could take over England but not destroy its civilisation.

Alfred, the first great ruler in English history, shows qualities which have come to seem typical of the better aspects of England. He was not only the war-leader of the Christian folk; he was a real shepherd of his people; conscientious, practical, persistent and wise. Handicapped by some nervous affliction, he yet made himself a great soldier lawgiver and educator, and his achievement was decisive. Behind him was the continental Carolingian 'renaissance', which had preserved some of the learning of Antiquity and introduced a clear script, and which had itself owed much to Northumbrian Anglo-Saxon influence. Alfred was determined to restore the education of well-born boys so that the natural leaders of the country could at least read English, and he used his bishops in this daunting task.[14] In his letter preparatory to the translation of Pope Gregory the Great's *Pastoral Care* into Anglo-Saxon – he called it *Hierde-boc* (herdbook) – Alfred cited what he thought were the essential texts. These were Orosius' *World History against the Pagans*, 'a word written to prove that the introduction of Christianity had not made the world worse

[14]Alcuin, in the eighth century, had remarked: 'Let the youth attend the praises of our Heavenly King, and not dig up the earths of foxes or pursue hares.'

than it had been before';[15] Bede's *Ecclesiastical History*, and the rather faint *Consolations* of Boethius, so influential at that time, as well as Gregory's lives of Italian saints. Alfred also, himself. wrote a commentary on St. Augustine's *Soliloquies*.

Yet his objects were extremely practical. Like Churchill in 1940, he asked for the 'tools and material for the work that I was charged to perform ... This, then, is a King's material and his tools for ruling with, that he have his land fully manned ... Also, this is his material which he must have ... sustenance for the three orders' (clergy, soldiers and workmen) 'in land to live on, and gifts, and weapons, and food, and ale, and clothes.'[16] With his own hand, for 'the prose is certainly Alfred's own',[17] he added a chapter to Orosius on Northern Europe incorporating the narratives of sea captains who had sailed beyond the North Cape and to the mouth of the Vistula in the Eastern Baltic, and he left an awesome yet popular reputation as one who 'ran through the fields of foreign lore'. He thus provided a compendious and simplified ideological background to the Danish wars, and he was a royal pioneer in the long struggle between English youth and a classical education. Moreover he probably encouraged the compilation of the *Anglo-Saxon Chronicle*, which depicts his later campaigns in detail, and which would develop into a full and vivid narrative, continuing, with many complaints, after the Norman Conquest.

So, well back in Old English history, is a king who fought and worked for civilised objectives; not, as generally at that time, for blood-lust and glory; who fostered – 'translating word for word' – a vernacular as well as a Latin culture among the leaders of the people, and who tried to bring England more into line with continental civilisation. Symbolically, the famous Alfred jewel has survived, picked up at Newton, Somerset, with the homely inscription '*Aelfred Mec Heht Gewyrcan*, Alfred had me made'.

[15] David Daiches, *A Critical History of English Literature*, Secker and Warburg, 1960, Vol. I, p. 25.

[16] Quoted D. Whitelock, *The Beginnings of English Society*, Pelican books, 1952, p. 66.

[17] Daiches, op cit.

V

The style of this splendid ornament shows the fine craftsmanship of the Anglo-Saxons. By the nineteenth century most of the English became rather Philistine, and that reputation has not much waned; but in a rural, Catholic, society this obtuseness cannot yet be discerned; nor for many centuries, until the rise of Puritanism and great industry, would it predominate. As in the rest of Christendom, the Church took the cultural lead, and, despite Aubrey, even in Bede's time stone churches were going up. The main Carolingian influences came from the Rhineland, as apparent from surviving Anglo-Saxon foundations excavated at Winchester and Ely; there were large buildings at Glastonbury, Durham and Exeter, and the churches at Bosham and Bradford-on-Avon, with their heavy arches and massive walls, would have been painted and ornamented in the Romanesque fashion of the day. Few Anglo-Saxon church buildings have survived, not because they were rare, or built in wood, but because the continental Norman lords and bishops, like the Victorians, had a rage for pulling old buildings down in accordance with modern ideas. And if nearly all the secular buildings have perished, for they were mainly of wood and thatch, they were certainly extensive and substantial.

The Church also gave scope to craftsmen in gems and silver and gold, vestments and tapestries, and the Old English illuminated manuscripts, interpreting the Carolingian tradition, were famous on the Continent. The superb Exeter book of the early tenth century shows what they could do; while the sculptors could early combine northern and Romanesque motifs, as in the stone crosses of Northumbria; the Winchester sculptors also enlarged the designs of Byzantine-influenced ivories, as in the Rood, Romsey. Anglo-Saxon embroideries were splendid and much in demand – the *opus Anglicanum* – English work'. Far from being a backwater of barbarism which the Norman Conqueror's panegyrists depict, Anglo-Saxon arts could hold their own with the best in Western Europe.

In defence at sea, however, the Old English were backward. The early settlers took to the sea because they had to; their poetry shows that, in general, they loathed and dreaded it. The

Anglo-Saxons had plenty to do colonising their own land and enterprise turned inward: their word for 'lord', so important in English history, does not mean war-leader: it derives from *hla-ford*, a contraction of *hlaf-weard*, 'guardian of the bread'; doubt-less what most of the people cared about was not glory or the sea but the 'wheaten loaf' – 'hwaeten hlaf'.[18] And barley was an even more popular crop than wheat, for it produced good ale, to be swigged from great drinking-horns, like the heady mead from the ubiquitous beehives – a drink not unlike a strong sweet hock.

The one and a half million Anglo-Saxons, the rich enjoying these good things and the poor making them, were less interested than the wolfish Vikings, swarming out of over-populated fjords, in the sea. And when the Scandinavians arrived, they came to settle and soon turned farmers: if the rich fisheries encouraged local seamanship, the trading ships were mainly foreign.

VI

Paradoxically for a country which would become the greatest sea power in the world, Anglo-Saxon England thus showed naval, not military, incompetence before the Norman attack. When King Alfred had built ships to fight the Danes twice as long as those of the invaders, their ambitious design had made them clumsy, and they had been manned by Frisian sailors. When Harold's Anglo-Danish government mobilised its fleet to inter-cept the Norman flotillas – whose transports were vulnerable un-decked 'saucers' for beaching, forty feet long with a draught of about four[19] – it could not keep the sea long enough, owing to defective supply and morale, to break up the convoy.

Yet Norman William plainly respected his adversaries and campaigned with caution. For he invaded in the old Viking way; seizing a base by the sea, consolidating his position and then ravaging the countryside. He did not even advance on London, though the way was open: and since the sea then came further inland both at Pevensey and at Sedlescombe, the Hastings area was still a peninsula: Harold's impetuous advance was, indeed, designed to shut him up there.

[18] Loyn, op. cit., p. 151.
[19] J. A. Williamson, *The English Channel*, Collins, 1959, p. 83.

The old belief that the Normans outclassed the Anglo-Saxons at Hastings, long accepted on the word of Freeman and Oman, neither of whom had seen a battle, is now superseded. If English tactics were inefficient, the Norman tactics were no better: the invaders were incapable of the shock tactics of disciplined cavalry pressed home in a charge, nor were the English capable of standing firm in a phalanx of pikemen to stop them. If the Bayeux tapestry is accurate, the Normans hurled their spears, like javelins, yelling '*Dex aie* – God help!', while their opponents, swiping with their axes, shouted 'Out, Out!' and '*Olicross!*'[20]

After his exploit in defeating the Scandinavians at Stamford Bridge, Harold was at Hastings within a fortnight, furious at the ravaging of his own estates. But William had seized the initiative and consolidated his base and the English fought a defensive battle with inadequate forces to stop him breaking out. Hastings, in fact, was lost – and only just lost – not through the obsolete tactics of a 'decadent nation on the outer fringe of European politics', but because Harold was both rash and outmanoeuvred by the cautious yet swift tactics of his opponent: '*Wyllelm him com ongean on unwear, aer his folc gefylced waere*', 'William came on them unexpectedly before the army was organised'. The defeat was incurred not through the obsolescence and inefficiency of an inferior culture, but strategically through the inefficiency of the fleet, and tactically through sheer overconfidence; and in defeat (the clergy at Winchester dead with their habits beneath their armour) the Old English showed the stubborn tenacity of their descendants at Waterloo.

[20] See R. Glover's conclusive article in *The English Historical Review*, LXVII, pp. 1–18. Snorri Sturlason, the thirteenth-century author of the *Heimskringla*, is vindicated against Oman.

Chapter 3

The Medieval Realm

THE foundations of England had thus been long established before ever the Normans subdued the island; now, within a manageable area the most compact and best-administered realm in Western Europe would be built, and the habit and institutions of self-government under law would come out of it. For over two and a half centuries after the Conquest there were, on balance, prosperity and expansion culminating in the climax of English medieval civilisation, before the French wars and Black Death brought recession. The military might of England was asserted first in, and then outside, the island, backed by the wealth of the wool trade and the tactical superiority of the longbow. Oxford and Cambridge Universities were founded and the Inns of Court; the precedent set, if strictly in feudal terms, for the control of public power in *Magna Carta* and its sequel, and the law consolidated by the statutes of Edward I. Institutions still in full vigour stem from this creative time and great cathedrals and castles still recall its vitality.

The mainspring of this achievement was the monarchy, working within a society 'which was rapidly becoming richer, more varied and more settled.'[1] The Crown could reach out and protect the small men against the great; already, even under the Angevins, it was able to supersede old cumbrous procedures by a royal justice available to all. The fiefs of the great Norman tenants-in-chief were enormous but not, in principle, a disruptive innovation: 'The Anglo-Saxon thegns were familiar with a dependent military tenure not easy to distinguish on any level from that of their "feudal" successors the knights'[2] – an Anglo-Saxon term (*cniht*) easily applied to the Norman *chivaler*. Indeed, it

[1] J. C. Holt, *Magna Carta*, C.U.P., 1965, p. 27.
[2] See J. O. Prestwich, 'Anglo-Norman Feudalism and the Problem of Continuity', *Past and Present*, November 1963, q.v.

was not by imposing new feudal arrangements but by exploiting the extensive if sometimes vague powers of the Old English monarchy that the Norman kings gave the history of England a new direction. Their courts and councils (*Curia* or *Consilia*) were in direct descent from the Households (*Hyreds*) and Witanage-mots of Edward the Confessor's time; they took the formal advice of their great men, and 'their joint authority inspires every act of state. The term 'folk right' dies at the Conquest but the *consuetudo Angliae* (Custom of England) takes its place.'[3]

This was the authority that William of Normandy had coveted and won. Immediately, too, he relied more on his own military household – the permanent professionals – than upon the already obsolescent Norman feudal host. William Rufus, like his father, hired mercenaries and would sign up on the spot a knight who had unhorsed him in battle: he was '*militum mercator* – a dealer in soldiers'. The parvenu Norman kings were savage adventurers determined to hold and to exploit, but though they used new methods of administration, neither the Conqueror nor Rufus was a great political innovator.[4]

But of course the Conquest altered English horizons; a ruling class which had looked to Scandinavia was ousted by one which looked to the Latin South. Crude and barbarous, the Normans were frenchified Vikings, part of a movement of European range; five years after Hastings other Normans completed their conquest of Southern Italy; twenty-five years later they had mastered Sicily, and they played a major part in the First Crusade. The languages of Court, ruling class and administration became French and Latin:

> *Now is the teaching abandoned and the people is lost,*
> *Now it is men of other languages that teach our people,*

laments Aelfric's *Grammar*:

> *Nu is theo leore forleten and thet folc is forloren,*
> *Nu beoth othre leoden theo laerath ure folc.*

[3] J. E. A. Jolliffe, *The Constitutional History of Medieval England*, Black, 1937, p. 177.
[4] See H. G. Richardson and G. O. Sayles, *The Governance of Medieval England from the Conquest to Magna Carta*, Edinburgh University Press, 1963, for a modern analysis. See pp. 1–22 on 'William Stubbs, Man and Historian', for an irreverent treatment.

II

The restive dangerous adventurers who had followed William formed a tense common interest, very few compared with the million and a half English. They at once clamped down their authority by palisaded strongpoints, transformed in the following century into barrack-like keeps, as at Rochester and Corfe. But they never achieved a continental anarchy; all land belonged to the King and sub-tenants owe him direct fealty. Moreover, the old administration was to hand; the tenth-century hundred and shire courts, now linked by the sheriffs to the Crown, were already 'new and efficient instruments of Government, to be used and extended as the King thought fit';[5] these courts could do justice even against high-handed magnates and find out what was going on. Thus the Conqueror began to get the substantial people of the country on his side; and his great Domesday survey was an astonishing effort of collaboration between sharp Latin-speaking clerks and knowledgeable local men.

The Norman kings thus knew where they were, and they were rich. Henry I, whose first act, on Rufus' death, was to ride hard for the treasury at Winchester, found an outstanding administrator in Bishop Roger of Salisbury, a tough cleric who based his power on Devizes castle. Henry put him in charge of the 'exchequer', so called because of its novel abacus and chequered cloth for calculation. Its officials, as one of them put it, were pioneers, 'cutting wood for rough edifices' to be 'improved by more skilful builders'; indeed, their successors would prove all too efficient. Today one official residence of the Prime Minister is still called 'Chequers', for it 'once belonged to the Angevin family de Scaccario'.[6]

All these Norman kings knew how to rule, which was more than any king had known since Canute; for Edward the Confessor, though no longer regarded as an incompetent *dévot*, at best managed, like Charles II, not to go on his travels again, and to 'hunt in tranquillity', his main concern.[7] When the Conqueror

[5] Richardson and Sayles, op. cit., p. 25.
[6] Keith Feiling, *A History of England*, Macmillan, 1950, p. 105.
[7] See F. Barlow, 'Edward the Confessor's Early Life, Character and Attitudes', *E.H.R.*, 1964. He was by descent a warrior from the royal House of

started to build the Tower of London and William Rufus Westminster Hall (both still extant) they were asserting a power
which had already made England invulnerable to attack and
would create a more impersonal routine of government. Gradually the judicial, financial, and administrative powers of the
Curia Regis – the King's Court – were developed by the restless
administrative flair of the Angevin Henry II, and England became the most close-knit realm in the West. It was strong enough
to survive the exactions of that glamorous absentee Richard
Coeur de Lion and of the tyrannic, temperamental but able
John; and it was consolidated, after the civil wars under Henry
III, by the legal-minded and formidable Edward I.

So from the King's household came the great officials: the
Chancellor, originally chief chaplain; the Steward of the Aula
(Hall); the Chamberlain of the private apartments; the Treasurer
of the Chest; the Constable of the stables; the Marshals who kept
discipline, and 'out of the household was slowly born the Civil
Service. The descent of the English bureaucracy from the Chamber in which the King slept and the adjacent closet, the wardrobe,
where he hung his clothes, is one of the curiosities of history.'[8]
Unlike the far-flung realms of France and Germany, with their
great provinces and dukedoms, the island became relatively well-
governed. That is the first and cardinal political aspect of English
medieval history – more important than any 'constitutional' experiments. By the thirteenth century 'wherever English law pre-
vailed ... there the King was supreme, his authority beyond challenge. Every jurisdiction was subject to his jurisdiction; every
local law was dominated by the common law.'[9]

III

This result was secured partly by luck. All the Norman Kings
were dynamic, able men, and Henry II was an administrative
genius. The Conqueror, a hard-bitten bastard – whose enemies to
the last, hanging raw hides over their timber defences, would

Wessex and from Viking-Norman Dukes, and as a youth he was reputed to
have carved Canute's horse in two in battle. He had spent twenty-eight
years in exile as a landless knight and was naturally continentalised.
[8] A. Lane Poole, *From Domesday Book to Magna Carta*, Oxford, 1951,
p. 9.
[9] Richardson and Sayles, op. cit., p. 41.

bawl 'hides for the tanner' in allusion to his maternal grandfather's calling – was a 'stark' man. He was of middle stature,
thick-set, baldish, 'fierce'; 'majestic when sitting or standing,
although the protuberance of his belly deformed the dignity of
his appearance'. He drove his eldest son 'little Robert Curthose'
from Court 'by the blustering of his terrific voice'.[10] William
Rufus was equally formidable, though reckless and prodigal. He
got his nickname not from his hair but from his face; he, too,
was immensely strong, thick-set, with peculiar eyes with an odd
glitter, a 'supercilious' look, a stammer and 'ferocious' voice. He
was the tough kind of homosexual, surrounded by martial and
raffish young men: 'troops of pathics and droves of harlots', declared the outraged chronicler, 'followed the Court'. After some
odd nightmares about streams of blood and gnawing a crucifix
that kicked him, he perished in a mysterious hunting accident
when one of his companions, by mistake or intent, shot down the
line. 'Yet in his wild way', writes Dr. Feiling, 'Rufus had done
well.'[11] Like his father, he had been a terror.

Henry I, the youngest brother, was abler than either since he
could even read. He, too, was shortish and thick-set: he 'preferred female blandishments' and sired many illegitimates.[12] He
conciliated the English by his marriage to Edith of Scotland,
though the match was derided by the barons, who called the
royal pair 'Godric and Godgifu'. Brought up at Wilton and
Romsey, 'singularly holy and by no means despicable in point of
beauty', Edith came of the Old English royal line through her
mother, St. Margaret, and through her the House of Windsor
descends from Cerdic. Henry was 'abstinent from war in so far
as he could be with honour'; a systematic ruler 'deliberate in

[10] William of Malmesbury, *Gesta Regum*, translated Sharpe and Stephenson. *Church Histories of England*, Vol. III, pp. 257 and 339.
[11] Feiling, op. cit., p. 115. He was extravagant, but sharp about money, as
when dealing with his Jews who had flocked to England to exploit the Conquest. One young Hebrew had turned Christian and when his father begged
the King to reconvert him, Rufus remained significantly silent. Taking the
hint, the older Jew offered him sixty marks down; whereupon the King
ordered the convert to recant. The youth asked Rufus if he were joking, but
though the King roared that he would not joke with the son of a dungheap,
the young man remained obstinate. Rufus, however, demanded the money,
and when the father said the service had not been rendered as per contract,
the King settled for thirty marks for his trouble.
[12] He had at least twenty, thus outdoing Charles II, who acknowledged
fourteen.

speech': he kept a zoo at Woodstock which contained lions, leopards, lynxes, camels and a porcupine – much admired. He would blind and castrate, as necessary, and in the course of governing England and Normandy at once, he had to delegate power. Roger of Salisbury became not only treasurer but Chief 'Justiciar' – 'second to the King' even when the monarch was absent; and in spite of baronial characters such as Robert Fitz-hamon who, cracked on the head with a lance, remained per-manently half-witted, and Robert of Belesme, who blinded his godchild with his own hands and had to be shut up in Wareham for life, the routine carried on.

Three terrifying kings in succession thus consolidated the Con-quest. But Henry's son William was drowned off Barfleur near Cherbourg, when drunken sailors ran his ship on a reef, and the succession lapsed to his arrogant sister Mathilda, Dowager Emp-ress of Germany through her marriage to the Salian Emperor, Henry V. She was successfully challenged by Stephen of Blois, the Conqueror's nephew, but the administration survived the confusion; Henry FitzEmpress, her son by her second marriage to the Count of Anjou, finally secured the inheritance.

A dynamic personality again took charge: another short stocky man, with reddish hair and grey eyes, Henry II had a devilish temper and restless energy. He was the greatest ruler in Western Europe, for his marriage to Eleanor of Aquitaine had added to rich Normandy the vine-clad territories on the Loire as well as large areas of south-western France – Poitou, the Bordelais, Gascony.

He consolidated and extended the administration, though he spent more than half his reign outside England. The momentum of impersonal government increased, while the royal writs pro-vided remedies available everywhere; increasingly the law of the land, the Common Law, came to exist in its own right, the ex-pression of the habits of a more settled society. A growing respect for the law would check even monarchy itself; power was not only established, it would be tamed.

Henry II also adopted the old Frankish procedure of empanel-ling 'lawful men' of the neighbourhood on 'juries' – at first to ascertain the rights and resources of the crown. Transplanted, this custom came to provide information about crime and devel-oped into 'trial by jury', a fundamental English right: by 1166

twelve lawful men were already indicting felons, and in time
would not merely swear to the facts but decide questions arising
from a case.

This historic procedure thus originated with government and
became part of a superior royal justice; 'a good article', as Maitland put it, 'that is to say a masterful thing not to be resisted'.
Yet responsibility rested not on royal bureaucrats, but on local
men, and all litigants came to have the right to demand to go before a jury. So the ancient and cumbrous oath-helpings and trial
by ordeal and even by 'battle' – a Norman innovation – were
superseded. And if conservatives felt it impious to transfer judgment from God to man instead of risking God's judgment by
ordeal or battle, a man could now 'put himself on his country'.

This innovation reinforced respect for the law of the land, and
this respect was confirmed by the famous *Magna Carta* of 1215,
decisive not so much for what is said, as for the way it would
later be interpreted. Naturally the celebrated 'free man', to whom
the justice of his feudal equals would not be denied, was no man
of the people; 'not a line gave any protection to the villein';[13]
and even the term 'Great Charter', used for the reissue two years
after, merely distinguished it from another dealing with forest
law, but the King himself had been brought to book by a politically articulate community of the realm. Although 'it is difficult
to concede to these men' (the northerners and Essex magnates
who were John's main enemies) 'or to many of the others...that
high sense of responsibility and public duty with which they have
often been credited...,' and 'for John's reign the constitutional
importance of *Magna Carta* is negligible', it did provide 'a practical assertion of existing law and customs, and it imposed limitations on the arbitrary power of the Crown. The King could no
longer override the law.'[14]

John of Salisbury, the mid-twelfth century author of the *Policraticus*, the first elaborate work of political theory by an Englishman, had already distinguished sharply, in the manner of Roman

[13] Feiling, op. cit., p. 160.
[14] A. Lane Poole, *From Domesday Book to Magna Carta*, Oxford, 1951,
pp. 470, 476. 'The leaders of the revolt', he writes, 'do not inspire confidence' and had no intention of keeping the terms; hanging round Staines on
the excuse of a tournament with a prize of a bear for the winner; (p. 478)
and even then raising rebellion, though the King tried to carry out the
Charter's terms.

law, between the *princeps* who rules according to law, and the *tyrannus* who governs by arbitrary will: now, in the thirteenth century, the ruler was bound not only by folk custom, by Christian obligation, and by feudal duty, but because he was a 'public power'. In its feudal idiom, *Magna Carta* brought this idea home: reissued and confirmed over centuries, it even took the place of the laws of King Edward the Confessor in general esteem. By the mid-fourteenth century the term 'free man' would become 'no man of whatever estate and condition he may be.'[15]

The third great political achievement, following on the establishment of better order and the attempt to tame public power, was the rudimentary beginning of government by consent. Bracton, the greatest English thirteenth-century jurist, has a strong sense of the ultimate authority of the whole realm; and the conflict between the King and the magnates to control the new administration which the Normans and Angevins had developed, led both sides to seek support from the lesser landowners and even from the towns. The Plantagenets and their often brutal baronage – *Barnagii sui* – would contend for centuries to control government, and therefore tried to bind lesser men, rural and urban, to their interests. The assemblies of King-in-Council now came to include knights of the shire and burgesses, summoned to provide information, assessment, and consent. Often they came reluctantly, 'living chessmen in the game of high politics';[16] naturally, they did not deliberate with the magnates, and the *colloquies* or *parliaments* went on after they had withdrawn or gone home; but a strong administration, eliciting support, brought wider horizons and responsibilities to those already experienced in local affairs.

Henry III, who succeeded John at the age of nine, proved the first really incompetent king since the Confessor; he was a rather petulant aesthete with large cosmopolitan ambitions in a century of great rulers – St. Louis of France and Frederick II, the spectacular Hohenstaufen Emperor. His mother had come from Angoulême and he married a princess of Provence; his brother became titular Holy Roman Emperor and his younger son tried to secure Sicily. His reign is remarkable for the arts, but he was over-ambitious and politically inept.

[15] See Holt, op. cit., pp. 3–18.
[16] E. L. Woodward, *History of England*, Methuen, 1947, p. 54.

In the resulting conflict between the King and his main opponent, his brother-in-law, Simon de Montfort, a predator who
has won too much credit as a founder of parliamentary government, both sides canvassed all the support they could get. A
standing Council to control the King was appointed by a commission of twenty-four, representing '*nos hauz hommes et prodes
hommes du comun de nostre reaume*', and as early as 1261
Henry was instructing the sheriff of Norfolk and Suffolk to divert
the three knights from each shire summoned by de Montfort to
St. Albans, to his own *Colloquium* at Windsor.[17] Already there
was competition for the support of the counties and the towns.

Thus the civil wars did not disrupt the realm into anarchy, but
even widened political consciousness; and Edward I, a great and
litigious man, was able to restore and consolidate government.
At thirty-five, he was already famous; during the civil wars he
had escaped from his captors by trying out a swift horse, shouting 'Hey guards, tell your friends...that England wins!' He had
then outmanoeuvred and butchered Simon de Montfort at Eve-
sham, and won renown on Crusade.[18] He became the greatest
law-maker of the Plantagenet Kings, his statute law decisive for
England's future. The Statute of Westminster the Second of
1285, for example, had profound social effects, in that the
custom of primogeniture, entailing land on the eldest son which,
in Maitland's words, had 'crept in with the Conquest', was extended from military to other tenures. In spite of vicissitudes,
great family dynasties thus went on, and their younger sons,
forced out into the world, did not come to form a caste of im-
poverished nobles, cut off from commerce and the law, but a
ramified establishment linked with the landed interest. Royal
justice was made swifter and more accessible by Judges of Assize
who tried cases before local juries; by the statute of Winchester
local commissions of array could enrol a militia, useful for local

[17] *Royal and other Historical Letters Illustrative of the Reign of Henry III.*
Selected W. W. Shirley. Vol. II, Rolls Series, 1866, p. 179.
[18] When attacked with a poisoned knife, he had seized the trestle of the
table and bashed in the assassin's head, then remarked 'Throw out this dead
dog and hang him over the town wall along with a live one.' *Cum nihil
haberet in manibus, assumpsit testellum quod supportabat tabulam, et in-
continenti percussit illum in capite: statim cervicatus est et mortuus . . .
Mox praecepit illis dicens, 'Ejicite hunc canem mortuum, et suspendite eum
super muros civitatis, adjuncto secum cane vivo.' Chronica De Monasterii
S. Albani*, ed. H. T. Riley, Rolls Series, p. 32.

defence, if not for warfare on the Continent. The King's government thus collaborated with the 'county'. Already by John's time 'Administratively and geographically it was the shire, the *comitatus*; socially and emotionally it was the native homeland, the *patria*. It could be represented, it could negotiate with the King, it could suffer penalties and it could hold privileges. It was the bedrock of English society and government.'[19] By Edward I's day 'Conservatores', later 'Justices' of the Peace, were being appointed to assist or check the Sheriffs, and by the early years of Edward III they would be assigned to every county, with more extensive powers. The long alliance between the Crown and the 'county' was consolidated.

Thus, by the early fourteenth century the pattern of English life had been largely determined for centuries. Within the framework of a strong realm the great landed aristocracy somehow managed, through the chances of descent, through attainder and civil wars, to adapt and survive, assimilating new wealth, whatever its origin; the country gentry became guardians of the peace throughout the land, increased their contacts with Parliament and the law, and controlled the levies of the neighbourhood; while the rich burgesses of London and the lesser towns were not grand enough to become an urban patriciate separate from the land, but were anxious to get back to it. This establishment was to persist into modern times; the Tudors would rule mainly through it, not by bureaucracy, and from it in unbroken descent the Stuart and Hanoverian oligarchy would derive.

Edward I also purged and reorganised the judiciary, and Year Books in legal French now recorded the arguments in Court. By the fourteenth century, also, the Inns of Court were established: concerned with the Common Law; situated between London and the Courts at Westminster, they were already privileged and expensive. These Inns took on the more genial attributes of Colleges and linked a secular legal profession with the establishment: this bulwark, with its exclusive jargon and tradition of good living, would be important in English life and strengthen the independence of Judges and of the legal profession.

Like most medieval rulers, Edward I was insolvent and died deep in debt, having pledged the customs revenues to a syndicate of Italian bankers; but the resulting crises increased the power

[19] Holt, op. cit., p. 27.

of the 'Commons', of the substantial *communities* (not the 'common' people) of the realm. In 1295, following the precedents of his father and of Simon de Montfort, the King had called a great Parliament to finance his Scottish and French wars, and 'out of these expedients of Edward I developed the Parliamentary system of modern England. The development was slow and could not have been foreseen.'[20]

It was thus in England, alone among the great European powers, that medieval institutions attained really decisive importance. Three things made this event possible: the compactness of the area, the strength of the administration, and the growing participation of the substantial men of the realm in national affairs, King and magnates bidding for their support.

V

Consolidated by an administration strong enough to survive civil wars, the English now asserted their predominance over the whole British Isles, and began to plunder the much richer and more heavily populated kingdom of France.

To the Angevin Henry II, with his immense continental possessions, it had not been worth while to mount major campaigns within the island itself. Richard I was an absentee; John unable to mount a major attack. Under Henry III the Welsh were still ravaging the Marches: 'know that Meredut ap Res, Res Vachan and Meredut ap Owein, with all the pride of Wales, went to the land of our Lord the King to pillage and destroy.'[21]

Edward I took the problem in hand. He built the great castle of Carnarvon, the birthplace of the first Prince of Wales; and though he never conquered Scotland, he was called '*Malleus Scotorum*, the Hammer of the Scots'. Bannockburn saved Scottish liberties; in conjunction with the French, the Scots would long be enemies; but they never had the resources for a substantial revenge. They had long, indeed, to wait the opportunities they were to find in England: since Edward I expelled the Jews, who did not officially return until the time of Oliver Cromwell, and the Scots did not infiltrate in force until the reign of James VI and I, the English were relieved of much competition.

[20] E. L. Woodward, op. cit., p. 55.
[21] *Royal and other Historical Letters*, op. cit., p. 368.

The new aggressive spirit now turned against France, the rich traditional stamping ground that attracted the English as Italy did the Germans. The Anglo-Saxons had been outpaced and out-classed by Danish armies; now the English had become the strongest people in the island, and by the fourteenth century the '*Goddams*' would be the scourge of the French. This insular truculence, indeed, would become innate and the English be-come the scourge of all their neighbours.

Civilisation, in the island, meanwhile, had greatly developed. The twelfth and thirteenth centuries, indeed, saw the culmination of English medieval culture, for the Normans had seized a rich land with well-organised market towns and a sound currency. The Conquest and the barbaric 'harrying' of the North had caused an immediate setback; and the coinage had badly de-generated, though Henry I, in the Norman manner, had taken it out of most of the moneyers for clipping and debasing it. But gradually the economic tide had turned: London, by far the greatest city, was an economic magnet with its civic institutions already well established. By Anglo-Norman times Aldermen were in charge of wards and 'wardmoots', their headquarters the Guildhall; here already questions of commercial law and proce-dure were decided. Henry I gave the Londoners authority – and hunting rights – over all Middlesex, and allowed them to choose their own Sheriffs; in John's reign they gained the right annually to elect their Lord Mayor, and their support or enmity was al-ready often decisive. The maritime city expanded and flourished; the young Londoners in Henry II's time were great on sport; the summer festivals all occasions for archery, jumping, wrestling and hurling – *arcu, saltu, luctu, jactu lapidem*; and in winter they would bait animals and skate on the marshes around a wider Thames. By John's time London Bridge was of stone; the whole great cosmopolitan city had long been the economic focus of England, as it has been ever since. The other towns, York, the capital of the North; Lincoln and Norwich; Durham and Chester, commanding the Scots border and the egress from North Wales; Canterbury and Bury St. Edmunds; Winchester and Exeter and Bristol, all were now well established, though none had a popu-lation of more than 8,000 and most of them much less. They were all rural, with pasture and arable, farmyards and gardens, part of their civic life.

By the late thirteenth century they were already dominated by splendid cathedrals – Romanesque and Gothic – still the most spectacular memorials of that time, though now far less splendid than they would have been then, lime-washed and painted in vivid colours: Durham, the most majestic Norman construction, with ribbed vaulting and huge carved pillars; Ely, the most intricately elaborate, towering over the black earth of the fens and symbolising the defeat of the last resistance of Hereward the Wake; Norwich, some thick columns patterned like a Spanish chestnut; the transepts at Winchester; the heavy arches of Romsey and Malmesbury, the impressive nave of Gloucester, the thickset work at Exeter. Like the Norman castles, these great buildings attest the conquerors' hold on the land.

The 'Early English' Gothic of the thirteenth century is still to be seen in purest form in Salisbury, most graceful of English cathedrals on the well-watered and well-planned site which had superseded Old Sarum on the upland chalk: Lincoln and Canterbury still dominate their cities. And contemporary with these great cathedrals were a host of parish churches, recalling the lives of more ordinary people and commemorating local families.

Many strategic fortresses, too, remain; Windsor was founded by the Conqueror, commanding the Thames on a strategic site; under Henry II the Round Tower was stone built, as were the outer walls to north, east and south. At Winchester, the Normans put up a big castle outside the West Gate, and the great hall was transformed by Henry III into a lofty and elegant structure, still standing, with slender clumped pillars and pointed arches, in style a secular equivalent of Salisbury. Ludlow, commanding great views away to the Welsh hills, was one of the earlier Norman strongholds, with massive central keep and Romanesque chapel gate. The contrast between the stark Norman keep and the later bastions and gate house at Corfe show how elaborate the military architecture became: it reached its culmination in the massive and efficient castles built by Edward I in Wales.

The Normans had also developed new monasteries, not only as places for the propitiation of God and the contemplations of Cluniac holy men, but as training grounds for men of affairs; Lewes and Reading were founded and the wealthy Benedictine Anglo-Saxon houses at Glastonbury and Westminster further en-

riched. The Cistercians came in during the twelfth century and
made for remote sites; Stephen Harding, who came from Sher-
borne in Dorset and had been prior of Citeaux, had laid down
the rules of this austere order. They concentrated on agriculture
and sheep farming, and the great northern abbeys at Fountains
and Rievaulx, Waverley and Tintern colonised waste places and
came to own enormous flocks, contributing to the main basis of
English prosperity.

VI

Culturally much more important, for they would survive the
Reformation enhanced, were the universities of Oxford and
Cambridge, destined to have so profound and lasting an influence in England and overseas. By the mid-twelfth century there
were scholars in Oxford, and when Henry II, contending with
his Archbishop, Thomas Becket, ordered all English students in
Paris to return, many came back there. A small, shifting, un-
disciplined population, they settled near their Masters, as they
had in Paris, and by the second half of the thirteenth century
they were more formally enrolled, often in 'Halls' under a
Regent Master. Cambridge was founded by a migration from
Oxford in 1209, during the Interdict imposed by Innocent III on
John; there were other migrations to Northampton and Salisbury
which did not take. The lives of these students are recalled in the
Goliardic poems – largely an English creation.

'*Nos vagabunduli, laeti, jucunduli*' they sang, '*Risu dissolvimur*
– we dissolve in laughter'. Already they drank all they could –
Angli caudati qui sunt ad pocula nati – English, with tails, born
for the bottle.[22]

These two independent typically medieval corporations, Oxford in the geographical centre of England, Cambridge a market
town in prosperous East Anglia, were not overshadowed by
London and the Court. Though many Oxford students, already
politically minded, supported Simon de Montfort by scurrilous
propaganda and even by arms, both universities were fostered by
successive Kings and cumulatively endowed by pious benefactors.

[22] See *Satirical Poets and Epigrammatists of the 12th Century*, ed. Thomas
Wright. Rolls Series, 2 vols.

Both were in meadowland, damp and hazy: indeed 'the climate of the old places of learning in England', it has been well observed, 'Eton, Winchester, Oxford and Cambridge, make one suspect that the Anglo-Saxons are so unbookish that they will only study when they are feeling slightly ill.'

But these mobs of Latin-speaking students had cosmopolitan horizons – the whole field of scholastic learning open to them – and their world is depicted in the first major work of English humour. The famous *Mirror of Fools* of Nigel of Canterbury anticipates the knockabout humour of Skelton and Butler's *Hudibras*.

'Once upon a time,' it begins, 'there was an ass with huge ears, who tried hard to have an equally long tail'[23] and though Dr. Gallienus insisted that he had a perfectly good one – King Louis of France hadn't a better – and that a longer tail would only get dirtier, the unconvinced and incorrigible ass, who was called Burnell, insisted on a prescription for a longer one, obtainable only at the medical school at Salerno. Hence a picaresque pilgrimage during which a monkey bit off half the tail. Undeterred, Burnell studied in the school at Paris and became a monk, until, reclaimed by his master, he again found his level. The sardonic humour is already recognisably English.

More seriously, in the new universities, small post-graduate colleges were now training an élite; at Oxford; Merton, University College and Balliol; at Cambridge; Pembroke, Gonville and Peterhouse. They taught not only theology, but Canon and Civil law. The Dominican and Franciscan friars came in: Grosseteste (c. 1175–1253), Chancellor of Oxford University and Bishop of Lincoln, was a patron of the Franciscans; he studied Greek to understand the Scriptures and the Fathers; he was also interested in optics and mathematics. Another Franciscan, his pupil Roger Bacon, though dominated by scholastic idiom and objectives, had an incongruously modern mind; he is the first Englishman concerned with applied science, a swallow who did not make a summer.

Born at Ilchester in Somerset, he studied at Oxford and in Paris, and survived much persecution. He knew Greek and was

[23]*Auribus immensis quondam donatus asellus,*
Institit ut caudam posset habere parem. (Op. cit., Vol. 1, p. 13.)

familiar with much of Aristotle, including the *Politics*; criticised the corrupt text of the Vulgate Bible, and even advocated experiment which 'tests by observation the lofty conclusions of all the sciences.' He speculated on lenses which would focus the sun and so burn up enemies at long range, 'for the perfect experimenter could destroy any hostile force by this combustion', and he foresaw that 'machines for navigating rivers' were 'possible without rowers.' 'Likewise,' he wrote, 'cars may be made so that without a draft animal they may be moved with inestimable impetus ... And flying machines are possible so that a man may sit in the middle turning some device by which artificial wings may beat the air in the manner of a flying bird.'[24]

William of Ockham, a Minorite Friar, also thinking in the scholastic idiom in the early fourteenth century, now developed the most characteristic tradition of English philosophy. He was a radical sceptic, insisting, like Hobbes, Locke and Berkeley, Mill and Russell, on the limitations of mind: '*entia*', he wrote, '*non sunt multiplicanda praeter necessitatem*' – entities should not be multiplied more than is necessary, a salutary maxim.

The historians, in the main, wrote in monasteries. Their Latin narratives are already vigorous, entertaining, discursive; even on occasion objective in the tradition of Bede; William of Malmesbury, Giraldus Cambrensis, Matthew Paris, Walter Map.

And there was by now a lively French-speaking court culture. The great were no longer, at least superficially, the ruffians of early Norman times, and their elegance was much imitated. 'Childer set to school', Higden's translator would write, 'after the coming of the Normans were compelled to construe French ... So much that the childer of noble men after they were taken from the cradle were set to learn their speech in French, whereupon churles, seeing that, laboured to speak French for all their might.'

French romances now elaborated the tales of King Arthur, popularised by Geoffrey of Monmouth in Stephen's time;

---

[24] *De Secretis Operibus*, quoted in Osborn Taylor's *The Mediaeval Mind*, Harvard and Oxford, 1959, Vol. II, pp. 532 and 538. Roger Bacon also indirectly influenced Columbus, who read, and acted upon, Cardinal Pierre d'Ailly's *Imago Mundi* which incorporated geographical theories from Bacon's *Opus Majus*.

Provençal and Aquitainian love songs, which came in with the southern foreigners detested by the more conservative barons, were fashionable at Henry III's Court.

But the future was with English, the rustic speech of the people, now simpler and enriched with French words. Books of devotion had never died out, and now religious and secular poetry adopted rhyming metres which the Anglo-Saxons never knew. The famous Cuckoo Song, composed in mid-thirteenth century Reading, then rural, evokes the land in spring.

> *Awe bleteth after lomb,*
> *Lhouth after calve cu.*

And the lyric

> *Blou northerne wynd*
> *Send thou my sueting*

has a pleasing lilt; while this verse of the reign of Edward I is already haunting:

> *Where be they that biforen us weren,*
> *Houndes ladden and havekes [hawks] beren,*
> *And hadden feld and wode?*

Chapter 4

Chaucer's England

S UCH were the lasting achievements of the medieval English, decisive for a future then unimaginable. They were made by a small minority, for most of the people were still peasants; *adscripti glebae*, bound to the soil by the routine of primitive agriculture; their 'silence can be heard'.

But by the thirteenth century this rural society was on the move; by the fourteenth, serfdom was becoming rare, and even the impact of the Black Death would improve the labourer's position. The English peasantry, though doomed in the long run, never lapsed into servile stagnation, often the curse of larger areas. They would remain for centuries a robust foundation for an expanding power, and when the Industrial Revolution transformed the country, their uprooted descendants would provide the manpower for a more dynamic England.

The Conqueror and his barons had exploited an already well-established civilisation; and it was now more wealthy and populous. A greatly expanded administration was already governing a society 'which was rapidly becoming richer, more varied and more settled . . . it was a world of great possibilities, but with no place for the economically naive.'[1]

The North had again become more prosperous and better controlled, and by the time of Edward I the population of England had probably doubled since the Conquest to three and a half million. As farming improved, the waste was colonised; already, even in the conservative South, the lord's demesne was generally compact; in many parts of England even twelfth century villeins were not all practising communal and conservative agriculture and crushed by manorial obligations. In East Anglia free peasants exploited their own farms, and in Kent the fruit crop was more important than wheat and barley. In the richer areas, indeed, the late thirteenth and early fourteenth centuries were 'a

[1] J. C. Holt, *Magna Carta*, pp. 27–9.

43

period of "high farming" when the great landlords were producing for the market on a large scale by the...intensive exploitation of their demesnes. Surviving records afford abundant
evidence of efficient estate management.'[2]

All sorts of things were sold besides cereal crops: 'stubble off
the corne lands, crops and setts of Withy'es, of osier rods, the
offal wood of old hedges, of butter cheese and milke, dunge and
soile, of bran, nuts, wax, honey and the like.'[3] England was, indeed, rich 'in corn and trees to be nourished, which is apt for
beasts, plentious of birds both in the sea and land of divers kinds,
and abundant in water full of fish, especially of pike and eels';
the fish so abundant that 'churls fed them to their pigs' and
with 'dolphynes and sea calues and baleynes, great fishes as it
were of whaleskynde.'[4]

The wool trade had been booming, with enormous flocks of
sheep on the downs and fenlands, as many as 16,000 or 20,000
on the estates of great abbeys; and there were now few 'wulphes',
though the main stock still lurked in Wales. Though liable to
local famine, to murrain, drought and flood, the high medieval
economy was often enterprising.

Already, too, the peasants had begun to stir: villeins and their
brood (*sequela*) could still be sold with the land; they were subject to death duties (often their best beast), to fines payable on
marriage – often to *leyrwite* payable if a girl had anticipated it;
to varying amounts of labour on demesne; but more men were
already buying themselves out: the enterprising, the lucky and
the laborious could rise in the world and the feckless and unlucky
go further down. Already the rising yeoman can be discerned as
well as the agricultural 'labourer'. Under Edward I 'the bonds
which held the villein to the soil were loosening almost everywhere, and the demarcation...into the three main strata, freeholders, tenant farmers and landless, or nearly landless, labourers
– which was to form the characteristic pattern of English society
until the end of the eighteenth century, is already clearly foreshadowed.'[5]

[2] M. McKisack, *The Fourteenth Century*, Clarendon Press, 1959, p. 315.
[3] Quoted ibid., p. 318.
[4] *Polychronicon Ranulfi Higden, Monachi Cestrensis*. English translation
by John of Trevisa and an anonymous fifteenth-century writer. Rolls Series,
Vol. II, p. 15. The writer is still beholden to Bede, op. cit., Bk. I, Ch. I.
[5] McKisack, op. cit., p. 341.

The English had long been united at least in a common passion for sport, even if most of them were officially excluded from it. Edward the Confessor in his casual way, had 'loved the coursing of swift hounds', but William the Conqueror had been obsessed by hunting. Following continental, originally Carolingian, fashion, he had created the 'New Forest' in Hampshire, a huge acreage, not all of it marginal land. Under the Angevins, Grovely, Chute and Clarendon in Wiltshire were forest; Savernake survives, its glades recalling 'great kings a-hunting the tall antlered deer'; Cranborne Chase, Bere, and all Purbeck in Dorset were forest. Huge areas of the fenland in Cambridgeshire and Huntingdonshire were forest; Mendip and Exmoor in the west. From Windsor the Kings could ride through unbroken royal forest to the Hampshire sea; Arden and Epping and Sherwood belonged to them, and in all this area the writ of the Common Law did not run.

The forest laws were, indeed, royal and arbitrary. Hunting, shared by all the privileged classes including the heartier clergy, stocked the larders of the itinerant Court; hence in part the ferocity of the forest laws. Deer and wild boars were the 'noble' beasts of chase, but rights of 'warren', to take hares and rabbits and keep down vermin, were eagerly sought. The verderers and game wardens who protected 'vert' and 'venison' were an unpopular crew, apt to bully the villagers, and enforce savage penalties on those who defiantly or secretly poached the game. One of the strongest grievances against John was the abuse of the forest laws by his officials.

Yet in England there never developed the fantastically artificial and elaborate rituals of many continental hunts, with their tariffs of kinds of game to be taken by the nobility in their degrees; and all the English, when they could, shared a rough camaraderie of sport, for large areas were beyond the control of the King and the great lords, and if one man was a verderer, another was a poacher. Most of those who could afford it also shared in the English cult of the horse. Riding was almost the universal means of transport, as among Chaucer's Canterbury Pilgrims, and it contributed, as in other civilisations, to the vigour of a pre-industrial society.

II

This prosperity and expansion of the high middle ages was checked by the recession which hit Western Europe during the fourteenth century, by the successive onslaughts of pneumonic and bubonic plague, by taxation for Edward III's Continental wars, and by popular revolt and heresy. The 'Black Death' – a contemporary term – originated in China, and came to Messina on the fleas of infected black rats in Genoese galleys from Asia Minor in 1347: from Messina it came to Pisa, and next year it was raging in Florence (where it occasioned Boccaccio's *Decameron*) and in France; by August it was in Weymouth, Dorset. The doctors were helpless; the considered but unhelpful opinion of the faculty of Paris was elaborately astrological, and since 'the Church abhorred blood', dissection had long been officially forbidden. There were no remedies save prayer or flight, both unreliable. By autumn the plague was in London and by the spring of 1349, in Norwich; it raged in Bristol and Somerset and the West Midlands. A second visitation followed in 1361-2, deadly to the children, and another, seven years after. The population was probably halved.

Naturally this disaster hastened social change: the shortage of labour became acute, wages nearly doubled; land went out of cultivation and whole demesnes were let on lease. Many villeins, surviving and immune, bought up cattle and goods cheaply; evaded their obligations or decamped, setting up for themselves; when landlords tried to enforce the old services, the peasants would open the sluices and drown the hay or leave the harvest to rot. It was against this background of recession, dislocation, social discontent and opportunity, and of taxes touching all, that a new aspect of England appeared – peasant and Lollard subversion, a prelude to later radicalism.

The Peasant Revolt of 1381 was all over in a month and mainly confined to East Anglia, the East Midlands and Kent; but it foreshadowed a new militant, proletarian, side of English life. It was made more against social than economic oppression, against foreigners and the higher clergy and unpopular advisers round the King – not against the monarchy itself. For the first time the peasantry became articulate, but not for long. Like the seventeenth-century Levellers, they were quickly outmanoeuvred when the establishment had pulled itself together.

The political background of the Revolt explains much. During the minority of Richard II, government had long been in a bad way. Half a century before, the old struggle of King and magnates to control an intrinsically strong administration had worsened; Edward II, large, handsome and lazy, had liked ease and his drink and doing things with his hands; he kept company with actors, *jongleurs*, thatchers, watermen and 'mechanics'. Apt to 'smite men for little trespass', he had declared that he 'would not have his servants chosen for him as if he were a lunatic'; and he had been susceptible to fascinating favourites – as Piers Gaveston, Earl of Cornwall; 'reckless' too, of Isabelle the Queen, well termed 'she-wolf of France'. Imprisoned in Berkeley Castle, which commanded the mouth of the Severn, he had been put down with 'a hoate broche (spit)...thro' the secret place posterialle.'[6] But many people thought him a martyr, and he lies under a fine effigy in Gloucester Cathedral, long an attraction for pilgrims.

His son Edward III, at seventeen, had hanged his mother's paramour Roger Mortimer, Earl of March, and proved a splendid, chivalrous and insolvent prince, the most popular of the Plantagenets: his bearded effigy in Westminster Abbey recalls the famous victories in France which marked the first phase of the Hundred Years' War. He founded the Order of the Garter, and rebuilt Windsor Castle in lavish style. But he sired too many children and fell into an early dotage; the fifteenth century would be made politically hideous by his descendants' feuds.

More significantly for the future, Parliament had become more important – in particular the '*communities*' or 'Commons', the main source of money. By 1336 they had demanded the repeal of a wool tax made '*saunz assent de la commune ou des Graundz*'.[7] They had been still entirely deferential to the aristocratic Council and the magnates; but by 1360 Lords and Commons had become distinct, the latter meeting separately in the Chapter House at Westminster with an 'Orator' (Speaker) of their own. In 1376 the first case of impeachment by the Commons had been tried by

[6] Higden, trans., op. cit., p. 325. Officially he had 'removed himself from the Government of the said realm by spontaneous wish '.

[7] McKisack, op. cit., p. 193.

the Lords: 'the classic distinction between the French *parlement*
– a body of professional lawyers – and the English Parliament – a
body of amateur politicians – is already clearly foreshadowed in
the reign of Edward III.'[8]

The royal Government had, of course, continued: 'The Commons did not want responsible Government or anything so
refined as this; they wanted good, honest, and, in particular, economical government by the King, and they thought the Council
the best means of ensuring it.'[9] They could sustain criticism, and
make difficulties over supply, but constitutional aspirations did
not yet exist.

III

Good, honest and economical government was not to be had
during the dotage of Edward III or the minority of Richard II.
The Poll tax which set off the Peasants' Revolt had roused everyone; not merely the freeholders, but those militant men, the
butchers (*carnifices, Johannes Bocher et uxor eius*) and the black-
smiths, as well as fullers, hedgers and ditchers, shepherds and
laborarii – John Trumpe, Thos. Yunge, John Drane and Walter
Mustard.[10] Tax returns were so badly cooked as to be farcical,
and in Kent tax gatherers replied by inspecting the girls to see if
they were virgins, for, if not, they were liable to tax. The preaching of itinerant Friars advocating social revolution also inflamed
the people.

In modern terms, the peasants were not, of course, communists; they wanted to be *kulaks*. They desired to remove the 'yoke
of servitude and villeinage', declared that they were 'for King
Richard and the True Commons', and tried to justify their revolution under forms of law. They seemed to have shown some
regional, even tribal, feeling, as in Anglo-Saxon times, and the
leaders may even have had vague ambitions to set up as regional
'kings'. The first risings were in Kent and Essex, but there were
big revolts in Suffolk, when the Prior of Bury St. Edmunds was

[8] McKisack, ibid.

[9] A. L. Brown, 'The Commons and the Council in the reign of Henry IV',
English Historical Review, January 1964.

[10] See Oman, *The Great Revolt of 1381*, Oxford, 1906, Appendix III, on
Essex Poll Tax returns.

hunted down in a wood near Newmarket and beheaded at Mildenhall; and Geoffrey Litster, a dyer from North Walsham in Norfolk, collected a great mob on Mousehold heath and dined in state in Norwich Castle. He did not last long, for Bishop Despencer got after him with a small but well found force and charged the rebels conclusively *'velut aper* – like a wild boar'.

The events in London are the most illuminating. The Kentish peasants, in conjunction with those from Essex, were led by an ex-soldier, Wat Tyler or Teghler, and by John Balle, a 'mad priest' who coined the notorious jingle

> *When Adam dalf and Eve span,*
> *Who was thenne a gentilman?*

They got into the City, where the merchant oligarchy were hated by the lesser craftsmen and apprentices; they camped outside the Tower itself, their bonfires glowing by Norman walls. The boy-King Richard II, his mother the widow of the Black Prince, and the detested Chancellor, Simon of Sudbury, Archbishop of Canterbury, were beleaguered inside.

The authorities were strangely helpless and supine. Richard, who was fourteen, had already parleyed with the rebels from a barge off Greenwich, and he now met the Essex peasants at Mile End, hoping to draw them off. Here, again, they made limited and precise demands: that serfdom be abolished, the game laws abrogated and that villeins should become tenants for rent. When other peasants got into the Tower, they only pulled the guards' beards; told them that 'all men were brothers' and that they merely wanted to punish the government. And when they destroyed John of Gaunt's Savoy palace, packed with the loot of France, got drunk and lay about under walls 'like hogs', and beheaded the Archbishop (the inexpert executioner took eight strokes to kill this well-intentioned man) and stuck his mitred head over London Bridge, they still protested that they only wanted to chastise evil counsellors and the vices of the rich. They already voiced a very English radical moral indignation – especially acute when plundering one's neighbour – and they hated foreigners and lawyers. So they killed Flemings, if they said 'brod and case' instead of 'bread and cheese' as the peasants pronounced them (however that was), and pursued elderly lawyers who proved 'agile as rats'.[11] Incited by idealistic Friars, they also attacked the wealth of the Church – 'Clerkes for welth' they said, 'werke hem wo'; or 'stonde manlyche togedyr in trewth', and 'God do bote (right) for now is tyme'. In the Delphic utterances of the leaders, 'Jakke Straw, Jakke Milner, Jakk Carter', the same signal runs – '*now is tyme*'.

The climax came in the cattle-market at Smithfield, dominated by the spirited young King, whose presence of mind saved himself and his company. Wat Tyler demanded that the huge Church estates should be given to the people; that all but one of the bishoprics be abolished and '*seigneurie proportioné entre tous genz*' – save for the Lord King. As Richard II parried these demands, Tyler laid hands on his bridle; then struck at the Lord Mayor, who at once cut him down. The rebel was then run through, deftly, by John Standwick, one of the King's squires, knighted that evening. Tyler had been arguing about the game laws, and how 'all warrens both for water and parks should be free for all, as much for the poor as the rich, and that they should take fish and game in all of them and course hares.'[12]

When Tyler collapsed, the peasant bowmen could have riddled the royal cavalcade, but young Richard spurred forward right hand raised, shouting 'Sirs, will you shoot your King? *I* will lead you.' They at once began to move off quietly behind him – 'like sheep' says one chronicler – while the belated forces of law and order deployed to contain them. Richard then told the 'stupid multitude' to disperse and ordered mercy, though, later on, in Essex, he remarked 'Villeins you are and villeins you will remain.' Finally, as King-in-Parliament, he had all the bogus charters he had issued rescinded. Not for the last time, popular revolution in England had failed.[13]

---

[11] *Tanta agilitate ascenderunt atsi essent ratones. Chronicon Henrici Knighton Monachi Cestrensis*, ed. J. R. Lumby, Vol. II, Rolls Series, 1895.

[12] Knighton, op. cit., p. 137. It was hot in mid-June, and Tyler, on horseback, had tossed a dagger from hand to hand – *Cultellum quem 'dagger' vulgus vocant, quasi pueriliter ludens*, before washing out his mouth 'coarsely' and downing a flagon of ale.

[13] The Parliament at Cambridge in 1388 decreed that the statutes of '*artificiers et laborers servaunts et vitayllers*' be '*fermement tenus gardes et duement executez*'; the peasants were not allowed to move from one hundred to another without licence, and anyone who had been a labourer up to twelve years old had to remain one – '*il demoure a tele labour sans estre mys au mystiere ou artifice*'. Knighton, op. cit., p. 303.

The Peasant Revolt is, of course, paralleled in more ferocious outbreaks abroad, Jacqueries in France and social upheavals in Italy also caused by dislocation and recession; but in England revolt was not communist or anarchic: already the English tried to remain respectable while making a revolution. Nor was the government's revenge ferocious by the standards of the time: Tyler's head replaced the Archbishop's on London Bridge, and Balle was hanged, drawn and quartered at St. Albans by the young King's express command; but no more than two hundred victims suffered, and most of them after due trial.

Another characteristic side of the revolt was popular hatred for learning and of 'intellectuals' as such. Already by 1355 in Oxford a mob of peasants under a black flag had tried to sack the university, crying 'Havoc!'; now, at Cambridge, town attacked gown. They sacked Corpus Christi College, a Lancastrian foundation which owned much house property, and burnt the university archives in the market place, 'a certain old woman named Margery Starre crying "Away with the learning of clerks! away with it!"'.

IV

In religion the critics of society were more constructive, and ideas more decisive for the future were put about. English puritanism, that world-influence, can already be discerned in the writings of Wycliffe and the Lollards – so called from the Flemish 'loellers' – mumblers. There had been discontent with the wealthy clergy in the twelfth and thirteenth centuries, expressed in many ribald and bawdy rhymes; but it was Wycliffe and his backers who first made it politically important, and who supervised the new translation of the Bible – the first since the Conquest – which now made the whole book available. He came from the Yorkshire estates of John of Gaunt, Duke of Lancaster, and since he declared that 'temporal lords might confiscate the goods of an habitually delinquent church', he won strong political support, for Lancaster in particular was against the great churchmen in the Government and had an eye on their property.

The hard doctrines of this early and all too dynamic Balliol man, whose love of paradox made him declare on occasion 'God had to obey the devil', were widely influential.[14] They foreshadow Calvin's ideas rather than Luther's, for Wycliffe discerned a predestined 'elect'; he also defied the authority of Rome – he even exhorted Parliament to renounce obedience – and attacked the orthodox belief in transubstantiation, claiming a spiritual but not a material presence in the sacrament: 'I knowleche that the sacrament of the auter is verray Goddus body in fourme of brede; but is in another manner Godus body than it is in hevene.'[15]

Wycliffe was a formidable scholar, but his Lollard followers, in plain russet garments and vowed to poverty, attacked the universities, the cult of saints and the artistic splendours of the Church. Their revolutionary views are expressed in *Conclusions for the reform of the Church of England (Ecclesiae Angliae)* that they affixed to the great door of St. Paul's in 1395.[16] The Church, they wrote, was 'blind and leprous' through the pride of its prelates – a *superbia* following the example of its 'stepmother' in Rome. It had become 'crazed with temporal riches', and faith, hope and charity were all gone; nor did the Papacy and its ritual represent the priesthood ordained by Christ for the Apostles. Further, clerical celibacy led to vice (*inducit sodomiam in totam Sanctam Ecclesiam* – experience proved it); indeed, if churchmen lived so high, they needed 'necessary purgation ... natural or worse.'

Next, they argued, even contradicting St. Thomas, that the 'feigned miracle' of the sacramental bread led to idolatry, and the blessings and exorcisms pronounced over bread and wine, buildings, vestments and even pilgrims' staves, were mere 'necromancy': this, too, was proved by experience, since the water blessed for curing illness did not work. Prelates, they declared, should not hold temporal office; no man could serve two masters, and they were no better than political 'hermaphrodites'. Special prayers for individual souls were also pernicious, and the whole realm could be prayed for much more cheaply *en masse*. Naturally they were iconoclasts, to whom the 'usual image of the Trinity was especially abominable', and confession led to lechery

---

[14] '*Confusio vulgi, hereticorum idolum, hypocriticarum speculum, schistmatis incentor, odii seminator, mendacii fabricator, J. de Wiclif.*'

[15] Knighton, op. cit., p. 158.

[16] *Annales Richardi Secundi, Regis Angliae*, ed. H. T. Riley. Rolls Series, 1866, pp. 174–82. All is set out scholastically: *conclusio, ratio*, and corollaries.

('*wooing*') and mortal sin. War, even through legal pretexts, was contrary to the New Testament; particularly as most men, after the first blow, lost their tempers, and so, if killed, went straight to hell.

The Lollards then turned, with some relish, to vice in nunneries: hotbeds of abortion, contraception, lesbianism and worse – sins all inevitably punished in hell. Finally, there were far too many *unnecessary* fine arts in the realm, which led to sins of '*Wast*' and '*disgising*' (fashion): these arts all ought to be abolished.

These conclusions, they said, were mere summaries; they had set them out much more fully in books in 'our own language' (*in nostro 'langage' proprio*); they implored God of His infinite mercy for radical reform. Here, it would seem, the Nonconformist Conscience was already alert.

V

The political crises of Richard II's reign – in part a sequel to the strain of the Hundred Years' War on the economy and on morale – centred, as before, on the control of the powerful administration; a conflict stepped up by the intelligent yet unstable personality of the King and by the ambitions and discontents of his variously repellent uncles. But the conflict led to a defeat of arbitrary royal power, decisive for England. The gallant boy of Smithfield became an early modern tyrant; neurotic, introspective and revengeful – so 'treacherous', said his enemies, that he was 'a disgrace to the whole realm.' Nor was he interested in campaigns in France. Artistic and extravagant – 'he kept the greatest port and maintained the most plentiful house that ever any King of England did . . .' He was also far too sensitive: brought back the body of his favourite, Robert de Vere, Earl of Oxford, who had been exiled in the Low Countries; opened his coffin, contemplated his friend's face, stroked the fingers and adorned them with jewels before a splendid reburial. He 'wallowed', it was said, in adulation; 'snorted' with rage; had his uncle Gloucester suffocated under down pillows and the Earl of Arundel decapitated: significantly, the headless trunk jumped to its feet and stood there 'for the length of the saying of the Lord's

Prayer.' He declared, with 'a harsh and arrogant countenance that the laws were in his own mouth, or sometimes, in his own breast';[17] he tried to pack Parliament; formed a corps of Cheshire archers and attacked property by 'arbitrary will';[18] he had become 'dangerous, perhaps dangerously mad.' Like others after him in England, he had to go.

For when his cousin, Henry of Lancaster, eldest son of John of Gaunt, 'challenged' the Crown, Richard was outmanoeuvred and tricked. The temperamental *quondam* King was confined to Pontefract Castle, where he was probably pole-axed after killing four of his assailants; though, in the official version, he 'fell into such a melancholy' that he refused to eat. His body was brought to London, the face exposed 'from the lower forehead to the neck': he had been only thirty-three.

So ended another attempt at royal tyranny in England and the elder line of the Plantagenets as well, leaving a vendetta that lasted into Tudor times. Richard II is better commemorated by the Wilton Diptych, which portrays him as an eager youth; by the magnificent full-length portrait in Westminster Abbey; and by Westminster Hall, rebuilt by his orders from Rufus' foundation.

The revolution was, of course, no 'constitutional' exploit. It was still not from the estates of the realm, sitting *qua* Parliament, that the sanction was invoked. On that October day of 1400, the throne in Westminster Hall stood vacant, covered with cloth of gold, for Richard had handed over his signet to the Archbishop: but the assembly was a convention of the estates, not a Parliament. Lancaster strode to the throne, took his seat, and was 'acclaimed'. There was no question of a Parliamentary title; he rather avoided it, though in his 'hasty and dubious proceeding', he was glad of the 'acclaim', with magnates and the estates to hand. The real right was of conquest and descent; indeed, the new-crowned Henry IV is said to have muttered to Sir Thomas Dymoke, the Royal Champion, 'If need be Sir Thomas, I will in my own person ease thee of thy office.'[19]

Richard II himself, when deposed, had no illusions. A deputa-

[17] *Annales*, op. cit., p. 267.
[18] McKisack, op. cit., p. 497.
[19] See E. F. Jacob, *The Fifteenth Century*, Clarendon Press, Oxford, 1961, pp. 16–19.

tion told him that the decision was 'not oneliche owre wurdes bute the wurdes and the doyng of all the states of this lond', so that they had full authority and 'plene powers'; but he replied tartly that 'he knew quite well they would say nothing but what they had been told to (wiste well that we wolde nought sey but as we were charged).' There was thus no Lancastrian constitutional experiment, but a collusive whitewashing of a necessary political crime. If, however, Henry IV did not claim his title from the law, he promised, in English, to enforce it:

'In the name of God,' he said, 'I, Henry of Lancastre, challenge this reiaume, this the corone, with alle the membris and the appurtenaunce therto, als that I am descendit be ryght line of the blode comyng of the Kyng Henry, and thorghe that ryght that Gode of hys grace hath sent me, with the help of my kyn and of my frendes, to recovere it; the which roiaume was in poynt to ben undon, for defaute of governaunce and the undoyng of the lawes.'

As William of Orange would do after him, he promised to respect property: 'Syres I thank yoe, espirituelx and temporelx, and all the estates of the lond, and y do yow to wyte that it ys nought my wil that no man think that by wey of conquest y wolde desherte any man of hys heritage . . . exept hem that han ben ageyn the gode purpos and the commune profyte of the reiaulme.'[20] The Lord Chief Justice had advised that any attack on property would infuriate the English (*Commovisset bilem totius populi contra eum*), and one of the main charges against Richard II had been that he 'most tyrannously and unprincely said that the lives and goods of all his subjects were in his hands.'[21] Murderous as had been the conflict and packed the assemblies, respect for at least the forms of law and for property is already plain.

VI

Against this political and social background, Middle English literature had greatly developed. The prose of Wycliffe and his

---

[20] *Annales*, pp. 281–2. With grand casualness the word for 'realm' is spelt three different ways.

[21] *Holinshed Chronicles*, Oxford, 1923, p. 34.

collaborators is vivid, the French words acclimatised, as in his sermon on the Prodigal son. 'And he seide to him, Thy brother is comen, and they fadir hath slayn a fat calf, for he hath receyved him ssaf. But this eldere sone hadde dedeyn (disdain) and wolde not come in; therefore his fadir wente out, and began to preie him. And he answeride, and seide to his fadir, Lo, so many yeeris y serve to thee, y passide never thi mandement; and thou gavest me never a kide for to fede me with my frendis.' The passage concludes with a fine cadence: 'For he, this thi brothir was deed and lyvede agen; he was perished and is founden.'

Middle English poetry reached its climax in Chaucer, a highly sophisticated courtier and man of business, who had travelled in France and Italy and was the first major poet in the language, unequalled until Shakespeare. As a narrative poet Chaucer is unsurpassed, and his insight into character, expressed often with a quiet irony, would have made him, in a different context, a master of the novel. This kind of insight would be expressed in their various idioms by Fielding, Jane Austen, Dickens and Hardy: it was to be one of the most characteristic achievements of English writers.

Chaucer is of European stature; a great craftsman in language, a subtle master of characterisation: he is unobtrusively accurate and deftly casual, getting effects with deliberate artistry. Bilingual in French and English, he knew both court and city, and he was as familiar with the latest Italian literature as with French and Latin poetry. He depicts for all time the panorama of late fourteenth century England, a cross-section of the society he knew well. And the types are already recognisable; set down with a tolerant understanding and humour which shows how mature his age could be; vigorous and confident, for all the political and social upheavals which had made the characters admired by Chaucer – the courteous Knight, the poor Parson, the honest Ploughman – already rare. Not that the poet grudges his jolly monk his good living,

A fat swan loved he best of any roost;

or the Prioress her French accent of Stratford-atte-Bowe; or the wife of Bath the pleasures of her youth: she was glad, she said, rightly,

'That I have had my world as in my time.'

He depicts with tolerance and relish most of the characters since thought typical of England as they jog along the chalk downs to Canterbury in the restless spring when *longen folk to go on pilgrimages.*

The discontent of the peasantry found a different voice in that haunting poet, probably John Langland, who wrote *Piers Plowman.* Here the Old English alliterative verse was adapted to a mystical, often profound, vision of society in a phase of social upheaval.

> *In a somer seson Whan soft was the sonne . . .*

the poem begins,

> *I was wery forwandred And went me to reste*
> *Under a brode banke At a bornes side.*

That May morning on Malvern Hills has lasted; and the closing petition

> *God give us grace here Ar we gone heunes*

expressed the Old English concern to set things to rights.

Chapter 5

Bastard Feudalism and Renaissance Kingship

THE politics of England from the usurpation of Henry of Lancaster, the invasions of France under Henry V and the confusion under Henry VI, to the revival of the monarchy under Edward IV hardly foreshadow the English genius for compromise. Under Henry V there was martial glory; under Henry VI aristocratic factions exploited the administration and the law; they invoked the argument familiar from the thirteenth century until the time of Henry VIII, that Conciliar government should be run by the magnates as of right; not by royal 'favourites' or abler upstarts of 'villein blood'. The King was expected to maintain 'good governance', but without the wherewithal to do so; and the magnates who were exploiting the confusion to 'bring the realm again into good order.'

Central and local government were thus terrorised and perverted by 'overmighty subjects' and their 'affinities'; they packed parliaments and jumped estates with the connivance of local juries, overawed or squared. It was only after Edward IV and Henry VII had put down these dynastic and local vendettas that effective government was gradually restored, the basis of successful Tudor administration.

The social, economic and cultural aspects of the age proved more important for the future: the increasing power of the lesser landowners and the townspeople; the rise of the great City companies and the expansion of London, Norwich, Bristol, Southampton and the rest; the growing prosperity of the yeomen; the use of English more like our own than the Middle English of Chaucer, and, later, the spread of a humanist Renaissance culture through print. This early modern age of foreign and civil war saw the foundation of the most famous English colleges and schools: Winchester and New College, Oxford, had been founded by William of Wykeham in the reign of Richard II; All Souls at Oxford by Archbishop Chichele in 1438 and Magdalen by Wayneflete twenty years after; King's College Cambridge by Henry VI in 1441, and 'the King's College of our Lady at Eton beside Windsor' the year after. The tone of the sumptuous Burgundian-influenced Court of Edward IV was urban and Renaissance; Henry VII, for all his business acumen, was a splendid prince, a patron of art and architecture; and the Court of the young Henry VIII was a brilliant centre of Erasmian learning. Cardinal Wolsey, that last corrupt and splendid embodiment of the old order, would found Cardinal College, to be developed by Henry VIII into Christ Church, Oxford; and Henry VIII would prove the greatest of all the royal patrons of learning, for he also founded Trinity at Cambridge, amalgamating King's Hall with Michaelhouse and adding a lavish endowment.

II

By the early fifteenth century the more enterprising English were a martial and predatory people, long seasoned in the wars in France. The Anglo-Saxons had not invaded Normandy; the Normans had invaded them: now, under a warrior aristocracy, led and conciliated by the glamorous and insolvent Edward III, the English had long diverted energies that would later find scope in sea power and colonisation to the plunder of France. This militant aspect of late medieval England, often forgotten in the affluent society whose citizens would not dream of attacking anyone, is paralleled in the record of the once ferocious but since exemplary Scandinavians. The tradition then created is behind the Elizabethans, and the eighteenth century and Victorian empires; and behind the sudden, unexpected, English capacity, when roused after decades of muddling through, to fight to a finish and win.

The glamour of war and heraldry, of shining plate armour, caparisoned horses and fluttering pennons, was stamped upon the English mind; but war had now become a business, with plunder and ransom as its dividends. Indentured service for pay, with elaborate provisions for sharing ransom and loot, had long superseded feudal arrangements; Edward III had got gigantic sums in ransoms and there was so much aristocratic protest when Henry V ordered the massacre of the valuable prisoners at Agincourt that two hundred common archers had to be detailed to do it.

The areas of France controlled by the English under the treaty concluded at Brétigny near Chartres in 1360, had been immense; the rich Poitevine country inland from La Rochelle, itself the great centre of the salt-trade; Bordeaux, the biggest Atlantic port, with the sunny vineyards of the Bordelais behind it; deeper into France, Angoulême and Périgueux and Limoges, the valleys of Dordogne and Garonne; Gascony, rich in wine and fighting men, if not in much else. Calais, Boulogne, and Ponthieu were springboards for attacks made in alliance with the cloth manufacturing cities of Flanders and with opulent Burgundy; the strategic basis for the Hundred Years' War. Rheims, even Paris, could lie open; and the Cotentin, opposite Southampton, the best southern English port, invited the invasion of Normandy, the wide cornlands of the Beauce and the valley of the Loire. No wonder that warriors, still half-continentals themselves, accustomed to the brilliant light and the luxuries of the richest areas of France, should turn their backs on the foggy island and, before these rich prospects, attempt the impossible. The classic remedy for discontent became another *chevauché* in France, an attempt on Rouen or Paris; although, after Agincourt, Henry V forbade his battle-dinted helmet to be borne in the procession to St. Paul's and ascribed the glory to God, he was acclaimed a popular hero.

The long war had begun in Cadzand and Sluys, commanding the mouth of the Scheldt and of the then navigable Zwyn; Sluys, a naval battle, had been won unchivalrously by archers and men-at-arms – '*moult orible*' says Froissart. Then in August 1346, at Crécy-en-Ponthieu, the French knights had charged into the evening sun with about as much chance as the infantry of the Somme in 1917 would have against machine guns and high explosive; they had been mown down by the Welsh weapon, the swift, cumulative arrow-storm, deadly even at two hundred yards. The blind John of Luxembourg and Bohemia, that pattern of knighthood, had fallen; while the Black Prince had annexed his ostrich feathers and the motto *Ich dien* – an exotic crest. His victory near Poitiers, after he had ravaged from Narbonne to the Loire, had been equally spectacular and more profitable – the French King himself captured and the ransoms unsurpassed.

Then had come anti-climax. Incompetent and corrupt governments, first of the ageing Edward III, then under the boy Richard II, had lost most of the French territories. But the Lancastrian usurpers had soon renewed the war; even Henry VIII would still be hankering for French conquests a century after; and if the future of England would be on the far oceans, naturally these rulers could not see it. Nor were they the kind of visionaries to do so; Henry IV's nephew, Dom Henriques of Portugal, with his eye on the West African shore and the Atlantic islands, now seems wiser than his cousin, Henry V; but the hard Lancastrian realists knew politically what they were about, when, taking advantage of the Burgundian-Armagnac wars, they again loosed their countrymen on the French.

For Henry IV had won a precarious kingship, crippled by debt and harassed by conspiracies: there was still danger from Scotland; the Welsh, under Owen Glendower, were again up in arms.[1] The new King, indeed, had a nervous breakdown by 1405; by 1411, when the first expedition left for France, he was too ill to go; he long fought a disgusting illness which he considered a punishment for his sins, and medieval doctors did the rest. By 1413 Henry IV was dead; not, as he had hoped, in Jerusalem itself, but in the Jerusalem chamber at Westminster.

His son Henry V was not the bluff patriot king of Shakespeare's plays; he was a dour and martial fanatic, obsessed by religion and his legal rights. He was the first heir apparent to attend a university, for he went to the Queen's College, Oxford, under the charge of his Beaufort uncle, later Cardinal of Winchester, whose resplendent effigy, hatted and robed, still lies in his cathedral. Seasoned in the Welsh wars, Henry V was also an

---

[1] The reign began in a sinister atmosphere. In 1402 the Welsh used 'magical devices'; their women committed obscene atrocities on the dead, and even the King was swamped out of his tent by the rain. The populace, that year, were terrified by appalling thunderstorms and the Devil appeared in Essex – *Diabolus quoque species visibiliter apparuit in Estsexia* – jumped on the altar and vanished, not with a melodious twang, but with an intolerable stench. *Annales*, p. 340.

expert and lucky soldier; *belliger quoque insignis et fortunatus*, with an unusual grasp of problems of logistics and supply. Though his contemporary Walsingham says he was 'suddenly changed into another man'[2] after his coronation (in an April snowstorm), he was not, it seems, a wild youth; indeed historic- ally 'the Boar's Head Tavern with all its engaging scalliwags will have to go.' If he could 'take a wilde bucke or doe at large in a park' without hounds, he loved music and had the fine man- ners of a great continental lord; he was 'certainly not the tradi- tional Englishman; there is something of an Este or a Gonzaga about Henry.'[3]

Henry IV, apparently guilt-ridden, once told his confessor that he could not renounce the throne because 'his childer would not suffer the regalye to go out of our lineage', and Henry V always particularly stressed his 'just rights' – at home and abroad. And immediately, his new attack on France harmonised the aristo- cratic Council and increased the much-needed 'coherence of the upper and middle ranks of society under the determined direc- tion of the monarchy';[4] more importantly, in the long term it created a patriotic legend fostered by the Tudors, which would long affect England. And indeed the Agincourt *chevauché* of 1415 was a memorable exploit, if a near thing. It was conducted with two thousand men-at-arms, six thousand archers, and some German master gunners, against forty or fifty thousand French, who again, stupidly enough, as at Crécy, attacked, instead of letting the English escape ingloriously to Calais. Henry V did not use Shakespeare's splendid rhetoric; he told his troops to avoid the mud; to 'see what could be done by swords and arrows in strong hands', and fought, himself, like a tiger. 'He was the first to fly at the enemy, and in his own person gave and took cruel

---

[2] Op. cit., p. 290.

[3] E. F. Jacob, *The Fifteenth Century*, Oxford, 1961, p. 126. The story of his escapades derives from the reminiscences of his contemporary, James, fourth Earl of Ormonde (d. 1452). These were incorporated, over sixty years later in 1513, by an anonymous translator of his official Latin biography, which had been written by Tito Livio of Forlì in 1437–8. Since, said the Tudor translator, Henry VIII had entered into 'semblable war against the Frenchmen', he had 'paind himself' to reduce the book into 'rude and holme English': in the process, he embellished the narrative. And the real Sir John *Fastolf* was a hard-bitten and successful soldier. See C. L. Kings- ford, *The First English Life of Henry V*, Oxford, 1911.

[4] Jacob, op. cit., p. 121.

blows.'[5] He got himself crowned in Paris, 'to set the two realms in coherent order', and he died with his thoughts on a crusade. But the Parisians who mocked the English and their fox-brush badges as they withdrew from the city, probably knew that Henry's ambitions had always been impracticable; even had the 'camp fever' not killed him, he could never have held France. He left a *damnosa hereditas* for the infant Henry VI.

After the judicial murder of Joan of Arc for alleged witchcraft, mainly to discredit the recent coronation of the new French King, there followed long disastrous campaigns and more intimate tragedy. Henry V's marriage to the Princess Katherine of France, rather tediously romanticised by Shakespeare, had brought in a strain of madness from the tainted Valois stock, and Henry VI proved intermittently imbecile.[6] So in disaster ended the Hundred Years' War. Yet it left a tradition of past glory and of the naval power of Henry V:

> *At Hampton he made the great dromons,*
> *The Trinite, the Grace Dieu, the Holy Goste.*

III

Another tradition, strengthened during the fifteenth century, to be politically reinforced under Edward IV and the Tudors, was very different. Over most of Western Europe the towns were pulling out of the economic depression of the fourteenth century, and laymen were taking a much more important share in government. Fortescue's *Governaunce of England*, written in English by a layman, not like the *Policraticus* in Latin by a cleric, has modern objectives – solvency, not chivalric panache; routine and foresight, not glory; insularity, not mirages of cosmopolitan domination and crusades; government under law, not by its bastard feudal perversion. It is significant also that in spite of the abuses described, 'by the end of the Middle Ages trial by jury

---

[5] *primus in hostes advolet, crudeles ictus infert et tolerat ... in persona propria*, Walsingham, p. 313.

[6] His grandfather, Charles VI, had fallen into a sudden frenzy and attacked those about him, until, says the chronicler, 'ingeniously tied up'. He would bite his own arms, and, particularly in hot weather, rush out into his orchard and hack down the trees until tired out.

had taken a deep root in the English system and had already become the theme of national boasting.[7]

Fortescue, that aged and experienced Lancastrian Lord Chief Justice, writing in the reign of Edward IV and anxious to make his peace with the Yorkists, wrote the first major work of political theory in English, and it is full of good sense. He wants to reform the Council, too long dominated by the magnates; record its proceedings in a book 'kept as a register or ordinarye'; make the King a solvent and efficient 'public power'; keep judges independent and impartial; see how 'the going out of the money may be restrained and bullyon brought into the lande'. He wants to augment sea power, and glorifies the masterly Edward IV 'who hath done more for us than ever did Kyng of Ingland'.[8] Fortescue wants government with consent of the estates of the realm and expresses a long habit of insular scorn at arbitrary rule and peasant poverty in France: 'thai drinke water, thai eaten apples, with brede right browne made of rye... But blessed be God, this land is ruled under better law.'

He represents not only the law but the substantial landowners and merchants, long so important in English life. The merchant oligarchies of London, Bristol, Norwich and Southampton – after Edward IV's accession at a new height of prosperity – now had a more powerful influence in English affairs; England was never, as Napoleon alleged, a 'nation of shopkeepers', but she was already producing an oligarchy of merchants and bankers with civic and maritime interests; working hand in glove with the great landowners, and, like them, beginning to accumulate the capital which would make the Industrial Revolution possible, and give the island the start over all competitors in the early nineteenth century.

These robust and high-living citizens and their wives, in their furs and velvets, their chains of office and snug, well-found houses, were much akin to the *haute bourgeoisie* of Antwerp and the Low Countries with whom they did their main business and conducted their main competition. In closer alliance with the great landowning peers and squirearchy, their descendants would

[7] Maitland, *The Constitutional History of England*, C.U.P. (1920 ed.), p. 213.
[8] See the Oxford edition by C. Plummer; also the author's *Western Political Thought*, pp. 221–7, for a short account.

form the establishment that would win decisive power in 1688, and they would then have oceanic horizons, like the merchants and bankers of Amsterdam. England, like Holland, would be a maritime business commonwealth; unlike Holland, she would have greater internal resources for lasting world power. Along with the martial and predatory tradition which derives from the wars in France, the mercantile interest and mentality is the second outstanding contribution of late medieval times.

It was based now, not, as in the thirteenth century, so much on the export of raw wool, as upon the even more lucrative export of broadcloth; on the kerseys and worsteds of East Anglia, the textiles of the North Riding in Yorkshire; on the 'blankets' made by Thomas Blanket in Bristol, and the close-woven cloths of the west country valleys in the Cotswolds, north Wiltshire and Somerset. Already they were made by Dauntseys at Trowbridge and Tames at Cirencester; by John Tame who 'built the fair new church at Fairford and his son Sir Edmund who finished it', with its splendid stained glass. Other merchants exported the raw materials for which England had long been well-known – hides and tin and lead, dairy produce and salt fish.

In exchange for this 'vent of cloth' and raw materials to the Low Countries, the Rhineland, the Baltic and Aquitaine, and, by Venetian and Genoese ships, to the Mediterranean, the 'feli-shippes adventurers' of the 'mercers' imported wine, velvet and silks, parchment and paper, spices, vestments and armour from the South; wheat, timber and furs from the Baltic. England and the Low Countries were, in fact, the main areas north of the Alps where merchant interests had fairly free play; there were still fifty toll stations along the Rhine. Further, now that the Scandinavians were throwing off the German monopoly of the Baltic, the Hansa cities had to allow the English 'free passage into the lands of Pruce'.

The range of this commerce is shown by the first treatise on sea power in English – the famous *Libelle* (Booklet) *of Englyshe Polycye*, written in 1436 to recall the incapable government of Henry VI to the policies of his father.[9] It lists the imports which England could already command: from Spain come figs, raisins and dates, 'syvyle oyle' and grain, now too often diverted to

[9] *Libelle of Englyshe Polycye*, a poem on the use of sea power, 1436, ed. Sir George Warner, Oxford, 1926.

Flanders for 'Fyne cloth of Ipre' and 'Cloothe of Curteryke made of English wool'.[10] From '*the Hyghe Duchmenne and Esterlynges*' come canvas, buckram, 'pych and terre', copper, steel and wax, while

> *Bere and bacone bene from Pruse ibrought.*

Here, again, the *Libelle* laments, the Flemings get their cut, in particular at the bacon and beer:

> *Thus are they hoggish and drynke well ataunte,*
> *Farewel Flemmynges, hay haro, avaunt!*

La Rochelle sends wine, and Brittany salt, as well as the worst pirates; they harry even the Norfolk coast. And the Genoese bring cloth of gold, silk and black pepper; while '*grete galees of Venees and Florence*' bring not only sweet wines, but also super-fluous 'chaffare', as

> *Apes and Japes and Murmusettes taylede.*[11]

And through marketing these luxuries,

> *They bere the golde owte of thys londe.*

The Irish, too, contribute hides and salmon, hake and herring, wool and linen cloth:

> *Skyns of otter, squerel and Irysh hare.*

Indeed, since the King of England is

> *Dominus also Hibernie*[12]

Ireland should be much better exploited; it could even become

> *for England a boterasse and a poste.*

Meanwhile, the English import *The comodius stokfysshe of Yselonde.*

The *Libelle* concludes with a famous exhortation for the sure keeping of Calais and the command of the Straits of Dover:

> *Kepe than the see,*
> *That is the wall of Englond;*[13]

---

[10] And shipped 'craftily' to Bruges by the haven at Sluys which is 'yclepted the Swyne'.

[11] Op. cit., p. 18.   [12] Ibid., p. 34.   [13] Ibid., p. 55.

men can thus *'live togedre werreless in unite'* – a naval *Pax Britannica.*

The profits of this extensive trade, now conducted by bills of exchange enhanced the prosperity of the great civic 'men of estate'. They were an oligarchy; the *potentiores*, as against the *inferiores* – craftsmen and apprentices. They bought land, married into aristocratic and county families and knew how to exploit the law: in a time of fairly well-controlled prices, their money talked.[14]

London was far the greatest centre of business, but many 'county boroughs' were now incorporated, and by 1447 Southampton appointed its own sheriff. Famous craft guilds and livery companies appeared – the Merchant Tailors, the Victuallers, the Glovers, the Fishmongers, the Brewers; they were rich, convivial, charitable and pious. The London Mercers had their coat of arms; 'Gules; a figure of the Virgin Mary with her hair dishevelled crowned, rising out of and within an orb of clouds all proper; motto *Honor Deo*'.[15] They laid on banquets, mystery plays, pageants and processions; they endowed city churches and began to found grammar schools and university scholarships and 'exhibitions'. The major towns were rich enough to carry on, in spite of political crises, and side with the winner.

These merchants had their business and often their family connections overseas; the East Anglians and Londoners with the Low Countries; the Southampton and Weymouth merchants – like the Russell ancestors of the Dukes of Bedford in Dorset – with Normandy and Bordeaux; all were economically outside the older feudal world, and the need of the Crown for credit and subsidies increased their political pull. Yet this bourgeoisie was not sufficiently differentiated and powerful to defy all comers, or

---

[14] 'That famose marchant and mercer Richard Whytyndon' (Dick Whittington) was not the penniless boy of legend. He came of a substantial county family in Gloucestershire; made his fortune selling damasks, velvets, and cloth of gold, and lent 1,000 marks to Richard II; repaid after the King's deposition, since the Lancastrians, too, wanted credit. The tale that he contributed his cat to his master's venture to Barbary to keep the mice down on the *Unicorn*, and that the animal was bought by the King of that country for ten times the worth of the cargo, is *ben trovato* but unsubstantiated; as, also, unfortunately, the legend of his hearing Bow Bells ring *'Turn again Whittington, thrice Mayor of London'*. But the story attests his wealth, his benefactions and his fame.

[15] E. F. Jacob, op. cit., p. 398.

spend its wealth and energy in conflict with other cities; as Ghent against Bruges, Florence against Pisa, Milan against the rest. Thus the great mercantile oligarchy reinforced the establishment and backed any administration which could bring security; they were not too humble, either, before the great landed magnates, most of whom had their own commercial interests so that there was mutual interdependence.

This plutocracy joined with the Court and magnates in love of good living, of tournaments, fashion and ostentation. The wealth of the City of London could already compare with that of Ghent and Bruges, and impress Florentine and Venetian envoys; their ramified trade by pack-horses and ships must have brought a certain widening of horizons. No wonder that the anonymous author of the *Libelle* could write

> *Cheryshe marchandyse, kepe thamyralte*
> *That we bee maysters of the narowe see.*

But beneath this civic prosperity was a growing urban and rural proletariat as well. There were prosperous yeomen, but many peasants, too, had long stagnated in rural squalor; some were now mere hired 'hands'. They lived in timber-framed hovels of clay and turf; they huddled over wood or peat fires; salted beef or pork were luxuries; they ate coarse bread, 'white meats' – dairy produce – cabbage and pease soup. They drank crude ale and cider when they could get them: 'Drink', wrote Dr. Lane Poole, 'was the principal solace of the village labourer'.[16] These illiterate and weather-beaten countrymen were the ancestors of the vast majority of the modern English, but their mentality can only be inferred – a dogged endurance, relieved, presumably, by bouts of drunkenness and rustic horseplay and wenching, along with the Catholic observances of the major crises of life.

The proletarian radical strain, too, was not stamped out. After the suppression of the Peasants' Revolt, a smouldering discontent is still apparent from the outlaw ballads of the fifteenth century. 'The streak of class violence which runs all through the stories of Robin Hood and the other outlaws is perhaps their most striking feature... The Robin Hood of medieval legend steps a good deal nearer the realities of his time than the emasculated

[16] Op. cit., p. 61.

version of him which we remember from nursery tales. In the ballads we are up against a full-blooded medieval brigand . . .'.[17] Yet, like the peasants in 1381, the outlaws, in outlook, remained conservative; loyal to the King, who may feast with them, and even take them into service. They were not real revolutionaries; their enemies were the rich landowners and fat abbots who had perverted the law or the corrupt sheriff who had denied poor men justice; not the social order itself. For in these popular fantasies Robin Hood, though an outlaw, is always a just man wronged – 'the theme of the righting of wrong done, of the lightening of the load of the peasant and the defeat of social injustice, which invests all the outlaws' acts with a kind of chivalry, does not really belong to the history of highway robbery'.[18] The outlaw becomes a folk-hero, the first of a long line of symbolic figures, ancestral to the bowdlerised heroes of nineteenth century historical romance, even to 'Westerns' in print and film. Thus the peasantry were not entirely inarticulate: with the social changes of Tudor times, they would become easier to understand; and in the plays of Shakespeare individuals.

IV

The physical background of fifteenth-century England still survives in a wealth of religious and secular building. The elaborate 'perpendicular' style was an English invention which had come in during the mid-fourteenth century; during the late fifteenth and early sixteenth it attained great virtuosity in fanvaulting and in the complex framing of stained glass, as in Henry VII's chapel in Westminster Abbey. Much of this architecture remains in Oxford and Cambridge, and it was still being put up in the 1630's when the Italianate Palladian style began to supersede it. Where stone was not easily available, brick was used, in a style brought over from the Netherlands, and it survives in many country houses, in much of Eton, and in many Cambridge colleges. Late medieval styles are widely translated into this medium, as the fortress became the country house, with

---

[17] Maurice Keen, *The Outlaws of Medieval Legend*, Routledge, 1961, p. 3.
[18] Ibid., p. 6.

large windows instead of arrow slits, and with token fortifications; but brick was seldom used, as it was in the Low Countries and Scandinavia, for churches and cathedrals. Ordinary glass, too, was now more common, though still often made in movable frames. Frescoes of 'Domesday' and episodes from the Bible became even more realistic and elaborate; England is still rich in architecture and decoration from this turbulent but wealthy time. More domestic and comfortable than the angular Early English style, this 'perpendicular' would become the model for a great deal of modern church and academic building through much of the English-speaking world.

All too little painting remains, save fine miniatures on illuminated manuscripts; the contemporary Italian masterpieces are vastly superior, and the portraits of the Lancastrian and Yorkist Kings are wooden rudimentary affairs: Henry VII, with a wary look and a red Tudor rose in his thin fingers, is the next English King after Richard II to be portrayed in a work of art.

V

Allas! my worthi maister honorable
This landes verray tresor and richesse!
Deth by they deth hath harm irreparable
Unto us doon . . .

wrote Hoccleve of Chaucer. In the short view he was right, for fifteenth century poetry shows a falling off, save in anonymous lyrics and carols, as

Mother and maiden
was never none but she;
Well may such a lady
Goddes mother be;

or in the late medieval plaint in an Atlantic climate,

Western wind, when wilt thou blow
That the small rain down can rain?
Christ, that my love were in my arms
And I in my bed again!

Laborious allegories and a clumsy self-consciousness set in, though Stephen Hawes, in Henry VII's time, could write,

> *After the day there cometh the darke nyght,*
> *For though the day be never so longe*
> *At last the belles ryngeth to evensonge.*

It is rather in prose that the age is remarkable: in 1474 Caxton marketed the first printed book published in England, a romantic *Recuyel (collection) of the Histories of Troye*, printed at Bruges that year; and, in 1477, the *Dictes and Sayings of the Philosophers*, the first book printed in this country. But Sir Thomas Malory's *Tales of King Arthur* – called by Caxton *Le Morte Arthur* and published in 1485, the year of Henry VII's accession – best foreshadows a terser, more accurate, prose:

> 'A, Launcelot,' he sayd ... 'Thou were the curtest knyght that ever bare shelde; and thou were the truest frende to thy lover that ever bestrade hors; and thou were the trewest lover of a synful man that ever loved woman; and thou wert the kyndest man that ever strake with swerde; and thou were the godelyest persone that ever cam emonge prees of knyghts; and thou was the mekest man and the Ientyllest that ever ete in halle emonge ladyes; and thou were the sternest knyght to thy mortal foo that ever put spere in the breste.'

The passage seems to echo the song of Maldon, and yet anticipate the epitaph on Thomas Hardy's Giles Winterbourne in *The Woodlanders*, who 'was a good man and did good things'.

Chapter 6

The Tudor English

THE government of Tudor England was authoritarian, not despotic; even Elizabeth I had to conciliate the nobility and play one magnate off against another. The founder of the dynasty, Henry VII, ruthlessly exploited the permanent revenues of the Crown; he minuted account books and awed his courtiers by making notes 'touching persons' in his own hand. The legend of his great fortune is false, but he left a considerable hoard of plate and jewels to his son.[1]

Henry VIII, under his apparent bonhomie, was just as calculating, even in his leonine rages; and remarked that if he thought his cap were privy to his council he would cast it in the fire. Elizabeth I, the one of his children most like him, told James VI of Scotland that those who 'perilled' him there 'should crake up a halter, if I were King'. All these able Tudors governed through their magnates, Parliaments and unpaid Justices of the Peace; they had no standing army. They improved the archaic yet adaptable machinery of central and local government; for even in the wilder counties some habit of responsibility had survived the terrorism and corruption of the mid-fifteenth century: that is the most decisive political aspect of the time.

The aims of Henry VII and at first of Henry VIII were, of course, traditional; and when the latter set England on a new course, had the administration radically overhauled, nationalised the Church and speeded up a social revolution which strengthened but finally undermined the monarchy, he was careful to act as King-in-Parliament: 'We are informed', he declared, 'by our judges that we at no time stand so highly in our estate royal

---

[1] He had spent heavily on ambitious diplomacy abroad; 'by the end of the reign the Chamber cash balance was completely exhausted and ... the issues of the new reign had to be used to pay the debts of the old'. B. P. Wolffe, 'Henry VII's Land Revenues and Chamber Finance', *English Historical Review*, April 1964, pp. 252 ff.

as in the time of Parliament.'[2] By 1589, Sir Thomas Smith, Secretary of State to Queen Elizabeth, would write: 'The most high and absolute power of the realm of England consisteth in the parliament...which representeth of the whole realm, both the head and body.'[3] All the successful Tudors understood how to adapt what was to hand. Above all, they imposed order; their 'greatest triumph' was 'the ultimately successful assertion of a royal monopoly of violence, both public and private, an achievement which profoundly altered not only the nature of politics, but also the quality of daily life. There occurred a change in English habits that can only be compared with the step taken in the nineteenth century, when the growth of a police force consolidated the monopoly and made it effective in the greatest cities and the smallest villages.'[4]

This ordered hierarchy they termed an 'empire', a sovereign state. Wales was now incorporated, Scotland subdued, Ireland cowed – a problem shelved if not solved. And if Henry VIII's ambitions were still continental, he was the founder of the modern Royal Navy; his forts still stand upon the coasts; he inaugurated Trinity House to train pilots and look after lighthouses and the interests of mariners, and he created the Navy Board, ancestral to the Admiralty.[5]

His achievement was timely: with the discovery of the Americas, England ceased to be a country cousin on the fringe of a continent that looked to the Mediterranean: though a late starter, she now became an oceanic power, well placed on great trade routes to the ends of the earth, her future not on the Continent but overseas. Vast new horizons were opening up, and if the earlier Tudors only occasionally noticed them, Elizabeth I, Drake and Raleigh thought strategically in modern terms. The begin-

---

[2] Prior Houghton before his execution at Tyburn declared that mother Church decreed otherwise 'than your King himself with *his Parliament*' (*quam ipse rex vester cum suo Parliamento*): 'I dare take that quarrel,' he concluded, 'to my death.' David Knowles, *The Religious Orders in England*, C.U.P., 1959, Vol. III, p. 471.

[3] *De Republica Anglorum*, II.

[4] Lawrence Stone, *The Crisis of the Aristocracy 1558–1641*, Clarendon Press, 1965, p. 200.

[5] See 'The Administration of the Royal Navy under Henry VIII', *E.H.R.*, Vol. LXXX, April 1965, pp. 268 ff. Far from losing grip in the closing years of his reign after Thomas Cromwell's fall, the King inaugurated a 'transformation of naval administration'.

nings of the British Empire were by no means made in a fit of absence of mind: 'its planning occupied the best brains of thinkers and men of action. They failed again and again, but they persisted, and their small successes were cumulative.'[6]

Further, Henry VIII's England broke away from the Catholic Christendom by which her people had been dominated since the conversion; this event 'changed the outlook of Englishmen even as they braced themselves to make their astonishing impact upon Western civilisation.'[7] Like the Scandinavians, the Dutch, the Protestants of Germany and Switzerland and powerful minorities in France and Eastern Europe, the English now repudiated an Italianate Papacy. But they did so without devastating wars of religion; Henry VIII could impose his will on the island, and Elizabeth I made a politic if at first precarious religious settlement, conservative, compromising, outwardly conformist. In the long run, as in Holland, this relative toleration would indirectly promote rationalism and a scientific outlook, and so contribute to transform Europe's place in world history.

Yet the sixteenth century witnessed no sudden social revolution; and the near-Marxist picture of eternally 'rising' middle class capitalists transforming a medieval society has had to go. As might be expected, 'relatively little structural change took place in English society between the fourteenth and the nineteenth centuries; what altered was the role of the various social classes within a fairly static framework.'[8] Within this frame, the territorial 'warlords' of the fifteenth century developed directly into the cultivated oligarchs of the eighteenth; consistently, 'the real new men, the rich merchants, were too concerned with scrambling aboard the old status band-wagon to have any wish to scupper it.'[9]

'A few great families of *nouveaux riches* entered and remained for the next half-century near the controls of government', but 'the new rich were not always new men'.[10] The magnates old or new who had bought up monastic lands, and the lesser men who had repurchased many of them, exploited their property with vigour; building up the already substantial resources which

[6] J. A. Williamson, *The Ocean in English History*, O.U.P., 1941, p. 85.
[7] A. G. Dickens, *The English Reformation*, Batsford, 1964, q.v.
[8] Stone, op. cit., p. 5. [9] Ibid., p. 11.
[10] Knowles, op. cit., p. 467.

would make England a great maritime power and financing wider enterprise. The long established cloth trade still dominated the economy, and its demands are behind the Elizabethan and Jacobean expansion. The merchant adventurers needed the markets of the Far East, but they found North America in the way: for nearly a century they largely ignored it, save for the Newfoundland cod banks. Then the English began to colonise. They also tried another route to Asia by the Eastern Arctic, and opened up trade with Muscovy and Iran instead; they entered the Mediterranean to get to the Levant and rounded the Cape in the wake of the Portuguese to trade with India and the 'Spice Islands' of Malaysia and Indonesia. All these new oceanic objectives went far beyond those advocated in the *Libelle of Englyshe Polycye*; and by the seventeenth century they would bring in substantial returns.

The turning-point in this momentous development was the English mastery of the North Atlantic, affirmed after the defeat of the Spanish Armada in 1588. It had been made possible by new designs in ships and ship-smashing guns, and it followed from a new conception of oceanic strategy after Drake's brilliant circumnavigation of the world. This new background also stimulated an astonishing late Renaissance literature and drama, which transformed the language and produced a galaxy of dramatists, poets and masters of prose, culminating in Shakespeare, the greatest writer in the English tongue. It created an intellectual capital for the whole future English speaking world – a process which went on through three creative centuries.

II

In spite of battle and murder, the ancient monarchy remained the driving force of the realm; in England, of all the great powers, medieval institutions best survived, and as the Crown took over new responsibilities, Parliament and local government worked in with it. The secret of Tudor success was a firm peace and good administration under the rule of law; both were brought about slowly by adjustment and consent; not, as in France and Spain, by absolute power and centralised bureaucracy. It was an achievement decisive for a vast future in space and time.

Henry VIII and Thomas Cromwell, his able and ruthless Secretary of State, overhauled, extended and modernised the administration; they nationalised the Church and they secured the dynasty. Efficient Conciliar government was the basis of their success, and the Secretary became its mainspring. Under Elizabeth the two great Cecil Secretaries, Lord Burghley and his son, Lord Salisbury – 'little bossive Robin' who would fix the accession of a Stuart King – would again make the office of decisive influence, though it would not survive the frivolous incompetence of the new Scots dynasty.

Thomas Cromwell, that self-made business man and bureaucrat, from whose sister Oliver Cromwell would descend, was the first layman to hold supreme power under the King; he promised to make his master the richest prince in Christendom, and where the King had himself taken council and 'done right' according to custom through various means, now government took on a more independent momentum. Through statutes made by King-in-Parliament it went ahead; old law courts were remodelled, new ones set up. From a compact and systematic Privy Council radiated the powers of Councils of Wales, of the Marches, of Ireland and the North, of Courts of Admiralty, Requests and Augmentations – the change symbolised by the clear Renaissance handwriting in which the first proceedings of the reorganised Privy Council are drawn up, in contrast to the frightful late medieval hand long current.

Unlike Wolsey, Cromwell knew how to manage Parliament; the Commons might grumble at taxation, hold up business, stand on privilege; but they did not grudge the strength and grandeur of the throne: they wanted 'good governance'; and on the whole they got it. Anti-clerical and insular, they abetted the plunder of the Church lands, whose purchasers obtained a solid interest in the new settlement.

In the counties, too, government worked closely with men of similar background. As already observed 'Guardians' or Justices of the Peace had been appointed under Edward II, and Quarter Sessions had been customary since the reign of Edward III, now these magistrates were linked with the Privy Council by Lords Lieutenant and their Deputies. Unpaid and representative men of substance, the 'J.P.s' were knowledgeable about their neighbourhoods; and they learnt law and procedure, if not always at the Inns of Court, at least through handbooks such as that popular work, Lambard's *Eirenarcha*,[11] which defined what Justices of the Peace were, what they did, and how they did it, and still illuminates a lasting aspect of England.

Their duty, Lambard emphasised, was not to 'reduce the people to an universal unanimitie (or agreement of minds)... but to suppresse iniurious force and violence.' They must be 'good men and lawful, not Barratours (litigious persons)'; '*meultz vailantz*', the best in the country, able to understand not 'loades, but stacks of statutes'; and they must swear to 'do *Egal* right to the Poore and to the Rich after (their) cunning wit and power and after the laws and customes of the Realm, and statutes thereof made.'[12] Nor should 'they *Let* [divert justice] for gift or other cause, but well and truly do their office... being soberly wise.' They should distinguish between *affray* – (*affrai del pais in timore populi*) 'which signifieth to terrify'; *assault*, 'which denoteth a leaping (or flying) upon a man', and *battery* – 'malicious strikings, thrustings into water and rape, all of which constitute a Breach of the Peace; though, naturally, 'a man may take his kinsman that is mad and put him in a house and bind and beat him with rods.'

Tudor governments also showed the concern for 'welfare' which would be so characteristic of England. The local constables not only helped to keep the peace; they tried to limit the effect of social and economic change and unemployment.[13] They had to apprehend sturdy rogues and vagabonds who 'beg, wander, or misbehave themselves'; make clothiers pay their dependants in lawful wages, not in 'pins, girdles and other such things'; 'take a view' of the aged impotent and lame and have them conveyed, on horseback or by cart, to the next parish and so by the

---

[11] *Eirenarcha: or of the office of the Justices of Peace*: in four books, gathered 1579, first published 1581 by William Lambard of Lincoln's Inn, Gent. London, 1591, with the motto from Virgil '*Hae tibi erunt artes, pacisque imponere morem*'.

[12] Op. cit., p. 59.

[13] Lambard, *The Duties of Constables Borsholders tything men and other lowe ministers of the Peace*, whereunto be also adjoyned the generall offices of Churchwardens, of Surveyors for amending highwaies, Distributors of the provision for noisome Foule and Vermin, Overseers and Gouernors of the Poore and of the Wardens and Collectors of the Houses of Correction, 1582 (ed. 1587). The title page is adorned with a woodcut of the Saviour bearing a heavy lamb – '*Periit et inventa est*'.

most direct way to the place where they were born, there to re-main. At hay and corn harvest they should direct all able-bodied men to labour and examine the quality of the malt from barley. Contributions for the upkeep of highways and bridges could only be exacted with their assent, or with that of 'two honest inhabitants'.

So rudimentary 'welfare' was already looked after, in a manner original at the time. 'Gradually', wrote Trevelyan, 'a proper system of Poor Relief, based upon compulsory rates, and discriminating between the various classes of the indigent was evolved in England, first of all the countries of Europe...'. In spite of corruption and casualness, the 'worst horrors of failure, of unemployment, and of unprovided old age were not suffered by the poor in England to the same extent as in the Continental countries of the *ancien régime*.'[14] After the disorder of the fifteenth century, the Tudor peace was thus gradually enforced; local militia mustered, unemployment and destitution assuaged, the local establishment collaborating with government.

The Tudors, who ruled by consent, were also alive to public opinion, and used calculated Renaissance splendour and aloofness. Flashing with gold and gems, served on bended knee – 'His Majesty' not merely 'His Grace' – Henry VIII had ruled by cunning and prestige more than force. For this cold-hearted *politique*, subtly aware of just how far to go, loved sport, women and high living and appeared the bluff and popular embodiment of Tudor Englishry. Mary I, for all her Iberian fanaticism, also loved and used calculated splendour; at her accession 'there was *Te Deum laudamus* with song and organes playhyng and tabuls in evere strett, and evere strett full of bonfyres and ther was money cast a-way.[15] And Elizabeth I, living in sophisticated luxury and a round of display, could also unbend and share the pleasures of the mob. On Mayday 1559, in boats decked with streamers and banners, flags and trumpets and drums, the Londoners 'shot eggs and oranges against one another with sqwybs, which by chance fell on a bag of gunpowder – the Queen watching out o' windows' (only one man was drowned). Elizabeth would have 'music to dinner and great cheer' and 'after to bull and bear baytying and the Queen's grace and embassadours

[14] *English Social History*, Longmans, 1946, pp. 112 and 230.
[15] *The Diary of Henry Machyn, 1550–63*, Camden Soc., 1848.

stod in the gallery looking at the pastime.' For all her Italianate culture, the Queen had a down-to-earth coarse-grained quality without which her legend would never have flourished.

Tudor society was indeed brutal and precarious, the minority culture thin above a seething world of illiterate poverty and crime – thieves, wrote an Italian observer 'taken up in coveys'; even the age of Elizabeth, so much romanticised, must have appeared one crisis after another. Yet in that century modern England became herself.

III

In Duke Humphrey of Gloucester's library in the Bodleian at Oxford still hang portraits of the splendid and confident prelates of the late medieval Catholic Church, in rich copes and holding great croziers; mitred and ringed, they contrast with smug Cranmer or wary Gardiner, austere in black and white, shorn of the pomp of cosmopolitan Christendom. Only after 1660 would the rich Anglican bishops regain something of the pomp of their medieval predecessors, and that in florid, insular fashion.

The change commemorated was profound. The English had been Catholic since the conversions, and when Henry VIII, in his own eyes always orthodox, seized upon the monastic wealth, he had intended little doctrinal change. The motive was dynastic, anti-clerical and national, not ideological, though Henry VIII succeeded because men's minds had changed. 'The Angevin Kings, Henry II and John, were as ruthless as Henry VIII and far less conventional by temperament and outlook. They too had overweening ambitions to control the English Church; they strove bitterly with Rome until at last the kingdom fell under an interdict. Nevertheless it seems inconceivable that in their day any ruler could have abstracted England, permanently, or indeed for many years, from Catholic Christendom. In the England of Henry VIII new psychological climates arose . . . and as this schism developed, it became increasingly clear that this was only the harbinger of changes far more fundamental.'[16] Henry was indeed playing power politics with a force beyond control, a European impulse separating the northern peoples from Rome, altering the social order and psychology far beyond England. The English

[16] A. G. Dickens, op. cit., vi.

schism or 'Reformation' was canalised, but not stopped; and if the *via media Anglicana* preserved more of the old ritual and doctrine than did the other Protestant Churches, Calvinist, Lutheran and the others, it altered the tone of England; of the Court, the universities, the cathedrals, the city and parish churches; of divinity, literature and family life. And when the comprehensive Elizabethan settlement broke down, and the Puritan sects, in revolt against bishops and ritual,

> *rolled the Psalm to wintry skies*

and hived off into Nonconformity, that schism, too, was equally decisive. If the upper classes still dominated the parishes, the Nonconformist cult of Bible, psalm and hymn, of a 'peculiar' people excluded from public office but not from trade; and fostering their own culture in independent schools, created a whole new aspect of English society and greatly influenced the development of North America.

Meanwhile, the insular Anglican hierarchy was consolidated by the threat of Spanish invasion, by attempts to assassinate the Queen, by the identification of the old religion with foreigners. The parish clergy were often no more effective than their medieval predecessors, but the established Church had the State behind it.

IV

The wealth of England, the basis of what would become the greatest nineteenth century commercial and industrial power in the world, can be discerned far back into medieval history; but late Tudor and early Stuart times saw an unprecedented expansion. Between the Dissolution of the Monasteries and the Civil Wars, English agriculture and technology caught up with and sometimes surpassed the standards of the Continent – a substantial prelude to the main Industrial Revolution of the late eighteenth century. In spite of the usual ups and downs of any economy, the surplus thus created was behind a brilliant many-sided culture, and a wide commercial expansion.

Tudor governments of the mid-century, caught in the current inflation, and crippled by the costs of defence and of Henry VIII's Scots and French wars, had spent most of the huge mon-

astic capital as income: the Crown had sold or otherwise alienated two-thirds of the monastic land and spent two-thirds of the
movable wealth outright; the currency was debased and credit
abroad obtained only at ruinous interest. By Elizabeth I's time
the crisis demanded new professional skills. Sir Thomas Gresham,
a financier long experienced on the Antwerp exchange, knew
how to 'bring the base money into fine'; in collaboration with
Secretary Cecil, he at last restored the currency; as early as 1569
his long-discussed project for a 'Royal Exchange' or Bourse was
realised; and with Antwerp ruined by religious wars, London
inherited its financial advantages. Gresham, a Cambridge man
from Gonville, was immensely rich and *rusé*. His uncle, Sir John,
had founded Gresham's school, Holt, in Norfolk and Sir Thomas
founded Gresham College in London, with chairs in modern
subjects; astronomy, mathematics, music and medicine; he was
a new type – 'a sort of combination of a Pierpont Morgan and
Keynes in his day.'[17] On his retirement, a Genoese, Sir Horatio
Palavicino, became a principal adviser to the government. He
had made a fortune in the alum essential for dyeing cloth, and
could transfer credit to pay the mercenaries fighting the Spaniards in the Low Countries, when Wolsey had to risk transferring
cash. Naturalised and knighted, this cosmopolitan figure ended
as a county magnate in Cambridgeshire, a forerunner of many
naturalised and ennobled financiers.

Other capitalists made their contribution: Sir Andrew Judde
from the Medway, founder of 'one notable free school at Tonbridge in Kent whereby he brought up and nourished in learning
great store of youth';[18] he was 'a Stapullar of reputation',
Master of the Skinners' Company and Lord Mayor. He had
made a great fortune in commerce and armaments which was
inherited by his son-in-law, 'Customer' Smythe, who reorganised
the customs, increasing his own revenues and the Queen's.

These men and their like adapted the economy to new demands of investment and finance; and if their Protestant benefactions were now no longer for masses and chantries but for
training men of affairs, the donors had a Catholic background.
They were not, of course, Calvinists obsessed by a mysterious
'capitalist' drive – a 'perversion', as Weber put it, 'of the human

[17] A. L. Rowse, *The England of Elizabeth*, Macmillan, 1950, pp. 117 ff.
[18] H. S. Vere Hodge, *Sir Andrew Judde*, privately published, 1953, p. 75.

spirit so mysterious that only the depths of the irrational can reveal its sources' – but merely a 'galaxy of adventurous risk and enjoyment-centred individuals.'[19] These hearty and cunning characters were, in fact, denounced by the Calvinists for their new-fangled ways as 'caterpillars' of the Commonwealth; and the 'reforming' preachers harked back to a past when nobles did their duty, gentry were not feckless, and yeomen and labourers worked hard at their callings.

Advised by these experts, Tudor government tried to plan for efficiency and expansion. In a context of creeping European inflation, stepped up in the second half of the century, and with more mouths to feed, England began to develop comparatively rudimentary industries. The government tightened up conditions of apprenticeship, put on tariffs to protect new enterprises, invited foreigners to impart new skills. The rudimentary coal mines were developed, particularly in the north-east – 'seacoal' their product was called in London, shipped round from Newcastle in colliers which began a school of seamanship that would train Captain Cook, the greatest of English navigators. The Yorkshire and Derbyshire coal, too, was better exploited, and South Wales mines now supplied Bristol.

German experts were brought in to design and drain the coal mines, to exploit lead in Somerset and tin in Cornwall; calamine for brass was found near Bristol. New blast furnaces were contrived, mainly in the Forest of Dean and the Sussex Weald; iron was smelted, guns and gunpowder made in England. Again the Germans were called in: Henry VIII had to buy cannon from Hans Popenruyter of Liége; Elizabeth's government had their own ordnance. Glass and paper and soap were made; woollen textiles already manufactured in Lancashire. England remained predominantly rural, but the population was now near five millions, and capital and man-power were beginning to combine for greater production.

[19] See C. H. and K. George, *The Protestant Mind of the English Reformation* 1570–1640, Princeton, 1961, for a long-needed criticism of Tawney's popularisation of Weber and the neo-Marxist interpretation of the age. There is, they say, 'no significant positive co-relation between the philosophy of the bourgeois, *qua* bourgeois, and the religious idealism of Protestantism, there is certainly no evidence of dynamic psychological causal connection between Calvinism and either Weberian capitalism or the far more significant capitalism of "this-worldly" predators' (p. 147).

Farming, also, began to improve: the 'jog-trot verses' of Tusser's *Five Hundred Points of Good Husbandry*, went into thirteen editions between 1573 and the end of the century.[20] Turnips were now grown for livestock in winter, peach trees and apricots were 'denizened'; that eccentric character, the Rev. Andrew Boorde (the original 'merry Andrew') sent Thomas Cromwell a novelty: 'I have sent your mastershepp the seeds of reuberbe, the which came oute of Barbary.'[21] Hops had been cultivated during Henry VIII's reign, though the monarch himself had disapproved of beer, commanding that ale only be served in the Household. The English cult of the garden, to persist into modern times, was now established. The cypress was acclimatised: lawns and hedges better kept.

There was now also a great demand for treatises on sport as well as on agriculture and gardening; hunting, fishing and swimming were all catered for. When in 1576 George Turberville published his comprehensive *The Noble Art of Venerie or Hunting*,[22] in the English way he got a poet to point out the moral worth of the sport:

> *And as for exercise it seems to bear the bell,*
> *Since by the same mens bodies be in health maintained well...*
> *A sport for noble peers, a sport for gentle bloods,*
> *The paine I leave for servants*
> *Suche as beate the bushie woods.*

Turberville describes the care and training of hounds and the ritual and music of the hunt. Yet, again in the English way, he is sympathetic to the quarry, in particular to the hare: 'It is a great pleasure', he writes, 'to beholde the subtiltie of the little pore beast'... and 'if, when she ryseth out of the forme, she set up her ears, and run not very farst at first, and caste up her scut upon her back... she is an old and crafty hare.' But the fox is

[20] A. L. Rowse, op. cit., p. 99.
[21] Ellis's *Original Letters*, Series III, Vol. II, p. 301. The purpose was medicinal; it took centuries for this repellent vegetable to become a popular adjunct to the English table.
[22] *Wherein is handled and set out the vertues, nature, and properties of Siventeen sundrie chases together with the order and maner how to hunt and kill everyone of them.* It is dedicated to the Master of the Queen's harthounds, and describes the 'nature and hunting of the Hart, Bucke, Reyndeer, Rowe, Wilde Goate, Wilde Bore, Hare, Conie, Foxe, Badgerd, Marterne or Wildcat, Otter, Wolfe and Beare'.

still vermin – 'as touching foxes, I take small pleasure in hunting them; like the badger, they stink': the 'noblest sport' was still 'to follow the hart that men hunt in the high woods.'

Turberville reflects the ancient cult of field sports that would dominate English life for centuries, and if hunting deer was a sport for Kings and aristocrats, the 'waste' still teemed with lesser game, taken freely with net, decoy and gun.

The reign of Henry VII had seen the first work on fishing in English. *The Treatyse on Fysshynge with an Angle* was written by Dame Julyana Bernes, prioress of a nunnery near St. Albans, and appeared in 1496 – one of the earliest books printed in the country. The angler, she writes, avoids the inconvenience and disappointments of hunting and hawking; he 'hath the wholesome walk, and merry at his ease, a sweet air of the sweet savour of the mead flowers that maketh him hungry; he heareth the melodious armony of fowls, he seeth the young swans, herons, ducks, coots and many other fowls with their broods, which beseemeth better than all the noise of hounds.' The Prioress is already expert on the making of the rods, on the use of live-bait for pike, and on making flies ('very artificial').

By Elizabeth's time Middleton's *Short Introduction for to Learne to Swimme*[23] was also popular. One should swim, it says, only from May to August, and then not if the wind is in the north or east. The bank should be free of briars or thistles, serpents and toads; one should also know the depth of water, beware of old stakes and sharp stones and swim in 'clear running water', not in a 'corrupt pool'. Once in, the swimmer should avoid 'unorderly labouring'; nor must he 'rudely leap in' when in a sweat, 'casting forth his legs, not close together'. He can learn the Roache Turne (to the right) and how to 'tumble' and 'roule upon his back'; a restful position which nature denies to any other creature. He can, of course, swim like a dog, and 'into this kind of swimming many do at first fall'; but to swim on the side, if more laborious, is faster. One can also 'hang by the chinne in the water', 'caper' with both legs, and swim under water or like a dolphin.

[23] Gathered out of Master Digbie's Booke on the Art of Swimming and translated into English for the better instruction of those who do not understand the Latin tongue, by Christopher Middletone, London, 1595. Woodcuts depict the different strokes in a winding, rural, river; Elizabethan undressing, as depicted, was complex.

V

Into this predominantly rural background the oceanic expansion brought a whole new range of experience. In the Middle Ages English sea-power had been tentative: Richard I had laid down the first dockyard at Portsmouth and tried to discipline his crusading fleets by the Laws of Oléron; his own royal galley from Southampton, with a crew of sixty, had retrieved him from Antwerp after his ransom and release from Germany. After the loss of Normandy, John had confirmed the charter of the Cinque Ports – Hastings, Romney, Hythe, Dover and Sandwich – exempting them from dues of 'tallage, passage, keyage, rivage, ponsage and wreck', and granting them the 'honours at Court' whereby the portsmen were 'coronation barons' who bore the canopy over the King.[24] John could muster fifty-one galleys: as already observed, Edward III had won the first major naval action in English history at Sluys, and Henry V commissioned 'dromons' at Southampton.

By the mid-fifteenth century, technical advance had opened new vistas of the world. Three-masted ocean-going ships, designed after the caravals developed by the Portuguese from the Arabs, could now work to windward, and hinged rudders on stern posts had superseded the steering oar. Magnetic compasses, too, were now common; an Arab or perhaps Scandinavian invention. This advance, behind the Portuguese voyages down West Africa and to the Atlantic islands and Columbus' landfall in the Bahamas, transformed the oceanic prospects of all the Atlantic states.

The first English explorations had been inconclusive, directed to find a north-west passage to Asia. When the *Matthew* under the elder Cabota, a Genoese, discovered Nova Scotia, this officially recorded landing in North America gave rise to later claims to possession, but the only (and considerable) immediate advantage was the exploitation of the cod banks off Newfoundland, a school of seamanship as well as a fishery. Rastell, in 1517, first described the North American continent in English verse – though he never got there, since his mariners refused to proceed beyond Cork:

[24] R. and F. Jessup, *The Cinque Ports*, Batsford, 1952, p. 20. The two ancient towns of Rye and Winchelsea also had their privileges confirmed.

Westward he founde new landes
That we never harde tell of before this;

but not till Elizabeth's time were they further explored from
England – rather, left to Jacques Cartier of St. Malo who pene-
trated Canada in the reign of Francis I. The Spaniards, mean-
while, had conquered the elaborate civilisations of Mexico and
Peru, and the Portuguese were exploiting the Persian Gulf,
India and the Far East.

Then, after the turn of the century, the English made up for
lost time. William Hawkins, in Henry VIII's reign, was already
trading for ivory in West Africa, and, in 1553, Captain Thomas
Wyndham died of fever off the Guinea coast in search of gold.
By the 'sixties Hawkins was running negro slaves into the Caribbean in collusion with the Spanish settlers of that forbidden area.
The English had thus obtained a good deal of the trade of the
mid-Atlantic.

While Wyndham was exploring the Gold Coast, the English
were also looking north-east. John Dudley, Duke of Northumber-
land, came to political disaster, but during his short rule under
Edward VI he backed the Muscovy company to send Willoughby
and Chancellor to Russia. As the ships dropped down river past
Greenwich, 'the courtiers came running out and the common
people flocked together . . . the Privy Council, they looked out at
the windows of the Court and the rest ran up to the tops of the
towers.'[25] Willoughby perished; but Chancellor got to the Court
of Ivan the Terrible – 'We, John Vasiliwitch, by the Grace of
God great lord, Emperor and Grand Duke of all the Russias, of
Volodamir, Muscovia, Novgorod, Emperor of Kazan, Tversky,
Vgorsky, Bulgaria and all Siberland, Great Commander of the
Northern Parts.'

With the backing of the Tsar, Anthony Jenkinson developed
the contact; penetrated to the Persia of the Safavid Shah Tam-
asp, 'the Sophi Shaw Thamas', as the English called him. In
Muscovy itself, by 1568, Thomas Randolph, an envoy seasoned
in dealing with the Scots, concluded in the small hours of the
night a major treaty with the Tsar. Turberville, turning from

[25] Quoted from Richard Hakluyt, *The Principal Navigations* (Everyman
edition, Vol. I, p. 271) by A. L. Rowse in *The Expansion of Elizabethan
England*, Macmillan, 1955, p. 168.

hunting to travel, went with him and described the Muscovites
without illusions:

> *Wilde Irish are as civil as the Russes in their kinde,*
> *Harde choice which is the best of both, each bloody, rude*
> *and blinde.*

> *Will*, he complained, *in Commonwealth doth beare the only*
> *sway.*

He concluded, with insular prejudice:

> *Loe thus I make my ende, no other news to thee*
> *Save that the country is too cold, the people beastly be.*[26]

Similarly unromantic views were taken of Persia and the East by
those who actually went there; Marlowe, who stayed at home,
wrote them up.

In the 'seventies Newbery got to the Middle East and Fitch to
India, followed, in James I's time, by Sir Thomas Roe's embassy
to Akbar, then the richest ruler in the world. Jacobean Englishmen also penetrated Siam and even Japan, when the first Toku-
gawa Shogun, Ieyasu, his supremacy still precarious, welcomed
the advice of the shipbuilder Will Adams, who settled in the
country.

While this expansion had been going on, in West Africa,
Muscovy and the East, the long understanding with Spain which
had lasted since the times of Henry VII had been disrupted;
after the Spanish attack on Hawkins' ships at San Juan de Ulloa
the port of Mexico in 1568, and upon the Netherlands in the
following year, the gloves were off. The strategic objective was
not to take over the Spanish American empire, but to defend
England, with as much profit as possible, and to explore new
lands in the 'South Sea'. Drake, with the Queen's connivance,
entered the Pacific, landed in California and returned round the
world; Sir Humphrey Gilbert annexed Newfoundland and
'planted' Nova Scotia; in the 'eighties, Raleigh 'planted' Virginia, an enterprise which failed mainly owing to diversion of the

---

[26] *Certaine letters in verse, written by Master G.T. out of Muscovia.*
Hakluyt, op. cit., Vol. III, pp. 124–35

supporting ships to fight the Armada. It was a prelude to the Jacobean settlement.

The main strategic purpose succeeded: 'Hawkins and Drake created an ocean-going navy, a new type of armament capable of striking hard blows thousands of miles from home.'[27] These well-found galleons that defeated the Armada with their formidable guns, were in principle the same kind of ships that won England the mastery of the oceans at Quiberon Bay, La Hogue and Trafalgar. Already 'the contrast is great between the petty oceanic interests of Henry VIII's early years and the swarm of English shipping when his daughter died, prying into every coast of the Atlantic, and seeking in all its four quarters for passage to the Indian Ocean and the Pacific.[28] The Muscovy company had been founded in the mid-century; the Levant company by 1592; by 1601 the East India Company was incorporated. In Jacobean and Caroline times a greater migration and settlement would follow, paralleled only in the nineteenth century, and decisive for North America.

These exploits altered the outlook of England; the glamour of Drake and Raleigh survives and Hakluyt's narratives are still enthralling. The oceanic expansion, as Dr. Rowse puts it, reflects 'the tremendous energy that has been generated in the southern half of the small island in the northern seas – lunging out north-east towards Siberia in an arc round the Arctic ice-pack to Greenland and the broken lands and passages north of Canada; down the African coast, into the Caribbean and southward along the Brazil coast through the Straits of Magellan into and across the Pacific; and lastly, tackling the long direct voyage round the Cape and across the Indian Ocean to the Far East.'[29]

VI

The contrast between earlier Tudor literature and the galaxy of brilliance in the last two decades of Elizabeth's reign reflects this expansion of horizons. Consider the rustic squalor of *Gammer Gurton's Needle*:

[27] J. A. Williamson, *The Ocean in English History*, p. 43.
[28] Ibid.
[29] A. L. Rowse, op. cit., p. 205.

> *As Gammer Gurton with many a wide stitch*
> *Sat piercing and patching of Hodge her man's brich,*
> *By chance or misfortune, as she her gear tost*
> *In Hodge leather breeches her needle she lost,*[30]

It comes out of village life in East Anglia, as had much of Skelton's knock-about verse:

> *He rumbleth on a lewd lute 'Roty bully joys'*
> *Rumble down, tumble down, hey go now now!*
> *He fumbling in his fingering an ugly good noise*
> *It seemeth the sobbing of an old sow!*[31]

Nor was Nicholas Udall's mid-century Etonian comedy, *Ralph Roister Doister*, with its characters Tom Truepenny, Margery Mumblecrust and Tibet Talkapace, much more sophisticated.

In prose, it is true, Roger Ascham of St. John's College, Cambridge, had already achieved a crystal clarity in his *Toxophilus* on archery, presented to Henry VIII in 1545, on his return from his last war in France. Consider Ascham's remarks on judging the wind when shooting; 'one of the first triumphs of modern English prose.'[32] 'To see the wind with a man his eyes it is unpossible, the nature of it is so fine and subtle; yet this experience of the wind had I once myself, and that was in the great snow that fell four years ago... The fields on both sides were plain, and lay almost yard deep with snow; the night afore had been a little frost so that the snow was hard and crusted above; the moving sun shone bright and clear, the wind was whistling aloft and sharp ...'

This style already bears out the opinion of Edward VI's tutor, the Hellenist Sir John Cheke, who wrote that 'our own tongue should be written clean.'

Ascham is a link between the relatively crude if effective prose of Malory and the full grandeur of Raleigh's eloquence, as deployed, for example, in his famous description of the last fight of

---

[30] *A Ryght Pithy Pleasant and meatie Comedie* ... played on stage not longe ago in Christ's Colledge in Cambridge. 1575. Probably written about the mid-century by John Bridges of Pembroke Hall, later Bishop of Oxford.

[31] Quoted by E. M. Forster in *Two Cheers for Democracy*, Arnold, 1951, p. 161. Skelton is writing of a musical kitchen boy, perhaps Lambert Simnel.

[32] Lawrence V. Ryan, *Roger Ascham*, Stamford and O.U.P., 1963, p. 68. The treatise became very popular, expressing a characteristic English feeling for a weapon which was already obsolescent.

the *Revenge*, with its long sentences evoking the 'wave and billow of the sea'; or in the famous penultimate paragraph of his *History of the World* – to 'eloquent, just and mighty Death! Whom none could advise, thou has persuaded; what none hath dared thou hast done; and whom all the world hath flattered, thou only hast cast out of the world and despised: thou hast drawn together all the far-stretched greatness, all the pride, cruelty, and ambition of man, and covered it all over with these two narrow words, *Hic jacet.*'[33]

In less than a century, Englishmen had learnt an unsurpassed skill in descriptive and meditative prose.

There is no need to stress the even more spectacular advance in poetry and drama; the lyrics, written to be sung, which derive from the Italian tradition of Wyatt and Surrey; the calm rhythms of Spenser, with his

Sweete Thames! runne softly till I end my song;

the far darting insight of Marlowe's thunderous line, sweeping the language into a new pace, as Byron in his more mundane fashion, would do after him. Looking at the wood-cut title pages with their crude lettering and phonetic spelling, one marvels at his range.[34] Finally there is Shakespeare's profound, yet reconciled, reflection of manifold reality and illusion; in love and war, in town and country, business and politics and the lives of common men. As Dr. Johnson put it, he is 'the poet of nature; the poet that holds up to his readers a faithful mirror of manners and of life'; who said, perhaps more comprehensively than any of the great geniuses, all that could in his day be said.

In England, as in fifth century Athens, the most brilliant achievements came early; the great Elizabethan and Jacobean masters were never surpassed even in the rich harvest of three succeeding centuries. It is in fact extraordinary that Shakespeare's complex, sophisticated, yet serene genius, the greatest intellectual contribution of England to mankind, should have rocketed up so soon, no more than two generations from the

---

[33] *The History of the World in Five books*, ed. 1687, p. 813.

[34] Tamburlaine the Great, *who from a Scythian Shephearde*, by his rare and woonderfull conquests, became a most puissant and mightye Monarque. And (for his tyranny, and terrour in Warre) was tearmed the Scourge of God! Or The Famous Tragedy of the Rich Ievv of Malta, written by Christopher Marlo.

homely if forceful early Tudor speech, and showered down such cascades of wit, beauty, and wisdom that the world is still dazzled. Here is the highest, yet representative response of a vigorous and eager people, already depicted to the life by Chaucer and still much rooted in medieval ways, to the stimulus of Italian humanism, to the new knowledge, the long-rumoured civilisations of the East, and the discovery of lands and oceans hitherto unimagined.

Chapter 7

The Great Rebellion

A FTER the political success of the Tudors, England lapsed into Civil Wars, her out-at-elbows refugees haunting Paris and the Low Countries; and the English set the precedent, followed in the French Revolution, of formally and illegally executing their sovereign. The Great Rebellion was a classic tragedy, a nemesis of conflicting characters; yet, like a fever, it purged the body politic and by reaction confirmed the rule of law. 'The result of the development of public law during the century was to create a state which differed from any other in Europe. The English people refused to identify King with state.'[1]

Despite the interregnum, the main trend of political, social and cultural development was confirmed, and at the Restoration decisions made before the conflict were accepted. The monarchy of Charles II in 1660 was not yet constitutional; it was mixed, despised by continental dynasts, politically unstable; but reflects the shift of social and economic power and confirmed basic liberties. The new absolute monarchy prevalent on the Continent, buttressed by bureaucracy, standing armies and heavy taxation, never took root.

Continuity was also preserved in commerce and colonisation, in agriculture and sport; in education, science, and literature. Despite the Civil Wars, a revolution of rising expectations went on; England was richer and more civilised in 1660 than in 1603.

As most contemporaries well knew, though some modern historians have argued against it, the Great Rebellion was made by rich men on their way up, not by desperate men on their way down, if adventurers exploited the general crisis of confidence. When Henry VIII had sold off the monastic lands, he had at first won support for his revolution; but in the long run he had

[1] Sir William Holdsworth, *A History of English Law*, Methuen, 1937 edition, Vol. II, p. 300.

consolidated a power stronger than the Crown. The great aristocratic landowners and city merchants were rich enough to resist
the alien Stuart claims; and both James I, with his favourites, his
dogs and his drink, and Charles I, with his fine taste and devious
mind, were politically inept. As Thomas Hobbes, who lived
through it all, observed, the King's enemies 'desired the whole
and absolute sovereignty and to change the monarchical government into an oligarchic.'[2] He also significantly placed on the title
page of his *History of the Civil Wars* a quotation from Lucretius:
'*Tantum religio potuit suadere malorum*' – so many evils can
religion bring about.

For the religious fanaticism which Henry VIII and Elizabeth I
had successfully contained had now broken out, and the back-
wash of the continental wars of religion, which had already
devastated France and were now devastating Germany, swept
briefly and less ferociously over the British Isles. The Rebellion
also released violent political discussion through pamphlets and
newsheets in which most of the radical notions which would take
on in the nineteenth and twentieth centuries were already canvassed. The various 'Independents' and religious visionaries were
often heirs of the leaders of the Peasants' Revolt and the Lollards, and spread their influence among the early colonists of
New England. But in the home country they were soon put
down; first by the Cromwellian sword Government, which asserted the rights of property with a heavy hand; and then by the
restored establishment, which after 1660 closed its ranks, and
even, after its casual fashion, made use of the new administrative
methods elicited by the war. As usual the perennial oligarchy,
not the people, won out; absorbing, in the English way, adventurers who had done well out of the war, discarding minor cavaliers who had not.

II

The English revolution, though it shocked Europe, was thus
no triumph for the common man. 'In these wars', writes
Hobbes, 'were very few of the common people that cared much

[2] *The History of the Civil Wars in England from the Year 1640 to 1660*,
by T.H., 1669.

for either of these causes, but would have taken any side for pay or plunder.'[3] Indeed, to most contemporaries the Civil Wars were a superfluous blunder, for the main point had been conceded before they began. If Charles I had declared of Parliaments 'as I find their fruit good or evil they are to continue or not to be', by 1641 that high claim had been abandoned and the Prerogative Courts of Star Chamber and High Commission abolished; the rule of Parliament asserted against the King. The Prerogative Courts had dispensed an uneven justice; when in 1631 the people of the Fenland assembled 'in hundreds and five hundreds' at the sound of a bell, demolished the work of Dutch engineers, and claimed 'common of pasture' and 'seizin time out of mind', someone had to fine them £2,000 and compensate the Dutch. But when Lord Savile accosted Sir John Jackson, 'Sirha, who gave you leave to hunt here?', drove him into a 'plash of water', then shouted 'Will you not draw?' and that 'a pott of ale was fitter for him than a sword', Savile was fined £1,000 in Star Chamber for the riot, a monstrous sum.[4]

The High Commission Court meted out a juster discipline. When young parson Vicars of Stamford made his pulpit a 'cockpit of contention', called a 'pore gentlewoman whore', taught 'new-fangles everyday', declared that God would not accept the repentance of old men (they had left it too late), and 'meddled with private matters of marriage in an undecent manner', he was, they felt, justly deprived and incarcerated.[5] And when parson Etsall affirmed his right from God to govern everyone in his parish, and that 'God sees no sin in his Elect', the Bishop of Rochester naturally exclaimed 'If I could prevail, I would send him to Bedlam.' Nor was it right that Richard Hickman of Waddington should with impunity 'use obscene talk and carriage' and make the churchwarden drunk on the communion wine, or that the parishioners of Hardwicke should 'Christen a cat'.

To those carrying on the King's archaic government, the Prerogative Courts were a bulwark of law and order; but to many Parliamentarians and the artisans who supported them, the

---

[3] Op. cit., p. 2.

[4] J. R. Gardiner, *Cases in the Courts of Star Chamber and High Commission*, Camden Society, 1886, p. 145.

[5] Ibid., pp. 220 ff.

Caroline Church and State thwarted productivity and enterprise. John Hampden, an astute politician, who refused to pay Ship Money, a reasonable tax, was extremely wealthy; Pym was 'a government employee and treasurer of a City company; Holles, son of a gentleman rich enough to buy an earldom. When the five members escaped from the King's attempt to arrest them in January 1642, they did not flee to the backwoods; they retired to the City of London . . .'[6] The Crown had alienated its natural supporters; all the big seaports were for Parliament, and the people of 'Leeds, Halifax and Bradford . . . naturally maligned the Gentry.'[7]

And the well-to-do Parliamentarians were in league with formidable lawyers. The antiquarian Lord Chief Justice, Sir Edward Coke, re-interpreted the Common Law peculiar to England, and long resisted the Crown's attempts to impose prerogative law in continental fashion. This old case-made law was now reinforced, often distorted, by medieval precedents; by the cult of 'Anglo-Saxon liberties' supposedly abused by 'Norman Colonels', and of Magna Carta itself, freely interpreted; for the 'supreme power civil' lay in the Commonwealth, and the monarch was a trustee, not the source of 'absolute and inherent right.' Like the barons of Magna Carta, the new oligarchy in asserting their own liberties set the precedent for the liberties of lesser men, if their immediate interest was their own. A Tudor monarch would have conciliated this interest; Charles I had no head for administration or flair for politics; he was an aloof, fastidious, royalty; the greatest art patron of the English Kings, much influenced by his Bourbon wife. He could read neither events nor men, nor assess power; still less, conduct a *coup d'état*.[8]

Against this background, the Rebellion proceeded in classic course to its macabre climax. Begun by civilian moderates, it was finished by grandees of the army, and, after a phase of near

[6] Christopher Hill, *Puritanism and Revolution*, Secker and Warburg, 1958, p. 11.   [7] Ibid., p. 204.

[8] Consider his ineptness when attempting to seize the Five Members in January 1642, 'Coming down to Wightehall . . . to the howse of Commons with armed men'. Always polite, he uncovered, bowing right and left; 'Mr. Speaker,' he said, 'I must for the time make bold with your chair.' But he brought no proper force and the 'birds', advertised of his coming, 'were flown'. 'Zounds, they are gone' said one of his amateur officers, 'and now be we never the better for our coming.' *The Journal of Sir Simonds D'Ewes*, ed. W. H. Coates, Yale Univ. Press, 1942, pp. 381–2.

anarchy, ended in military dictatorship and the rule of major-generals 'behaving themselves most tyrannically'. Indeed, after the murder of Charles I, the army had defied most public opinion: 'Think what justice', the King had warned them at his 'trial', 'other men will have'. The army won a decade of power, but no security: if the administration made by Thurloe and his colleagues to prosecute the war survived, with a system and order the old régime had not been able to command. At the Restoration what seemed sanity was reasserted, and Samuel Pepys and his kind salvaged a bureaucracy from the Interregnum, more efficient than that created under Henry VIII by Thomas Cromwell.

But the English were left with a deeper hatred of arbitrary power, whether of Crown or army, and a deeper class-consciousness, worsened by religious prejudice. Unhorsed and offered his life by the Parliamentarians, Spencer Compton, second Earl of Northampton, had 'scorned to take quarter from such base rogues and rebels as they were' and died defiant. The rebels were bitterly despised; their hangers-on, who often manned the Committees for Sequestration on royalist estates, detested. On the other side, the old Puritan capacity for moral indignation was confirmed: the Cavaliers were familiarly known to their opponents as the 'Dammees',[9] and the cult of sermons and sabbath, of family prayers and being a peculiar people was intensified by victory and by defeat.

The English Sunday ('The Lord's Day, commonly called Sunday') made its official appearance only by 1642, in an order of the House of Commons which forbade 'Tippling in Tobacco Shops and Ale Houses', and fruiterers and herb women to 'stand with fruit' or milk women to cry 'milke' in any streets. But, socially, Parliament was not radical: it was much concerned that the books and records of the College of Heralds should be kept from 'demolishing, defacing, embezzlement or purloining'.[10] Indeed, both sides were united in the desire for economic expansion, if the conflict, and the legend it left first fully expressed two lasting aspects of the English character: Cavalier panache and

[9] Christopher Hill, *Society and Puritanism in Pre-Revolutionary England*, Secker and Warburg, 1964, p. 419. 'Damn me,' cried one, dying in battle, 'I'll go to my King.'

[10] Husband's *Collections*. Of the publicke Orders, Ordinances, and Declarations of both Houses of Parliament. March 1642–Dec. 1646 (1646), p. 7.

Roundhead austerity, symbolised in our own century by Sir Winston Churchill and Clement Attlee.

III

'It is not our conquests but our commerce, not our swords but our sails', wrote a mercantilist in 1643, in the midst of the First Civil War, 'that first spread the English name in Barbary and thence into Turkey, Armenia, Muscovia, Arabia, Persia, India, China, and, indeed, over and about the world.[11] In spite of domestic conflict, the oceanic horizons opened up by the Elizabethans were exploited in the seventeenth century; and when Blake's Cromwellian battlefleet passed Gibraltar into the western Mediterranean, the English asserted a new dimension of naval power. With that behind them, they developed the far flung commerce which the Elizabethans had begun. The resounding exploits of Drake, who had 'encompassed' the world, the belief that the Spanish empire was a 'colossus stuffed with clouts'[12] and that the Protestant English had a mission to extirpate Spanish cruelty and fanaticism, had taken deep root: 'The righteousness of the Elizabethans remained still a part of English religion in Kingsley's time and produced a last romantic echo in Tennyson's *The Revenge*.'[13]

In spite of the growing riches of the well-to-do, unemployment had increased, and 'plantations' were now thought a sovereign remedy: the settlement of Virginia was designed to produce commodities hitherto bought in continental Europe, though in fact it soon had to live by tobacco; New England – the 'Plymouth Plantation' – was colonised because the Foundling Fathers in 1620 fetched up on the sandy beaches of Cape Cod too late in the year to proceed to part of Virginia, itself pitched upon because in Guiana they would have had to fight the Spaniards and Portuguese if they were to practise their Calvinist religion.

The sporadic and casual Caroline attempts to promote colonial trade and settlement were resumed much more efficiently by the

---

[11] See R. W. K. Hinton, 'The Mercantile System in the time of Thomas Mun', *Econ. History Review*, Second Series, VII, No. 3, 1955.

[12] J. A. Williamson, *The Ocean in English History*, p. 116.

[13] Ibid.

Commonwealth and Protectorate. 'Whereas the Plantations in New England', began an order of the House of Commons in 1642, had attained 'good and prosperous success without any public charge on the state...' and were likely 'to prove very happy in the propagation of the Gospel in those parts', all customs duties, either way, were to be abolished.[14] The Navigation Acts of 1650 and '51 gave British shipping the monopoly of the Atlantic trade; and when Cromwell – a neo-Elizabethan – became Protector, he deliberately took up what Drake and Hawkins and Raleigh had begun.[15] He had already secured from the Portuguese freedom of trade in Brazil, West Africa and the East; and he tried, and failed, to overthrow the Spanish-American empire: Jamaica, then no asset, was all he obtained. Royalists and Parliamentarians were thus united in mercantilist objectives, and the Restoration Government at once reinforced the Navigation Acts by another in 1660 and a Staple Act in 1663. This rivalry with the Dutch united all parties: Mun, Selden (whose *Mare Clausum* was published in 1637), Cromwell, Albemarle and James, Duke of York. For according to mercantilist ideas England could thus expand her trade. All colonial produce had to be shipped in English vessels and, if further exported, to pass through England. The consequent smuggling and discontent in the plantations were more than offset in the eyes of the government, whatever its political views, by the overriding importance of maintaining the seapower, now recognised as England's trump card in the game of European politics, on which all oceanic enterprise must depend.

Atlantic expansion was paralleled by the exploitation of India and the Far East. The influx of Spanish-American silver had increased the purchasing power of Europeans in Asia; the Portuguese who, in 1580, had come under the hand of Spain, lost grip on their Eastern empire, and Dutch and English East Indiamen could cross the Southern Indian Ocean direct to the East Indies, independently of the seasonal monsoon. The East India Company, rich with the profits of the Spice Islands – the 'lacquered' as opposed to the 'feathered' Indies – now turned to the

[14] Husband's *Collections*, op. cit., p. 6.
[15] This aspect of his régime was highly popular: in 1666, after the Restoration, Pepys could write 'It is strange how everybody nowadays reflects upon Oliver, and commends him, what brave things he did, and made all the neighbour kingdoms fear him.'

mainland of India, where they developed a lucrative trade in cotton fabrics, which 'besides serving for ornament supplied the growing need of European civilisation for washable under-clothing.'[16] Indigo for dyes and saltpetre for gunpowder both proved lucrative, 'as the musketeer drove the pikeman from the fields of Europe ... However other trades might fluctuate, there was hardly a time from the Defenestration of Prague to the fall of Napoleon when a cargo of saltpetre would fail to arrive on a rising market.'[17] After the Restoration, the East India Company, with Government support, became immensely rich, and its 'interest' important in eighteenth century politics. In the Levant and the Persian Gulf, also, the Company's factories were established; from Mocha directly, and later from Surat, near Bombay, a new luxury was imported and the 'coffee house' came to play its decisive part in London trade and politics.

Such, in brief, was the expanding commerce which forms the background both to the political and social conflicts and the diffused prosperity of seventeenth century England, and such the decisive settlement of 'plantations' across the Atlantic. Whatever their own internal dissension and social divisions, a still hierarchical society looked down upon the colonials and regarded emigration as a last resort; but the English were now intensely sea-minded, and owed their political power and their growing prosperity to the navy and to the great joint stock companies which were exploiting markets hitherto the monopoly of Spaniards and Portuguese. The Dutch, engaged on a similar enterprise, were their chief rivals; at first their superiors, in time to be outclassed. Already, by the Restoration, England was on the threshold of the vast empire attained, and partially lost, in the mid-eighteenth century. The financial developments behind this expansion, decisive for the mentality of the nation, will later be described; suffice it that the still elementary banking services of the Goldsmiths of London were developing techniques for loans, deposits, drawn notes – cheques – and bank notes by the mid-century. It was a ruthless, wealthy establishment that emerged out of the Civil Wars into the Restoration.

[16] J. A. Williamson, op. cit., p. 107.   [17] Ibid., p. 109.

IV

The seventeenth century was thus not all civil war and religious rant; in a chequered, inflationary, but expanding economy the poor were poorer, but ambitious families were doing well. Wealth to population greatly increased and, apart from the fantastic expenditure of the Court and magnates, there were new standards of comfort; of silver instead of pewter, of carpets and feather beds; of elaborate furniture carefully itemised. 'One high chair ymbrodered with yellow twist upon black velvet'; a 'canopy of green cloth laced and fringed'; one 'large chair seated and backed with scarlet fringed with yellow silk'; a bedstead of 'walnutree' and 'five curtains of red and yellow say, with the curtain rods and five gilt knobs'; vast quantities of linen; table napkins by the dozen.[18] These people were houseproud, like the Dutch, whom they admired: 'homeliness', that northern quality, was coming in, often strengthened by the piety of the head of the household, taken over from the father confessor.

The great magnates accumulated vast estates and the prices of land doubled during the century; they built gigantic palaces, still famous; Elizabethan Hardwick in Derbyshire with its vast display of glass and fantastic towers; Longleat in its wooded amphitheatre near Warminster in Wiltshire; Montacute with its honey-coloured Somerset stone; Knole in Kent, a huge medieval palace adapted to Stuart taste; Jacobean Hatfield in brick, built by Sir Robert Cecil, the first Earl of Salisbury; Wilton, rebuilt in the mid-seventeenth century from its Tudor original by Inigo Jones and John Webb, its elegant south front facing across great lawns on to the Nadder, the cube and double cube rooms displaying the masterpieces of van Dyck. The manor houses of the gentry and the town houses of substantial merchants became more comfortable. Gardens were already an English cult; they were now more extensive, with long walks, parterres, flower borders and ornamental fishponds and canals. Orangeries and even hot houses came in – 'what was very ingenious was the subterranean heat'. *Parkinson's Paradisus Terrestris* lists a great variety of flowers and vegetables grown for the market; already the 'Piazza' at Covent Garden was established.

[18] From the Will of the Auditor to the Earls of Bedford, 1627.

This prosperity reflected more capital investment and new East Indian fortunes laid out in land, as well as an increased acreage of arable, as against sheep runs. Books on farming acclimatised Dutch methods of cultivation; marling and manuring were better understood and root crops further developed; and although the English long objected to the potato as 'windy meate', by the mid-century Sir Richard Weston was advocating the 'Husbandry used in Brabant and Flanders'.

The gross plenty of the diet of the Tudor well-to-do now became more varied, the main meal now at mid-day, 'when "the English eat a great deal at Dinner; they rest a while, and to it again...Their supper is moderate; gluttons at noon, and abstinent at Night."[19] The sequence of soup, fish and meat now superseded the meat-fish Tudor custom; with cheaper sugar, the English love of 'pudding' began. 'Blessed be he that invented Pudding', wrote Misson, and he praises 'Christmas Pie', the ancestor of Christmas Pudding, a 'most learned mixture'.

The English still drank vast quantities of ale and beer and consumed quantities of cheap oysters: they also now took to the Dutch custom of drinking gin and to Irish '*Aqua vitae*, vulgarly called Usquebagh' – or whisky.

The Tudor cult of sport continued; and the English, writes Trevelyan, were already 'notorious' in Europe for their devotion to horses and dogs. The Tudor books on sport already cited, had their often elaborate successors, and in 1636 Gervase Markham issued the final version of his popular treatise on the horse.[20] 'Every horse', he writes, 'has his due temperament'; from the hot choleric horse, the cold dull horse, the dry mischievous horse, to the moist cowardly horse – the best horses having a proper balance of humours, of 'power natural', that virtue belonging to the liver, and 'vital spirits', from the heart. 'Travail not your horse too late', he advised, 'lend him not, keep his stable sweet, have a plain green for him to tumble himself thereon.' And exercise him to prevent 'choleric humours in the panicles of the brain', nightmares from the raw digestion of the stomach, and the inward wet cough. 'Tyred' horses will revive after a quart of

---

[19] *Misson's Memoires*, quoted in *The Englishman's Food* by J. C. Drummond and Anne Wilbraham, Cape, 1939, p. 129, q.v. for the best account.
[20] *Markham's Maisterpiece*, containing all knowledge belonging to Smith, Farrier, or Horse-leach.

strong ale brewed up with a half ounce of elicampane. And never
buy a horse if he turns up the whites of his eyes or lays back his
ears when ridden; he will prove 'a sullen jade, full of naughty
qualities'.

Izaak Walton's *Compleat Angler*, published in 1653,[21] is the
classic of fishing, still famous. Walton, a London merchant, and
pioneer biographer, who retired to the country during the Civil
Wars, was expert not only in taking fish, but in cooking them;
knowing how to stuff a pike with oysters and anchovy, and just
how to dress an eel with sweet herbs, good butter and salt – 'a
most excellent dish of meat'.[22] Natural dialogue and apt inser-
tion of rhymes and songs combine with good practical instruction
on tackle and bait, and on fishponds and how to order them.

These and many other works reflect the English passion for
outdoor sports, later expressed in games with mass popular appeal, as in cricket and football – one of the most original and
pervasive influences of the island on the world.

Thus, beneath the political, social and religious upheavals
which in retrospect loom so large, the continuity of English life
went on, little interrupted save by heavier taxation. There was
not the devastation and massacre occasioned by the Wars of
Religion in France and in the Thirty Years' War in Germany.
Mercenaries and foreign invaders were not let loose on a great
scale, nor did widespread famine and disease follow in the wake
of the armies. Society was already too well grounded in a manageable area; wealth and productivity beginning to increase.

V

In education, also, a creative continuity was preserved. On
medieval foundations Renaissance had been reinforced by Reformation; ancient schools and colleges were now re-founded, and
great merchants no longer endowed chantries but grammar
schools. Between 1550 and 1660 they poured out their wealth in

---

[21] *The Compleat Angler*: or contemplative man's recreation. Being a dis-
course on Rivers, Fishponds, Fish and Fishing. The fifth edition, 1676, was
supplemented by Charles Cotton's treatise on how to angle for a trout or
Grayling in a clear stream. (The edition of 1760 by John Hawkins is dedicated to Edward Popham of Littlecote, Wilts, on the Kennet.)

[22] Ibid., p. 210.

these Anglican endowments. To medieval Eton and Winchester and the great London schools, Westminster and St. Paul's, were now added the originals of Harrow and Shrewsbury, of Rugby, Merchant Taylors', Charterhouse, Felsted, Repton and Blundell's. As Eton with King's, Winchester with New College, Westminster with Christ Church and Trinity, Cambridge, so Merchant Taylors' was linked with St. John's at Oxford, Blundell's with Balliol. And a net of grammar schools caught local talent and brought the sons of gentry, clergy, yeomen and tradespeople together in a way now thought happy, though at that time some critics disapproved and advocated foreign travel for the better born. There were in fact more schools to population than at any time until the late nineteenth century, and the Caroline Court was a centre of intelligent patronage.

The greatest schools thus educated a close élite, widely recruited but remote from the people, and these schools survived the Civil Wars. After the Restoration, in May 1661, wrote John Evelyn, he 'heard and saw such exercises at ye election of scholars at Westminster School to be sent to the University in Latin, Greek, Hebrew and Arabic, as wonderfully astonished (him) in such youths.'[23] Boys conversed and acted in Latin, for this Anglican learning was still based, to the concern of some Puritans, on the literature of pagan antiquity; and 'while youth do learn the language of the heathen', wrote one moralist, 'they do also learn the wickedness of that language.'

This esoteric culture, common to the ruling classes, was variously interpreted. Dr. Richard Busby, for example, the famous Head Master of Westminster, to whom families on both sides in the Civil Wars continued to entrust their sons, was a strict and scholastic conservative. He prayed for Charles I on the day of his execution, and was rumoured – falsely – to have kept on his hat in the presence of Charles II lest his boys should think anyone more important than he was. When the Speaker of the House of Commons showed arrogance, he was accused of behaving 'like a Busby among so many schoolboys'. Busby ruled by the birch and expurgated many classical texts.

Thomas Farnaby, on the other hand, the most famous schoolmaster of the previous generation, was more liberal. The son of a

[23] See W. A. L. Vincent, *The State and School Education, 1640–1660*, S.P.C.K., 1950, p. 19.

carpenter, of Cornish and probably Italian descent, he was educated by the Jesuits in Spain; but being 'very wild' and 'minded
to take a ramble', says Anthony Wood, he had been with Drake
and Hawkins in the Caribbean. Reduced to schoolmastering, he
founded an immensely successful academy in London; then
moved to Sevenoaks in Kent where it flourished: 'more Church
and statesmen issued thence than from any school taught by one
man in England.' He edited Juvenal, Martial, Ovid and Petro-
nius, and taught more on the lines later proposed by Aubrey in
his *An Idea of the Education of Young Gentlemen* – in which
continental notions of the 'complete man' were advocated.[24]

The blend of strict still scholastic discipline and disputation
with more secular learning had been already apparent under
Elizabeth I. Ascham, besides writing on archery in his youth, had
popularised humanist theory in *The Scholemaster*: 'Young
childer', he wrote, 'are sooner allured by love than driven by
beating to attain good learning'. He had wanted his boys versatile as well as learned; 'merry and pleasant' as well as able;
though precocious quick wits, he observed, were apt to be 'carried away by riots and unthriftiness'. Richard Mulcester, of Eton
and Christ Church, headmaster of Merchant Taylors' and St.
Paul's, had shown similar psychological insight: education should
go with the grain of personality, not against it. The end, he had
said, was 'to help nature to her perfection'.

So strong and respected was this élite culture that it easily
survived the distractions of the Civil Wars. In the English way,
the system took its conquerors captive: the intruded Presbyterian
Provost of Eton, Francis Rous, soon succumbed to the place,
'which hath my dear affection'; the Warden of Winchester,
though he had 'preached against those who had taken away the
Church beautifyings', took the Covenant and kept his office; and
when Cromwell, who had sent his sons to Felsted, in his prosperity sent his ward to Eton, he followed a very English precedent.

It was, of course, taken for granted that the mass of the people
were left illiterate. During the Interregnum, government con-

[24]Aubrey, however, was always against French education: 'like the shear-
ing of Hogges,' he wrote, 'they make great cry and little wool ... their
minds do chiefly run on the propagation of their race.' Unlike Busby,
Aubrey objected to beating: 'I would have no such thing as the turning up
of bare buttocks for pedants to exercise their cruel lusts.' Anthony Powell,
John Aubrey and his Friends, Eyre and Spottiswoode, 1948, pp. 282–7.

sidered plans for a comprehensive state-directed education – 'all the people instructed, none neglected'. The famous Czech educationalist Commenius was asked to advise, but he left, disillusioned, after six months. Samuel Hartlib, a 'very communicative' Pole, who had written *Macaria*, an optimistic Utopia, did better; he obtained a pension of £300 a year, when the salaries of many schoolmasters were about £15: perhaps he deserved it, since he had written that 'I see the cause is not in God but in man's fooleries that his people live in misery in this world.'

The attempt at a national system of education proved premature, but at least the bone was not lost for the reflection: the theorists were not let loose; existing élites were not destroyed, standards maintained. The schools continued to train men for Church and State, and were behind the scholarship of the age of Bentley in the early eighteenth century.

The universities, too, continued to flourish and expand in their new Anglican guise. By the end of Elizabeth I's reign, all undergraduates belonged to colleges through which alone they matriculated: hence the lasting contrast with universities abroad. The Reformation had 'made the fortune' of Cambridge, 'hence its Tudor look compared with the medieval appearance of Oxford'.[25] The Great Court and Neville's Court at Trinity had been completed by 1615: St. John's, the college of Cheke and Cecil, was greatly enlarged. Dr. John Caius, the most eminent doctor of his time, a Norwich man who had studied under Vesalius at Padua, and a widely travelled President of the Royal College of Physicians, refounded Gonville as Gonville and Caius: he is commemorated by the Italianate gates of Humility, Virtue and Honour, 'copied from the sepulchral monuments of the ancients'. Two puritan colleges, Sidney Sussex, which harboured Oliver Cromwell, an 'ardent footballer', whatever that then implied, and Emmanuel, important for New England, were now established. At Oxford, Jesus, St. John's, Trinity, all flourished, and Sir Thomas Bodley, a retired diplomat, refounded the most ancient university library in England. Already the peculiar English humour and sentiment for their ancient universities is expressed in Aubrey's account of Trinity at Oxford and its eccentric President, Dr. Ralph Kettel: he had a 'terrible gigantic aspect... but dragged with one foot a little, by which he gave

[25]A. L. Rowse, *The England of Elizabeth*, pp. 513–18.

warning (like a rattlesnake) of his coming'. He was a legend, a forerunner of many famous characters.[26] Aubrey thought Oxford and Middle Temple the 'greatest felicity' of his life: 'Ingeniose youthes', he wrote, 'like rosebuds, imbibe the morning dew'. Thus medieval English education was Anglicised.

VI

During the Interregnum, too, the new Baconian vision of applied science was first assimilated. After the first Civil War the numbers of undergraduates increased, the places left by ruined royalists filled by the sons of those who had done well out of the upheaval. John Wilkins, a famous Warden of Wadham, brother-in-law to Oliver Cromwell and first President of the Royal Society; Seth Ward, Savilian Professor of Astronomy, and later Bishop of Salisbury; Dr. John Wallis, Professor of Geometry, were all new men: it has even been said that 'modern science entered Oxford behind the New Model Army'.[27] In spite of these origins, rudimentary scientific experiment became fashionable during the Restoration, when Charles II founded the Royal Society. So a new aspect of English genius now became important – a flair for scientific hypotheses and inventions which would extend English influence throughout the world and contribute greatly to the seventeenth-century rise of Western Europe to a phase of world supremacy.

Indeed, Francis Bacon's vision of organised research into the 'truth and nature of things' for the 'relief of man's estate', paralleled by Descartes' ambition to 'render ourselves the lords and possessors of nature' was decisive for all mankind. The society Bacon depicts in his *New Atlantis* is dynamic and productive; applied science mounting an attack on the poverty hitherto taken for granted. The French Encyclopedist Diderot would take the *Novum Organum* of '*L'immortel Chancellier d'Angleterre*' as

---

[26] He was 'irreconcilable to long hair', and would on occasion cut it off with the knife from the buttery. 'I will show you,' he would say, 'how to inscribe a triangle in a quadrangle. Bring a pig into the quadrangle and I will sette the college dog at him, and he will take the pig by the ear; then come I and take the dog by the tayle, and so you have a triangle in a quadrangle. *Quod erat faciendum.*'

[27] Christopher Hill, op. cit., p. 29.

a model, and Saint-Simon, who would insist on the amelioration of the lot of the most numerous and the poorest class, would consider Bacon 'as great a man as he could be for his time.'

A lesser man than Bacon, George Hakewill, who championed the 'Moderns' against the 'Ancients', understood the idea of progress and even of world-commonwealth as early as 1640; attributed the pessimism of the 'Ancients' to the 'morosity and crookedness of old men and the overvaluing of Antiquity', and pointed out that had mankind been degenerating ever since Adam they would now be no bigger than rats. The Wiltshireman Thomas Hobbes, the most original and powerful of English political philosophers, a great master of ironic and pungent prose, was convinced, after the nominalist medieval school of Ockham, of the limitations of mind; but he had a fine sense of responsibility and the optimism to try to clean the slate; to start afresh with a man-made political morality, based on a hard appraisal of the latest psychology and of human folly and fate. He provoked bitter attack for alleged atheism and for 'vilifying the human nature', but he is behind the philosophies of man-made improvements of the nineteenth century, and one of the makers of the modern outlook.

Less redoubtable minds were pessimistic at the loss of the old faith; declared that creation was coming to its final climacteric year, that nature was poisoned and 'out of tune', and preached to eager congregations swingeing sermons on original sin.

With the modification of the Laudian censorship, these controversies now got into print and a strident war of pamphlets broke out. For the first time the power of the press affected the mass of the people, and Richard Baxter's relatively liberal Calvinistic *Call to the Unconverted* sold 20,000 copies on publication. Revolutionaries and cranks, clapped into gaol, were not denied pen and paper: John Lilburne, that irrepressible eccentric who, though born a gentleman, 'could neither make a leg with grace nor put off his hat seemly', and whose appetite for martyrdom made him famous, anticipated a perennial strain of English radicalism, though he ended up, disillusioned with politics, as a Quaker. Other 'Leveller' propagandists spoke out in print: 'I do extremely indulge the building of Christian societies on a small model', wrote William Walwyn, deeply 'concerned' for social justice. More raucous, in the manner of Skelton, Richard

Overton, alias *Martin Marprelate* or Claw Clergy, attacked the Presbyterian divines; and Gerard Winstanley, a mystical pantheist, inspired the Diggers to attempt a simple life of agrarian communism. All these eccentrics have been claimed as forerunners of modern radicalism and even communism; 'they had more in common with William Langland than with Thomas Paine or Karl Marx.'[28] They stemmed from the Lollards and from the Anabaptist and Millenarian movements of the sixteenth century; from the uncritical reading of generations brought up on the translated Bible; and they broke out from the Anglican and Presbyterian Churches, even from the theocracy of New England, where the frontier enabled the spirit to blow where it listed and Roger Williams at Naragansett to try to convert Red Indians.

This tradition of Bible reading, preaching and pamphleteering was gathered up and simplified by a Baptist tinker. John Bunyan's *The Pilgrim's Progress* became a best seller and remained so; in plain speech and homely detail he immortalised spiritual experiences among classes hitherto inarticulate and outside the culture of Court and universities. 'The people in scorn called Quakers', inspired by George Fox – who told a magistrate to *tremble* at the name of the Lord – began another English movement which would spread. Unlike the more ascetic visionaries, they accepted life: after his revelation Fox could write that 'all things were new, and all creation gave another smell unto me than before, beyond what words can utter.' Discarding ritual and social distinctions, they hit upon a psychologically powerful meeting in silence, until they were inspired to testify by the subconscious or the spirit. A firm benevolence and humane concern for suffering inspires them still, and their enterprise is world-wide.

VII

The range of English self-expression was thus greatly widened during the Interregnum, but the established literary culture remained unimpaired. At the Jacobean and Caroline Courts lyric poets expressed the vicissitudes of love in words of crystalline beauty.

[28] See W. Schenk, *The Concern for Social Justice in the Puritan Revolution*, Longmans, 1948, pp. 106–8 and 161, for a clearing up of that controversy.

Free beauty, wrote Campion, *if you strive to yoke, you lose,*
And for affection strange distaste you breed.
What nature hath not taught, no art can frame,
Wild will be wild still, though by force made tame.

Raleigh had written,

Passions are liken'd best to floods and streams
The shallow murmur, but the deep are dumb;

and an anonymous poet could ask,

Weep you no more, sad fountains;
What need you flow so fast?

Andrew Marvell, who loved life, was obsessed with time.

But at my back I always hear
Time's wingèd chariot hurrying near,
And yonder all before us lie
Deserts of vast eternity.

Of these many brilliant poets the profoundest was John
Donne, who also brought the elaborate Jacobean-Caroline pulpit
eloquence to its climax. Courtier, doctor and divine, Donne was
a realist, well aware of that 'subtle knot which makes us man':

To our bodies turn we then, that so
Weak men on love revealed may look;
Love's mysteries in souls do grow,
But yet the body is his book.

He gave full rein to love:

Licence my roving hands, he wrote, *and let them go*
Before, behind, between, above, below,
O my America, my new-found-land,
My kingdom, safeliest when with one man man'd.

Yet he could write

Batter my heart, three person'd God,

and conclude the most splendid of his *Devotions* thus:

Perchance he for whom the *bell* tolls, may be so ill, as that
he knows not it tolls for him ... No man is an *Iland* intire

of itself; every man is a pebble of the *continent*, a part of
the *maine*; if a clod bee washed away by the sea, Europe is
the less, as well as if a Promontorie were, as well as if a
mannor of thy *friends* or of *thine* owne were, any man's
death diminishes *me*, because I am involved in mankinde;
and therefore never send to know for whom the *bell* tolls;
it tolls for *thee*.[29]

Milton, the greatest English epic poet, still towers above his
age. He was immensely learned in the European culture of his
time, classical and modern. On the outbreak of the Civil Wars,
he was in Italy; but he abandoned a visit to Sicily and Greece
and returned to ruin his eyesight in the secretariats of the Interregnum. When his political hopes vanished, he set himself to
justify the ways of God to Man and created the thunderous
cadences of *Paradise Lost*, the supreme English seventeenth century poetic exploit; 'like the painted ceilings of Italian palaces,'
as G. N. Clark brilliantly puts it, 'with their clouds and deities,
except that it was vaster and sombre and, in spite of its myth-
ology, real.'[30]

An elaborate prose, too, culminated in Robert Burton's *Anatomy of Melancholy* and in the *Religio Medici* and *Urn Burial*
of Sir Thomas Browne; the recondite learning, the elaborate
quotations, the complex antithetical sentences, touched with the
pulpit eloquence long popular. Consider Burton on Heroical
Love[31], or on Superstition; or Browne on Time, 'which antiquates
antiquities and hath an art to make dust of all things . . .' so that
'the iniquity of oblivion blindly scattereth her Poppy . . . the night
of time far surpasseth the day, and who knows when was the
Equinox?'

These masters, like their contemporary, Rembrandt, painted
with a broad and evocative brush, in a world of mysterious
shadows and sudden dramatic light. They summed up a whole
world of complex North Renaissance Humanism and their elaborate constructions, like the masques of Inigo Jones, perhaps best
symbolise their age.

[29] See John Donne, *Complete Poetry and Selected Prose*, ed. John Hayward,
Nonesuch Press, 1929, for the great range of his mind.
[30] *The Later Stuarts, 1660–1714*, Clarendon Press, 1934, p. 350.
[31] *Anatomy*, III, II, Mem. I, Subs II, I ff.

VIII

So between 1603 and the Restoration the English went through a political revolution which, after a decade of 'sword' government, was limited by the strength of older, more fundamental trends in their society. The ancient rule of law was asserted against the absolute, dynastic, state, and the monarchy refashioned to suit an oligarchic business commonwealth. The 'Glorious Revolution' of 1688–9, when the Catholic James II was evicted, was merely the sequel to a decision made much earlier in the century: the men of great and small property had their liberties secured, and, in principle, the liberties of others were asserted as well. The vigour and enterprise of the eighteenth century would rest upon the political and social victories of the seventeenth.

Further, economic and colonial expansion was not disrupted; rather it increased. English military and naval power was better organised and deployed under the revolutionary government than ever before, and the intellectual life of the country went on in full vigour. The brilliant Elizabethan culture became more mature, deep-rooted and widespread; and the natural bent of the English for science and invention was now, for the first time, revealed.

Chapter 8

Restoration and Horizons of Empire

WHEN, in 1660, Charles II had come into his own again, the basic strength and continuity of English life were unimpaired; but politically England was still riven by factions and religious strife and, compared with the great continental states, a second-rate nation. By the end of the Marlborough wars and by the accession of the Hanoverian dynasty in 1714, the country had become a great oceanic and military power, following long and arduous campaigns: the defeat of the French navy off La Hogue in 1692 and Marlborough's victory in 1703 at Blenheim in Bavaria, deep in the Continent. By 1694 the Bank of England had been founded and London had superseded Amsterdam, itself the heir of Antwerp, as the greatest financial centre in Europe. The Union with Scotland in 1707, though 'most of the Scots middle class and lower classes' were 'hot against it',[1] proved a long-term success. The West Indian islands now produced great wealth; the North American colonies expanded and, after the second Dutch war, included the Dutch American settlements, in particular New Amsterdam, renamed New York. The East India Company also prospered, and in 1688, the year of the Glorious Revolution, Dampier made the first English contact with 'New Holland' – now Australia. During those decades and the early Hanoverian years, modern English prose was created by Dryden, Swift and Defoe, while the Elizabethan and Jacobean theatre was revived in a new style after the long Puritan repression. London, much of it gutted by the Great Fire, was transformed by Wren; the Whig principles of

---

[1] Feiling, op. cit., p. 613. It was particularly difficult to collect the new excise duties on liquor: there were riots in Glasgow and, thirteen years after the Union, the maltsters threatened to 'go to prison and leave off brewing' and went. There was confusion in relating the Scots and English gallon, for the Scots was much larger, and the Commissioners of Customs in Edinburgh complained that their low salaries subjected them to 'too much temptation'. *Cal: Treasury Papers*, 1720–8, p. iii.

political liberty were stated by Locke, and the laws of the cosmos were apparently explained by Newton. England pulled out of the frustrations and fanaticism of the Interregnum and, save for the religious intolerance of the Anglican Church, the restored establishment was not vindictive. After the expulsion of James II in 1688 and the settlement of the succession by Act of Parliament on William III and Mary II, there was growing prosperity and self-confidence. In spite of the strain of continental wars, the foundations of the first eighteenth century British Empire were laid, and the oligarchy confirmed its victory over the Crown; a victory of the propertied classes which, within its limitations, asserted basic liberties. And if the submerged masses were still illiterate and poor, the articulate minority often flourished.

II

Even before the Great Rebellion the English had refused to tolerate a continental kind of absolutism, but the Sovereign still appointed the executive; indeed, until far into the eighteenth century he was expected to govern. Disgusted with faction, the country had accorded the restored monarchy wide powers: James II's position was originally strong. But with his Catholicism, his standing army and his apparent threat to establish absolutism on the French model, he was overthrown by a combination of Whigs and Tories, united in defence of the constitutional and religious settlement of 1660. Even then, the luck which attended William of Orange's expedition in 1688 – the 'Protestant' east wind keeping the English fleet in the Downs and bringing William of Orange's expedition intact into Torbay – had to be ascribed to Divine favour, when cited to justify a Revolution 'glorious' because successful.

The franchise remained medieval, the constitution unwritten; and the English continued to work apparently unworkable institutions; they also invented a rudimentary myth of 'party' politics and improved a still archaic administration. The first – and it is a mere prelude, since there were no highly organised 'parties' in the modern sense until the late nineteenth century – crystallised round the old religious animosities beneath the Restoration Settlement. By 1680 two great political interests were in being, the 'Whigs' and the 'Tories'. The first were, in general, an alliance of great magnates with the rich dissenters in the leading towns; the second represented the landed gentry who supported the monarchy and the Church. Originally the 'Tories' were so-called from Catholic bandits in Ireland, on whom, it was alleged, the succession of James, Duke of York, would depend; the original 'Whigs' from Scottish Covenanters who in 1641 had fought Charles I, after 'that unlucky business of imposing upon the Scots our book of Common Prayer.' Within the politically conscious minority of the nation, a habit of organised contest thus grew up, with manifestoes, badges – 'red rosettes for Tories and true blue for Whigs'[2] – and even rival newspapers. Within a new setting the political pamphleteering of the Great Rebellion took on a more sophisticated venom, expressed in a brisker prose. Factions are nothing new anywhere, and loyalties remained shifting and personal; but the English early practised a civilian way of letting off political steam, destined to spread over vast areas of the globe with varying success.

More immediately important, not only had the administration improved, for the Civil Wars and the Interregnum had forced Parliament to devise new boards and committees; but a neo-Elizabethan foreign policy had demanded the first real regiments in the army and a more systematic concern for the fleet, upon which the nascent world power of England would depend.

In this contest a representative and engaging Englishman is Samuel Pepys, most famous for the intimacies of his earlier diary, but professionally, at the climax of his career, a great civil servant of a new kind, laborious and adroit, proud of his position, impatient of muddle.[3] 'Never till now', he wrote, 'did I see the great authority of my place, all the Captains of the fleet coming cap in hand to me.' He enjoyed 'getting an account ready against the Parliament' and the 'infinity of business to be done on a sudden'; in particular, his own *tour de force*, when, primed with half a pint of sack at the Dog, he began his defence 'acceptably

[2] Feiling, op. cit., p. 557.

[3] 1633–1703. The son of a tailor, and educated at St. Paul's and Cambridge, he rose through his family connections with Admiral Edward Montagu of Hinchingbrooke – one of Cromwell's 'generals at sea' – who helped bring in Charles II and became Earl of Sandwich. By 1673 Pepys was Secretary to the Lords Commissioners of the Admiralty: in 1684, Permanent Secretary to the Admiralty. His greatest work was done under James II.

and smoothly ... all my reason about me as it had been at mine own table'. He found his performance 'cryed up' and received the congratulations of the King himself. There was still no independent civil service – Pepys was a Member of Parliament and dependent on the shifts of patronage – but he was the kind of administrator who, in spite of casualness and corruption, enabled England to become a great naval and military power.

This relatively efficient administration was based both upon the Tudor reorganisation and the expedients of the Civil Wars. It now became more professional: for the first time experts were called in to sit on particular commissions; for instance Locke, Davenant, Wren and Newton served on commissions for plantations and recoinage in the 'nineties. It could launch and sustain Marlborough's well-found armies upon the Continent – the first major English intervention since the Hundred Years' War and now made in terms of vast oceanic and colonial enterprise. The wars of William III and Marlborough mark a new scale of ambition: not only to stop Louis XIV's attempt to dominate Western Europe, but to avert the ruin of English and Dutch trade and colonisation which would have followed, had the French and Spanish empires been combined. The future of South America and the Pacific as well as of Central America, the prized West Indies, and the entire North American continent was in question; the fate of India and the East Indies. Hence the importance of the war of the Spanish Succession, of Marlborough's successive victories commemorated in Vanbrugh's great palace of Blenheim – the English answer to Versailles, with a column enumerating European triumphs. It was the first English monument to an imperial ambition, and to a subject who obtained virtually supreme power; the greatest general in English history, whose charm, courage and humanity did not prevent him becoming a millionaire.

The Treaty of Utrecht in 1713 hardly achieved all that the war party had desired, but it secured the main objectives of the Alliance; got the Spaniards out of the Low Countries (now transferred to Austria, the traditional enemy of France); kept the French out of North Italy at the price of Austrian domination. The naval base at Gibraltar also established English power in the Western Mediterranean, as well as in the Caribbean and in the north-western Atlantic.

At home the historic *Habeas Corpus* Act of 1679 had already secured the subject from arbitrary imprisonment without trial. Any person, it provided, who stood committed for any crime, except for treason or felony plainly expressed in the warrant of commitment, was to have the writ in the legal vacation as well as term; the Chancellor or the judge was even liable to a fine of £500 if it were withheld. And since the fines imposed went to the injured party and not to the Crown, the Crown could not intervene. Further, no person could now be sent into prison out of the kingdom, and even traitors and felons had the right to a speedy trial. Juries, moreover, could not be fined or imprisoned for 'false verdict' or one made against the direction of the judge. Thus the time-honoured custom of imprisoning subjects *incommunicado*, and leaving them to rot without trial, habitual in many otherwise highly civilised states, was prevented and one of the fundamental liberties of England confirmed.

These liberties had also been theoretically justified by the most influential of all English political philosophers, John Locke. Cautious, pedestrian, without illusions, practical and deeply insular – as witness his diary of his travels in France[4] – Locke's quiet genius made him a decisive influence in England and, more directly, in the United States. A formidable man of the world as well as a physician, he achieved fame as a philosopher expounding the limitations of mind, and as a proponent of originally medieval doctrines of the supremacy of the community or 'commonwealth' over government, as reinterpreted in the seventeenth century. Locke thought of the public power as a trustee, dedicated to protect property and to promote the well-being of subjects, and not as a patriarchal institution of divine origin, sacred in itself. The ruler was responsible to the governed, and liable, if he failed in his trust, to dismissal by them. Influenced by Socinian and Dutch thought; tolerant in religion; zealous, in the English tradition of Ascham, for an education which would liberate personality and foster 'health, reputation, knowledge, doing good', and a shrewd economist as well, Locke shows a deliberately limited good sense, typical of the English

[4] 'Take the leaves of kidney beans and put them under your pillow... they will draw all the puneses (fleas) unto them and keep you from being bit.' The tiles of Provençal roofs reminded him of 'an Oxford cap on a scholar's head'. See *Locke's Travels in France 1675–1679*, ed. John Lough, C.U.P., 1953.

political classes who made the Revolution of 1688. Like Bacon, he deeply affected the writers of the French Enlightenment, with their European and world influence,[5] and he encouraged a radically sceptical philosophy.

Another English view of politics was racily expressed by Lord Halifax, the 'Trimmer'; so called from one who 'trims' a boat to keep it on an even keel. Halifax's realistic views are spiced with humour: 'the government of the world', he admits, 'is a great thing, but a very coarse one too, compared with the Fineness of Speculative Knowledge.'[6] In the English manner, he finds tyranny not only sinister but absurd: even monarchy itself is a symbol not to be taken too seriously; necessary, as Bagehot would concur, since the 'rules of commonwealth are too hard for the Bulk of Mankind to come up to.' To Halifax Louis XIV was not sublime but ridiculous; 'a mistaken creature, swelled with Panegyricks and flattered out of his senses, not only an encumbrance but a *nuisance to mankind*.' This weapon of ridicule, employed with some effect against Napoleon and Hitler, has proved a good weapon in the English political armoury, and appeals to other peoples who have developed the Anglo-Saxon tradition.

Sustained thus by an insular prosperity and self-confidence, manifest at home by the successful taming of the sovereign's power and abroad by victories on land and sea, which the prosperity of the island could – under raucous protest – well afford, the England of Queen Anne became symbolised by a characteristic figure. 'John Bull' was invented by Dr. John Arbuthnot, a friend of Swift, in a blistering Tory satire on the war and the events which led to the Treaty of Utrecht.[7] He 'drew the charac-

---

[5] See Maurice Cranston's *John Locke, a biography*, Longmans, 1957 – the best account; also the present writer's *Hobbes and his Critics*, Cape, 1951, for the political theory behind Locke.

[6] See *The Complete Works of George Savile, First Marquis of Halifax*, ed. Sir Walter Raleigh, Oxford, 1912.

[7] *John Bull still in his Senses, or The Law is a Bottomless Pit*, (in the *Life and Works of John Arbuthnot*, ed. G. A. Aitken, Clarendon Press, 1892, pp. 44 ff.), exemplified in the Case of Lord Strutt, John Bull, Nicolas Frog and Lewis Baboon, who spent all they had upon a lawsuit. Printed from a manuscript found in the Cabinet of the famous Sir Humphrey Polesworth, 1712. Reprinted in 1727 as the *History of John Bull*. Lewis Baboon was Louis XIV; Nicolas Frog, 'a cunning sly whoreson', though reliable in business, the Dutch; Lord Strutt, the King of Spain. Marlborough is *Hocus Pocus*, an old cunning attorney, who involved Bull in the lawsuit.

ter which has ever since been accepted' and it at once took on.
Bull was what many Englishmen liked to think they were; 'an
honest plain-dealing clothier descended from as good a stock as
any in the neighbourhood.' He was bold and choleric; 'quick,
and understood his business very well; but no man was more
careless at looking into his accounts or more cheated by partners,
apprentices and servants. This was occasioned by his being a
boon companion, loving his bottle and his diversions, for to say
truth no one kept a better house than John, nor spent more
generously.' He was a civilian figure, plump and ruddy, with
cheeks 'like a trumpeter'; but he was formidable as well;
'dreaded not old Lewis either at backsword, single falchion or
cudgel play.' He was, however, very 'apt to quarrel with his best
friends, especially if they pretended to govern him', and 'his
spirits depended very much upon the air.' He was also no fool, a
fact which the rivals of England have often forgotten, for 'the
Bulls though seemingly plain and well-meaning yet are cunning
enough to turn most Accidents to their own private advantage.'[8]

Such is the character that stood for early eighteenth century
England; it remains an image still widely accepted, and still
perhaps not far out.

III

The self-confidence symbolised by John Bull was based on
economic facts. For already, by the late seventeenth century, the
foundation of the Bank of England had marked a new era of
government finance. The goldsmiths had long kept deposits, advanced loans, and honoured cheques, as well as doing business in
plate, diamonds, pawnbroking and shipping; but now, for example, the goldsmith-banker Sir Francis Child, founder of
Child's Bank, began to shed that side of the business and work
financially with government. Since Parliament controlled taxation, particular public funds could now be assigned as a guaran-
tee, and 'annuities' became a new way of investing in government
'securities'.

The Bank of England had been founded to finance William
III's wars. For decades the reform had been demanded: in 1694,

[8] *History*, p. 4.

advised by a Scots financier, the King set up a joint stock bank for subscribers to a loan of £1,200,000 at 8 per cent. Two years later, Locke and Newton were set to carry out a total recoinage of the debased and clipped silver current; then, in 1709, the Bank of England got the monopoly of Government loans and the City were further committed to the political settlement. As another expedient, the National Debt had been instituted, with important results. It 'hastened the capitalistic development of the country's economic resources, while, at the same time... virtually ended the long-drawn antagonism between the Crown and the Commons over questions of taxation.'[9] During the Interregnum, moreover, the Jews had been allowed to return, and financiers from Holland and Portugal had since expanded their interests in England; banks also grew up in the provinces founded by local men of substance. By the 1720's the stockmarket was important in England's life.

The economy was further stimulated by Scottish infiltration, for the Act of Union had now fully opened the 'road to the south'. As well as developing a vigorous culture in Edinburgh, the Scots would greatly contribute to the economic and intellectual life of England.

Apart from Locke's contribution, political economists now gained prestige: Sir William Petty, for instance, an adventurer from Romsey, who had 'lived in his youth on two-pennyworth of walnuts', and read Vesalius on anatomy in Paris with Hobbes 'who loved his company', had made a great fortune under the Commonwealth as Surveyor of Ireland; better informed than Gresham or Palavicino, his *Political Arithmetic* made him a pioneer of economic theory and rudimentary statistical method.

Against this background, a solid class of investors, with their money in Government Funds and East India and South Sea stock, were already a political and social force, and London the greatest financial centre in the Western world.

IV

The élite of this vigorous society, emancipated from the religious conflicts of the sixteenth and earlier seventeenth centuries,

[9] G. N. Clark, *The Later Stuarts*, Oxford, 1934, p. 168.

intent on practical objectives, and well aware that fanaticism is bad for business and that power must be bridled in the common interest by law, achieved a great deal in science, the arts and literature.

Sir Isaac Newton was the greatest scientist of his time in Europe. The son of a Lincolnshire farmer, he formulated his epoch-making law of gravitation at twenty-three, when rusticated from Trinity College, Cambridge, because of the plague: over two decades later, he thought it worth while to publish the discovery, and his *Principia Mathematica* gave a new picture of the universe which was to dominate men's minds for centuries: 'It seemed indeed that Newton had settled the main principles of mathematics, physics, astronomy and optics once and for all. [10] The Hon. Robert Boyle, too, opened new horizons: he emancipated physics and chemistry from the alchemical notions which haunted even Newton, and his investigation of the atmosphere set these sciences on a more practical course. Halley, the astronomer, who reached the peak of his career in the reign of Anne, carried further the work of Kepler and Galileo. John Ray, at Cambridge, made advances in botany, and travellers to America and the East acquired plants hitherto unknown: the Botanical Garden at Oxford was founded after the Restoration. Following on the pioneer vision of applied science described so forcefully by Bacon, the English now developed this new side of their genius, which would have a greater future and was already winning European prestige. The Dutch mathematician Huygens thought it worth while to make three journeys to England, and such was the reputation of English shipwrights and navigators that, ten years after the Revolution of 1688, Peter the Great, the young Tsar of Russia, came on from Holland to England to study their methods himself. If his entourage leased and 'damnified' Sayes Court, John Evelyn's house at Deptford, and if, as the bailiff put it, they were 'right nasty' about the house, broke three hundred window panes, burnt out the warming pan, made 'pot-holes' in the lawns and 'broke several hollies', all was in the cause of progress.[11]

---

[10] G. N. Clark, op. cit., p. 359.

[11] The legend that the Tsar thought it fun to be trundled in a wheelbarrow through the holly hedge, or, as B. H. Sumner more cautiously put it, himself trundled his wheelbarrow through it (*Peter the Great and the Awakening of*

From the Restoration to the death of Queen Anne English architecture greatly developed; projects postponed or interrupted during the Civil Wars and the Interregnum were again taken up, and great magnates, as Edward Hyde, Earl of Clarendon at Charlbury, celebrated their triumphant, and, in his case, short-lived return. The magnificent naval college at Greenwich, with its splendid ceilings, was originally a naval hospital built under William III, who also enlarged Kensington Palace and Hampton Court, where he found better air than in London. Architects were now expected to have wider theoretical grasp, and the more successful were men of the great world. Sir Christopher Wren, the best of them, the son of a rector of East Knoyle in Wiltshire, afterwards Dean of Windsor, was a typical late Renaissance character; a scientist and a humanist turned architect. Educated at Westminster under Busby and at Christ Church, he became a Fellow of All Souls and Savilian Professor at Oxford before he was thirty. His first, and amateurish building, was the Sheldonian Theatre at Oxford; but he found his full scope in the world of London and the Court. Inigo Jones had designed the classical Banqueting Hall at Whitehall before the Civil Wars; now the new 'Palladian' style swept the board. Although admirable medieval building was still going up on the eve of the Civil Wars, as Laud's quadrangle at St. John's College or the roof of the staircase to Christ Church hall, the disparaging term 'Gothic' had now become fashionable. 'Both for natural imbecilitie of the sharp angle of itselfe and likewise for their very uncomeliness [it] ought', connoisseurs considered, 'to be exiled from judicious eyes and left to the first inventors, the Goths and Lombards.'

The fire of London gave Wren his greatest chance. Many of his elegant City churches survive, and his masterpiece, St. Paul's, in spite of recent outrages threatening to dwarf it, still dominates the Thames and the City, surviving the blitz of the Second World War. Sir John Vanbrugh (van Brook), the son of a sugar merchant of Flemish descent but English by his mother, a daughter of Sir Dudley Carleton, started life as a captain of Marines, and went on to write brilliant comedies: he then turned to architecture

---

Russia, p. 37), is apocryphal. The hedge was 400 feet long and 9 feet high and 'mocked the rudest assaults'. See H. W. G. Hiscock, *John Evelyn and his Family Circle*, Oxford, 1955.

and built Castle Howard and Blenheim: 'military glory in stone'.[12] Hawksmoor, best known for the western towers of Westminster Abbey and the inner quadrangle of All Souls, retained a pleasing medieval fantasy in the new style: but in church and secular architecture the Palladian style became predominant, exemplified in the well-proportioned rooms and elaborate ceilings and fire-places of country houses all over England; houses which have at once a Dutch homeliness and a touch of a French-Italian panache, without the un-English exuberance of baroque.

Henry Purcell, 'one of the most celebrated Masters of the Science of Musick in the kingdom and scarce inferiour to any in Europe', now also attained a continental fame. He was expert in making and repairing instruments and, though he died at thirty-six, he is the first great English composer; for although the English had always been a musical people, and the best lyric and Jacobean poetry had been written to be sung to viol and lute, it was not until the late seventeenth century that an Englishman could compete with such continental masters at Monteverdi and Lully.

In scholarship also England now obtained European reputation. Richard Bentley, the son of a Yorkshire yeoman, and born 'remote from town and bred among the peasantry when young', was sent to St. John's College, Cambridge, by his grandfather, a master builder. Following the Dutch Lipsius and the great French-Italian Scaliger, he set new standards in European learn-ing. His *Dissertation upon the Epistles of Phalaris* (1697) proved that they were not the work of a seventh century Sicilian tyrant, but the clumsy forgery of an Hellenistic 'sophist, whoever he was, that wrote a small book of letters in the name and character of Phalaris . . .' This character, wrote Bentley, 'had not so bad a hand at humouring and personating, but that several believed it was the tyrant himself that talked so big, and could not dis-cover the Ass under the skin of the Lion.'[13]

[12] A. L. Rowse, *The Early Churchills*, Macmillan, 1956, p. 330. Vanbrugh hit it off well enough with Marlborough, another soldier, but with Duchess Sarah became a 'cat on hot bricks'.

[13] *Dissertations upon the Epistles of Phalaris etc.*, ed. Rev. Alexander Dyce, London, 1836, p. 89. Bentley made his main reputation as a critic of the Chronicle of the Byzantine Malalas: for his 'brilliant and elaborate production digresses into numerous interesting enquiries and his wonderful felicity of conjectural emendation were first displayed to the world' (p. xix). The *Dissertation* was occasioned by an edition of the *Epistle* undertaken, casually

The resulting controversy set new standards in academic warfare: Bentley annihilated his critics with elaborate learning, citing the anachronisms and dialect that abounded in the *Letters*. 'Had all other ways failed of detecting this imposter, yet his very speech has betrayed him, for the language is Attic ... But he had forgot that the scene of these epistles was not Athens, but Sicily, where the Doric tongue was generally spoken and written.'[14] Bentley also threw in dissertations on Greek drama and drinking cups and depicted a whole panorama of Greek society in a new way. Though the controversy was satirised by Swift (whose patron was involved) in the *Tale of the Tub* and *Battle of the Books*, Bentley came off best.

Bentley was also a formidable innovator: as Master of Trinity, Cambridge (1700–42), he managed, after running feuds with the Fellows, to landscape the 'Backs' and institute examinations and 'prizes seriously awarded'. 'Claret', said this robust Yorkshire character, 'would be port if it could': polyglot, far-ranging, yet deadly accurate, with an inspired commonsense expressed by an efficient style, his scholarship was unrivalled.

Nor was Bentley alone: medieval studies were now consolidated; already William Dugdale, the Warwickshire antiquary, had written his *Baronage* and *Monasticon*; Thomas Hearne, a labourer when a boy, became underkeeper of the Bodleian Library at Oxford; George Hicks and Humphrey Wanley were pioneers of Anglo-Saxon and old Scandinavian studies; while the austere and short-lived Henry Wharton, from Paston Grammar School in Norfolk and Caius, collated chronicles on which later medieval studies were based. 'Vigorous in their humour', writes Professor Douglas, 'encyclopaedic in their interests, they were driven by that abundant vitality not only into the hidden places of obscure learning but also out into the world of practical endeavour. By the energy of their strenuous lives they gave the seventeenth century some of its most distinctive qualities ... they were powerful agents in the formation of the English character.'[15]

enough, by the Hon. Charles Boyle of Christ Church, who insulted Bentley as Royal Librarian for alleged churlishness over lending a manuscript. The Christ Church dons took Bentley's criticism as an 'affront to their whole society' and 'heaped such insults on him' as to make their reply 'a curiosity of literature'. *See* R. J. White, *Dr. Bentley*, Eyre and Spottiswoode, 1965.

[14] Op. cit., p. 355.

[15] David C. Douglas, *English Scholars*, Cape, 1939, p. 15.

In spite, therefore, of the pedantry, vendettas and easy good cheer in the ancient universities,[16] the hard-hitting scholars of the age set standards for what would be a vast English-speaking world.

V

The Courtiers of the Restoration had introduced a new, frenchified, drama; its idiom different from that of the Elizabethan stage. Banned under the Commonwealth and Protectorate, the brilliant Jacobean and Caroline drama revived, but it now took on a more restricted 'classical' form; women now took the parts formerly assigned to boys and the conventions of the French tragedy and comedy came in. Witty, urban and cynical, concerned with ingenious cuckoldries and farcical mistakes, with brilliant dialogue and social rather than human values; this kind of drama reached its climax in the Irish-educated Congreve, who could never, he confessed, 'look long upon a monkey without very mortifying reflections', and who perfected in *The Double Dealer* and *Love for Love* a style of which the echoes are still discernible in the social comedies of Wilde.[17]

Meanwhile the 'long-eared rout' of Puritans had been sent packing in Samuel Butler's immensely popular *Hudibras*. '*Written in the time of the late Wars*', its rhymed jog-trot verses, after the manner of Skelton, satirised the exploits of *Sir Hudibras* in a

---

[16] The Fellows of All Souls, 'unreformed' under their old statutes, were already celebrating their emblem, put up out of a ditch when the foundations were being laid,

> *Then let us drink and dance a Galliard*
> *In the Remembrance of the Mallard;*
> *Oh by the Blood of King Edward,*
> *Oh by the Blood of King Edward,*
> *It was a swapping, swapping, Mallard!*

[17] The simian qualities that Congreve satirised were denounced in a best-selling contemporary tract, *A Short View of the Immorality and Profaneness of the English Stage, together with The Sense of Antiquity upon this argument*, by Jeremy Collier. 'Being convinc'd that nothing has gone farther in Debauching the Age than the Stage Poets and Play Houses', he begins, 'I thought I could not employ my time better than in writing against them.' ' 'Tis not safe for a man to trust his virtue too far', writes this censorious pedant, speaking for all his kind, 'for fear it should give him the slip; and such entertainment 'sinks Reason into Appetite and breaks down the Distinction between Man and Beast. Goats and Monkeys, if they could speak, would express their Brutality in such language as this.'

parody of Don Quixote. This sanctimonious prig, who went 'a-colonelling',

> Could raise scruples dark and nice
> And after solve 'em in a trice,
> As if Divinity had catch'd
> The Itch, on purpose to be scratch'd.

His own

> Beast was sturdy large and tall
> With Mouth of Meal and Eyes of Wall,

and the Colonel was dragged, in the manner of Burnell the Ass, through farcical adventures, pointed by excellent Annotations, suggesting, for example, that High Dutch was the language that Adam and Eve spoke in Paradise.

This homely satire was rooted in the past; but a new idiom of verse and prose now became more fashionable, also getting its most telling effects by mockery and invective. Dryden was immensely versatile, a master of a brisk explanatory prose, contrasting utterly with the elaborate effects of Sir Thomas Browne or Burton. 'You might', it was said, 'as well compare the flight of the great Bustard to that of the swallow or eagle as Dryden's imagination to that of Milton, yet for traversing plains with undiminished vigour he is matchless'; 'like a nimble Spaniel' he can 'beat and range through the field of memory' till he 'springs his quarry'.

Some lyrics in his dramas are still fresh as dew, as

> Love and Time with reverence use
> Treat 'em like a parting friend,

and

> How sweet it is to love
> And how gay is young desire.

Accurate, too, in describing pleasure, as

> Whilst Alexis lay prest
> In her Arms he lov'd best,

and

> . . . found the fierce pleasure too hasty to stay.

But Dryden's fame was won by the most powerful satire ever

written in English. The dash and insight of *Absalom and Achito-phel*, the humour and pace, is apparent in the opening, when *David* (Charles II)

> *Wide as his command,*
> *Scatter'd his Maker's Image through the Land.*

It goes on to pillory politicians and literary hacks, as Shaftesbury and Shadwell, in a spate of sustained brilliance:

> *A fiery Soul, which, working out its way,*
> *Fretted the Pigmy Body to decay;*

or

> *Og, from a Treason Tavern rowling home,*
> *Round as a globe and liquor'd every chink*
> *Goodly and great he sails behind his Link.*

Dryden's plain fashion of prose was wrought to perfection by Swift, whose baleful genius is remembered mainly through *Gulliver's Travels*, a scarifying satire disguised as a children's tale. But his greatest effects are obtained by a deadpan simplicity; as in the *Modest Proposal for preventing the Children of Poor People from being a Burden to their Parents*. Here he advocated breeding children for the table: 'I have been assured', he writes, 'by a very knowing American of my acquaintance in London, that a young healthy child, well-nursed, is at a year old a most delicious, nourishing and wholesome food...'; he points out also that infants' flesh would be in season throughout the year. Again, in his *Serious and Useful Scheme to make an Hospital for Incurables*, he provides for the future of 'all incurable Fools, Knaves, Scolds, Scribblers, Coxcombs, Liars and Whores.'

Swift's psychological conflicts have been much debated; but 'if the source of his terrible driving force is obscure, there can be no denying the high order of his art. He obliterated the distinction between journalism and literature by the power of his genius; and by creating a language of uncanny naturalness succeeded in making the Augustan style seem to us a development of the natural order of things, rather than an artifact of tremendous consequence.'[18]

This kind of limpid yet deadly prose was given a milder turn by Addison and Steele, pioneers of a sedater journalism congenial

[18] *Times Literary Supplement*, 30 January 1964.

to the well-to-do; and the idiom of poetry would be set for decades by the artificial yet sparkling verse of Pope. But it was Defoe, the Dissenter, the father of the English novel, who portrayed a wider panorama of England, outside the ruling class. He was sixty when, in 1719, he wrote his famous work *Robinson Crusoe*, a tale of adventure set out in the plainest, most commonsensical, terms; and his *Moll Flanders*, written three years later, describes, with accurate sympathy, the vicissitudes of low life. This master of plain prose also wrote a *Tour thro' the whole island of Great Britain*,[19] with a sharp eye for scenery. For Wiltshire with its 'vast continuous body of high chalky hills whose tops spread themselves into fruitful and pleasant Downs, upon which great flocks of sheep are fed'; and also for business and people. For Poole, then 'famous for the best and biggest oysters in all that part of England', and Dorchester, 'where I saw the Church of England clergymen and the Dissenting Minister or preacher Drinking Tea together and conversing with civility.'[20] Defoe's picture of England, halfway between the Jacobean economy and the Industrial Revolution, is a classic of its kind.

V

Such are the main political, economic, and cultural contributions of the creative, forthright and confident epoch between the Restoration, the Marlborough Wars and around the Hanoverian succession: they have all survived as living influences. The hard hitting vigour and eye for the main chance is remarkable, and remarkable, too, how many men of genius came from the people – Newton and Bentley, Samuel Butler and Defoe. The Court was still exotic under the Stuarts and alien under William III; Charles II and James II came of Bourbon-Medici blood through their mother, and of Scots-Danish stock from Charles I. William of Orange was a Dutch royalty of French-Stuart descent; only Mary II and Anne were half-English, from minor Wiltshire gentry through their mother, Anne Hyde. And with Anne, the Court became more dull and homely, for her Danish consort was

[19] By D. D. Gent. The best edition is edited by G. D. H. Cole, Peter Davies, 1927, 2 vols.
[20] Ibid., p. 210.

not enlivening: 'I have tried him drunk and tried him sober', Charles II had remarked, 'and, 'Od's fish, there is nothing in him.'

After 1660 the Anglican Church drew in upon itself: the Nonconformists who, during the Interregnum, had close contacts with the Continent and, in the manner of the English Left, had been imposed upon by many continental charlatans, now settled down to their own self-sufficient way of life; many rich enough to add a certain worldly complacency to their spiritual self-satisfaction.

But the social and economic power of the dominant classes was still based on land; for the first ambition of the successful tradesman was still to buy an estate; as usual the 'rising middle class' continued its ascent until it woke up to find itself gentry. Outside London, the pomp of English civic life remained faintly comic, and no English merchants as such had the grandeur of their prosperous equivalents in the greater continental towns. Most of the really great landowners, their resources enriched by judicious marriages, remained on top, and would somehow stay there until well into the nineteenth century. Civilians ultimately controlled the military and naval might of England; religious enthusiasm became unfashionable, and the Bull family settled down to turn 'most accidents to their private advantage'. In doing so, they let themselves in for a great deal more than they had bargained for, for they acquired the first British Empire of the high eighteenth century.

Chapter 9

The Triumphant Oligarchy

THE eighteenth century was to see the climax of the civilisation of a mainly pre-industrial England and the culmination and partial disruption of the first British Empire. Above the world of mass poverty and crime depicted in Gay's *Beggar's Opera*, there flourished a vigorous and restive society which combined rudimentary internal order with the liberties secured in 1689 and consolidated by the Hanoverian succession.

This oligarchy was long depicted as exclusive and corrupt; battening on an 'unreformed' administration and holding archaic institutions sacrosanct; in fact it well enough represented the politically conscious nation at the time, and 'pocket boroughs'[1] gave able young men their chance. Even the much-maligned George III was representative; and his policy towards America reflected 'the will of the House (of Commons), and so preserved intact the system of mixed government which was ultimately to develop into constitutional government. For that he deserved well of his people', even if 'the price the nation had to pay for preservation of its system of government was the loss of the American colonies.'[2]

The Hanoverian monarchs still had great power and their Court was the centre of political and social life. 'Fortunately', writes Dr. Plumb, 'they were crassly stupid, and they could not grasp, as the Stuarts and William III had grasped, the complexities of either foreign or domestic affairs. Both George I and George II, though obstinate, domineering, and excessively prone to interference in detail, were incapable, totally incapable, of

[1] Most notoriously Old Sarum, the preserve of the Pitts; 'a place', as Hobbes had put it, 'where (as last I got a sight of it) a stranger that knew not what the word Burgesse meant . . . would think it were a couple of Rabbets.' *Collected Works*, 1750 ed., p. 650.
[2] *History of Parliament*. The House of Commons, 1754-1790. Sir Lewis Namier and John Burke, H.M.S.O., 1964, p. 204.

forming a policy.'[3] Policy and administration thus fell to their ministers: Walpole, 'a fixed star', as Dr. Johnson observed, where the Elder Pitt was 'a meteor', was the first great Prime Minister – the title originally 'a term of mild abuse'. He created an inner circle – the two Secretaries of State, the Lord Chancellor, the Lords Privy Seal and President of the Council and the Chancellor of the Exchequer, who met informally but regularly to transact business. And if they ruled only as the King's servants, keeping shifting political groups in line by patronage and taking care of local interests, the monarch, too, had to work within this medium. George III had to go into politics, not to 'be a King', but to carry on government; he was in fact the greatest borough-monger of them all, conciliating because he could not coerce. And the system was adaptable in crisis; during the 'fifties, the King had to allow the Elder Pitt – 'that mad Pitt' he called him – to take charge. Thus the power to govern was secured but circumscribed: the contrast, already apparent in the seventeenth century, with the rise of centralised bureaucracy abroad confirmed.

For within this loose framework, the high aristocracy and their dependants, the gentry; London merchants, West Indian nabobs, and the élite of the armed services and the law contended for advantage. In the counties, of course, the landowning gentry remained predominant. Wiltshire, for example, was 'famous for its independency'; Penruddockes of Compton Chamberlayne and Goddards of Swindon could keep out the nominees of aristocratic Pembrokes and Ailesburys for forty years.[4] In Norfolk, too, the great aristocrats were curbed; if Thetford was in the pocket of the Graftons as Wilton of the Pembrokes, Norwich, like Salisbury and Devizes, was independent. In Dorset Bonds of Creech, Banks of Corfe Castle and Calcrofts of Rempstone formed a solid front; and Bridport was dominated by the Pinneys and their West Indian fortune, Lyme Regis by the Fanes. Over most of rural England, the gentry, not the Court

[3] J. H. Plumb, *England in the Eighteenth Century, 1714–1815*, Pelican History of England, p. 50.
[4] In 1772 on a poll of 2,925, Ambrose Goddard beat Henry Herbert by 815 votes. The contest was in part regional, North Wilts voting pretty solidly for Goddard. At Wilton, in South Wilts, not one voter dared to oppose Herbert: Westbury and Warminster were divided; Trowbridge solid for Herbert. *The Poll of the Freeholders of Wiltshire*, 1772.

magnates, were in control. There Court influence was kept well within bounds.

So land still meant power and would mean it until the late nineteenth century; the landowners, great and small, continued to assimilate success. When a merchant bought a large estate, he was, and he knew it, buying his way out of his class at a premium.[5] That premium had always been willingly paid: in England 'the word tradesman does not', wrote Namier with a continental eye, 'sound so harsh as in other countries.'[6] Rising professional men, too, were accepted: 'no eminent German lawyer or professional man would have been made Count or Baron': in England they could become peers. And in England only the heir, following the old custom of primogeniture already described, took the title; his brothers and younger sons being accorded only 'courtesy' styles, while on the Continent all were nobles. Nor was even the greatest English estate a vast territory, cut off from the capital and cultivated by serfs. Landowners were neither potential rebels nor officials of the Crown: they formed an independent and predominant interest; any gentleman of coat armour had the right to wear a sword and to call out a Duke.

This spirited class, 'voracious', says Namier unsympathetically, 'and a-moral', was behind Pitt and the drive for Empire; it checked government but it did not paralyse it, and within a closely restricted franchise it preserved the basic English liberties.

II

This ruling yet representative minority had launched England into world power. In 1640 ninety per cent of England's exports had been of cloth; by 1700 this proportion had been reduced to forty per cent, the difference made up by re-exports of calicoes, tobacco, and sugar from the colonies. The mercantilist policy had succeeded and England had replaced Holland as the greatest entrepôt trader in Europe, indeed the world. Merchants and colonists, now often backed by government, further spread the influence of the small, rainy island in the eastern Atlantic over

[5] J. H. Hexter, *Reappraisals in History*, Longmans, 1961, p. 97.
[6] *England in the Age of the American Revolution*, Macmillan, 1930, p. 7.

huge sun-drenched and static civilisations. In North America, also, in snowbound prairies and forests hitherto unknown to Europeans, English trappers padded in Amerindian 'mocassins' through primeval woods and penetrated vast rivers in Amerindian 'canoes'. In competition with the French, who were handicapped by European ambitions, the English found themselves committed, in part against their will, to a vast empire not only in India but in North America. Such conquests are normal in history but seldom so far flung. And in India the English did, more systematically, what Turki and Mongol and Afghan predators had done for centuries: they gradually took over the great Mughal empire after the conflict between Mughals, Sikhs and Mahrattas had brought it to decline.

So, by the mid-eighteenth century, England had become the greatest of all the European maritime powers, dominating the East and securing a whole new 'Anglo-Saxon' civilisation in North America. English was now becoming a world language; already by the end of the Seven Years' War the first empire was in being: much of it was lost, and in the nineteenth century the English would create another.

First they seized the Carnatic from the French; after 1757 they took over Bengal, its rivers stretching into the heart of northern India; they defeated the Mahrattas and consolidated their power in less than half a century, but they were still merged into the civilisation of the sub-continent. In America two versions of English life had already been established: in the north the Puritan settlement, derived mainly from Norfolk and the West Country, and, intellectually, from Puritan Colleges in Cambridge – Emmanuel and Christ's; in the south the owners of the great plantations had established an easy-going, sub-tropical version of English country house life and exploited their tobacco and cotton fields by negro slaves – creating an appalling problem for the descendants of all concerned.

Though after 1759 they took over eastern Canada, the English themselves still prized the then pestilential West Indian sugar islands more than the American colonies. They were also now prospecting the Pacific; eighty years after Dampier's discoveries, Captain Cook took the *Endeavour* to New Zealand, south-east Australia and the Great Barrier Reef, and explored huge areas of the ocean, north and south. The English, since Elizabeth's time, had been oceanic-minded; now the world power glimpsed by the Elizabethans was becoming a fact.

Against this vast background, even the greatest colonial blunder in English history was not ruinous. The Americans were driven out of the Empire; they did not break out of it, for 'the idea of an independent American republic did not appeal overwhelmingly to more than a fraction of the American people'.[']
But secession was probably inevitable, given the facts of distance, economics and ways of life; and it was mainly the strength of their outraged feel for liberty that pushed the colonists into rebellion. Viewed in purely constitutional terms, the American Revolution may be seen as the last act of the constitutional dramas of the previous century. Though the colonists and Burke often used the political arguments of the Parliamentarians ('No taxation without representation') for instance, they had always been insistent that loyalty to the Crown was not in question, merely obedience to an English Parliament. George III, on the other hand, in insisting that this obedience be enforced was really fighting the battle of the legislature. The conflict thus showed the King and Lord North as the true heirs of the Whig Settlement of 1689. And it is revealing that while in England Parliamentary sovereignty has to this day remained unlimited and unchallenged, the colonists resurrected in their Supreme Court something remarkably like the old English principle of fundamental law as an ultimate restraint on their legislation.

Social prejudice and casual administration on the one side; growing wealth and self-confidence on the other; the timely support of France, all contributed to what in fact proved a good solution. And the struggle had provoked in England a new sense of imperial tolerance and responsibility. For he did not, said Burke, 'know the method of drawing up an indictment against a whole people'; 'a great empire and little minds' went 'ill together' and 'magnanimity in politics . . . (was) not seldom the truest wisdom'. These memorable words, like the eloquence of the dying Chatham, were lost on the mediocrities in power; but they crystallised, for the first time in terms of Empire, a tradition of tolerance and understanding. The Commonwealth often today

[']*Cambridge History of the British Empire*, Vol. I, p. 763. Trees in the Province of Maine, said the English, were His Majesty's property, whether standing or felled.

reflects after two centuries ideas enunciated by Burke. In apparent catastrophe, he made the most memorable affirmation of political liberty then current; while, on the other side, the signatories of the Declaration of Independence derived their ideas largely from John Locke and expressed them in lapidary phrases; not to be lost on the Revolutionaries in France.

The eighteenth century both at home and abroad, far from being an age of indolent corruption, maintained, within its inevitable social limitations, the liberties of England, and, directly and indirectly, spread these principles far beyond the island.

III

Pepys, writing after the Restoration, had considered that the Anglican Church 'would never heartily go down with the generality of the Commons of England.' In fact that hazy compromise suited temperament and climate; harking back, perhaps, in spirit to Anglo-Saxon times, it produced good scholars, if not now saints. Nothing is more English than the Anglican Church, whether in the incomparable dignity of a coronation or in the bleat of village congregations singing slightly out of tune. And the ancient universities, steeped in Anglican tradition, had come a long way from their medieval Catholic origins.

If the Anglican schools and universities fell off from the vigour of the previous century, neither Gibbon's comment on the Magdalen Fellows 'whose dull and deep potations excused the brisk intemperance of youth', nor the raffishness of the richer undergraduates, in fact give the whole picture. The lethargy of celibate Fellows, the snobbery of Heads of Houses, the quiet malversation of endowments formed a perennial satiric theme: Amherst in his *Terrae Filius*[8] alleges that Oxford outdoes Billingsgate in 'water language', and makes play with 'Dr. Drybones, the reverend old Clergywoman and the Hanover Turnip': reflects, too, upon the 'corpulency' of 'foaming divines', whose endowments alone keep them decent. But this kind of satire can be vamped up in any age: curricula were narrow, undergraduates often idle, yet there were still 'dons' – the term is already used by Amherst – of deep learning. The poet Gray found the life of

---

[8] *Terrae Filius or the Secret History of the University of Oxford*, by N. Amherst of St. John's College.

a Fellow-Commoner at Peterhouse, Cambridge, convenient for study: not only 'laden tables and well-stocked cellars, the sleepy afternoons of port and tobacco in college parlours',[9] but libraries and learning were at command; and when some undergraduates 'going a hunting... thought it no bad diversion to make Gray bolt', and scared the poet with a false alarm of fire, he could easily transfer to Pembroke and remain there for life. In the modern academic world there might have been no room for him. Samuel Johnson, who went up to Pembroke College, Oxford, in 1728, and had then little cause to be loyal to his university, spoke of his tutor with affection,[10] and was gratified to be given honorary degrees, which he accepted in impeccable Latin.

Philosophical debate in the universities was violent, but not sluggish. Locke's *Essay Concerning Human Understanding* had expressed an empiricism characteristic of the English mind, and created a tradition which has gone on unbroken up to Moore and Russell and beyond. His opponents knew what he was up to: his theory of ideas implied strict limitations on the range of mind, and would lead, they vigorously declared, to man being but a 'species of Machines'; thought would become but an 'operation of Matter, qualified with a knack of thinking.' The attacks mounted against Locke may have been wrong-headed, but they were to the point.

The confidence which orthodox Anglican divines and philosophers felt in the natural order directed by a beneficent Providence was sincere, and often ably expressed. That it now appears complacent does not mean that these able academics could not think. Archdeacon William Paley, whose portrait at Christ's College in Cambridge shows the force of his mind, was a considerable worthy in his time: his *Political Philosophy* and *Evidences of Christianity* settled conservative opinion for decades, and his influence lasted far into the nineteenth century.

Nor should one accuse the eighteenth century universities of torpor when Oxford produced in Sir William Blackstone, of Pembroke and All Souls, the most influential lawyer of his age. Blackstone, whose massive learning and powerful historical sense were expressed in a commanding, lucid and attractive style, depicted law as the expression of the existing social consciousness,

[9] R. W. Ketton-Cremer, *Thomas Gray, a biography*, C.U.P., 1955, p. 70.
[10] Boswell's *Life of Johnson*, O.U.P., 1927, Vol. I, pp. 178–9.

emerging and changing with the times, rather than the *fiat* of some omniscient legislator or revealed code. His historical intuition and commonsense are very English; and though his conservatism exasperated Bentham, his *Commentaries* (1765–69) were vastly influential, not only in England but in America, for he had apparently explained the British Constitution.

Moreover, the age is famous for great orators, and the eloquence of Chatham, Fox, and many lesser but notable politicians, is rooted in the classical learning of the ancient schools and universities. If the Latin quotations bandied about the House of Commons were as much a tribute to the birch as to the book, they testify that conventional learning sometimes stuck, and that the Eton saying that the shadow of lost learning at least protects one from many illusions was already apt.

The antiquarians of the time who, with more zeal than system, were now investigating the English past, and whose theories and discoveries are already recorded in the transactions of the Society of Antiquaries, came from the universities; Bishop Tanner of St. Asaph with his great manuscript collection, still important; Dr. Percy, Bishop of Dromore, whose *Reliques of Ancient English Poetry* – 'shewing the first effects of ancient genius',[11] became a landmark in the Romantic movement. Thomas Warton admirably edited Milton's shorter poems and became Professor of Poetry at Oxford.

Beyond the pale of the Anglican Church and the universities, the ancient traditions of Nonconformity went on; preserved in well-found dissenting families and in surprisingly efficient 'academies' which taught a wider range of subjects than the Anglican schools, still bound close to an often pedantic Renaissance learning. The Nonconformists, in fact, had far greater influence overseas than the Anglicans, and the greatest hymn-writer in the English speaking world was a Baptist from Southampton. Isaac Watts, whose mother, Sarah Taunton, had a Huguenot strain.[12]

---

[11] Consisting of old Heroic Ballads, Songs, and other pieces of our earlier poets. London, 1765, 3 vols. Percy used many ballads, which Pepys had pasted into five volumes of folio, from the Pepys Library at Magdalene College, Cambridge.

[12] His upbringing was oppressively pious, but his maternal grandfather was a successful brewer, and he had a fighting strain from his Watts grandfather, one of Blake's sea captains, who was said, when in India, to have 'drowned a tiger'.

He wrote hymns which can compare with Luther's *Ein Feste Burg*, that Marseillaise of the Reformation; and if

Time, like an ever-rolling stream,
Bears all its sons away,

today *O God our help in Ages Past* is still sung throughout the Christian English-speaking world.

Watts was also a redoubtable advocate of a broad and liberal education: 'take a wide survey now and then', he wrote, 'of the vast and unlimited regions of learning, and then reflect how few of them you are acquainted with in any tolerable degree'. *Watts on the Mind* was long widely popular.

Joseph Priestley, who first isolated oxygen, also came from a dissenting academy, and many inventors came of similar background. They formed 'philosophical' groups; the Birmingham Lunar Society, for example, which included Priestley, Wedgwood and Arkwright. Nonconformists tended to free thought and Socinian views, originated in Poland by a Sienese, Sozzini, had long come in from Holland, where Locke had spent years as a refugee. Locke had been considerably influenced; Newton, too, had become 'unsound' on the Trinity, though he never let on: John Biddle, also, the founder of Unitarianism, had 'ungodded Jesus Christ'. The Saviour, he declared, was just a good man.

Politically, the Nonconformists were often radical – at least highly critical of government. They cherished 'natural rights'; 'substantially', it was supposed, 'enjoyed in the time of the immortal Alfred'. Not everyone was enthusiastic for the consequences of the Glorious Revolution, and the old republican ideals of Harrington and Milton were not forgotten. A deep distrust of government, as such, was behind the surprisingly violent support that Wilkes could command. Even that unattractive demagogue was a champion of freedom of the press and political liberties, and he exploited old traditions.

Nonconformists and humanitarians helped to make brutal eighteenth-century England notable for prison reforms and charitable endowments. General Oglethorpe, who described the siege of Belgrade to Dr. Johnson with a 'wet finger' in a little wine upon the table, was a famous philanthropist. Horrified at the condition of the gaols, he had started a colony at Savannah in Georgia for the deserving poor. A dissenter, John Howard, also dedicated his life to penal reform; he wrote *The State of the Prisons* (1777) and made his 'circumnavigation of Charity' through most of continental Europe and the Levant. Like the Italian prison reformer, Beccaria, he was indefatigable and he is still remembered.

Many great London hospitals were founded in the mid-century – Guy's, St. George's, the London and Middlesex; St. Thomas's was rebuilt and Bart's extended. Captain Coram started the Foundling Hospital and schools were founded – as Taunton's at Southampton, endowed by a cousin of Watts' to train boys for the sea mainly with the proceeds of successful privateering. In spite of the callousness of most public opinion, philanthropy and humanitarian good works were already a well-established aspect of England.

Gradually the more prosperous classes took to a more 'genteel' way of life; indeed, by the later part of the century 'respectability' was coming in. The rural gentry, as depicted in Fielding's Squire Western, were often genially barbarous; the Court aristocrats dolled-up in conscious sophistication, like dancing masters. But as the century went on the contrast diminished. 'Polite' – urban – standards were diffused at 'Spas' attended by the country gentry at Tonbridge, Droitwich and Bath – the latter frequented since Elizabethan times. 'Taking the waters' was supplemented after the mid-century by sea-bathing; at Weymouth George III would emerge from the waves to 'God Save the King' played by the local and loyal band. This novel custom, with its ritual 'bathing machines' and rival 'bathing women', took on among those to whom the ocean seemed friendly; if not among those who lived off the 'hungry sea'. The 'watering-place' was mainly an English idea.

But the customary gormandising of the English well-to-do did not diminish: as Thackeray wrote, 'Swift was fat; Addison was fat; Gay and Thomson[13] were preposterously fat' (he might have added Gibbon). 'All that Club and Coffee House boozing, shortened the lives and enlarged the waistcoats of men of that age';[14] and when Lord Chancellor Northington replied to George

---

[13] James Thomson wrote *The Seasons of the Year*, containing the representative lines

> *Thus solitary and in pensive guise,*
> *Oft let me wander o'er the russet mead.*

[14] Quoted in A. S. Turberville, *English Men and Manners in the Eighteenth Century*, Oxford, 1929, p. 103.

III's 'They tell me you love a glass of wine', with 'Those who have informed your Majesty have done me great injustice; they should have said a bottle' and probably meant two,[15] he was representative. Gambling was frenetic – vast sums changing hands; whole estates put under the hammer, timber cut down, dependants ruined. Cock-fighting, bear- and bull-baiting – 'a mad bull let loose to be baited, with fireworks over him and dogs after him' – enabled the mob to place their bets; and gin celebrated or assuaged the sequel. Smallpox ravaged rich and poor, checked by the introduction of inoculation from Turkey, but not defeated until the last decade of the century, when Edward Jenner devised vaccination, one of the many great medical discoveries made in England.

IV

Against this chequered and vigorous social setting, the condition of the people remained brutal, all the worse for the growing civilisation of the upper and middle class. Yet the achievements of the creative minority in literature and the arts were to be outstanding for the whole English-speaking world. English painters could now first compare with the continental masters. Sir Joshua Reynolds[16] and Thomas Gainsborough[17] worked in the tradition of Van Dyck, but both are intensely English. Reynolds was the first great native portrait painter, with a homely, sometimes sentimental touch, and a subtle perception of character. Gainsborough, a pioneer of landscape in the Dutch tradition, broke away from the conventions of Claude and of the French pastoral artists; he liked to catch his sitters in the poses of ordinary life, though he had a rare feel for the sheen of a brocaded

[15] Ibid., pp. 84–5.

[16] Reynolds (1723–92) was the eleventh child of a Devonshire clergyman, who was a Fellow of Balliol but of 'guileless disposition'. 'This is done by Joshua out of sheer idleness', he wrote of a sketch in a notebook for Latin grammar. Joshua studied in Rome and Florence, and early made his mark in London. When the Royal Academy was founded in 1769, he became the first President, and inaugurated the annual Academy dinner, still an occasion for the establishment. He was extremely popular; entertained lavishly; made £5,000–£6,000 a year and left £100,000.

[17] Gainsborough (1727–88), whose father was in the wool trade, came of dissenting stock in Suffolk, the youngest of nine children. At nineteen he married a beautiful girl, a year younger than himself, who also possessed a comfortable annuity. He first made his reputation in Bath; then set up in London, where he was 'beloved for his affability', though without Reynolds' social ambitions.

waistcoat or the sweep of a woman's dress. He is grounded, more than Reynolds with his wide continental experience, in the Suffolk landscape which he had depicted when a boy.

In architecture, also, the eighteenth century enriched the island. The austerity of Holkham on the Norfolk coast gives a northern flavour to the Palladian style, originally deployed along the hinterland of Venice; and Adam interiors and Sheraton furniture show a similar restraint.

A new 'landscape' gardening now swept aside continental formality, and created parks with lakes and plantations artfully designed for a climate of changing light and seasons. Lesser Georgian houses in town and country are well designed and convenient, in contrast to the enormities of the Victorians; and the tradition was long decisive for 'colonial' architecture both of New England and the southern States.

The vivid and concentrated life of eighteenth century London, still small enough for coteries, was reflected in the clubs which now became an important and original aspect of England. They were sporting, gambling, political, gastronomic, bibulous or literary or all these. The club, leathery, masculine, informal, is different from either the salon or the beerhall; it is an English invention.

This vigorous, compact, society produced great literature in many facets. The predominant European culture was French; but the English had created the novel. Defoe's realism was carried on by Fielding, whose *Tom Jones* (1749, the year of Voltaire's *Candide*) is both picaresque satire and a vindication of good-heartedness and good sense; Smollett, whose *Roderick Random* appeared the year before, had seen life in the raw as a surgeon's mate in the Royal Navy – the names of his characters, Captain Trunnion, Humphrey Clinker, Peregrine Pickle speak for themselves; he depicts the grosser aspects of eighteenth century life with precision. But Richardson, a printer who began to write in middle age, was the greater innovator, with an oblique way of feeling himself into his characters; and Sterne's tricks with time and odd introspection first explored more private worlds, as in the memories of the immortal Uncle Toby in *Tristram Shandy*.

The sharp eye and sharper pen of Horace Walpole ('though our present minister, notwithstanding he has the monkey disposition of Heliogabalus, is happily without his youth or lusts') can compete in brilliant insight and malice with his most sophisticated contemporaries in France. Consider his character of the third Duke of Grafton: 'A very extraordinary man; with a very good common sense and knowledge of mankind, he contrived to be thought a fool, and, by being thought so, contrived to be always well at Court... He had the greatest penetration in finding out the foibles of men that ever I knew, and wit in teazing them. He were insensible to misfortunes of his own or of his friends... betraying was never his talent, he was content to be ungrateful.' Malice is made convincing by apparent accuracy.

Walpole's miniatures contrast with the European panorama of Gibbon, the greatest writer among English historians, still compulsively readable; his majestic prose pointed with epigram. 'It was in Rome', he began, 'on the 15th of October, 1764, as I sat musing amidst the ruins of the Capitol, while the bare footed fryars were singing vespers in the Temple of Jupiter, that the idea of writing the decline and fall of the City first started to my mind.' 'It was the day, or rather night, of the 27th of June, 1787', he concluded, writing at Lausanne, 'between the hours of eleven and twelve, that I wrote the last lines of the last page, in a summer house in my garden. After laying down my pen, I took several turns in a *berceau*, or covered walk of acaceas, which commands a prospect of the country, the lake and the mountains. The air was temperate, the sky was serene, the silver orb of the moon was reflected from the waters, and all nature was silent.'

If Gibbon's later background was continental, Dr. Samuel Johnson, the great lexicographer, only once left the island. He remains the embodiment of English common sense; a tremendous 'character', with his Midland accent – 'poonch' for 'punch' – and 'deliberate and strong utterance.'[18] 'I dogmatise', he said, 'and I am contradicted, and in this conflict of opinions and sentiments I find delight.' Through Boswell's inspired skill no one in the literature of the English-speaking world lives so vividly as Johnson. Boswell (of an undergraduate peccadillo): 'That Sir, was great fortitude of mind'; Johnson: 'No Sir, stark insensibility.' Asked how he felt after the failure of his tragedy, *Irene*,

---

[15] Even if the tenth Lord Pembroke did remark to Boswell at Wilton that Dr. Johnson's sayings would not appear so extraordinary, 'were it not for his *bow bow* way.' Boswell's *Life*, Vol. I, p. 569.

he replied 'Like the Monument'. Of noble savages he remarked, 'as to care . . . they are not above it, but below it, like bears'; and when Bishop Berkeley tried to prove that the universe was merely subjective, he answered 'striking his foot with mighty force against a large stone, till he rebounded from it, "I refute it thus".'

The drama flourished in a more kindly idiom than that of the Restoration dramatists, and Shakespeare, often in garbled form, was greatly appreciated. Johnson's fellow townsman Garrick, who came of French descent, was a versatile genius who could interpret character even in the melodramatic style then the fashion, and Goldsmith and Sheridan – who wrote *The Rivals* and *The School for Scandal* before taking to politics – were humane if subtle observers of society.

In music, then, as always, England received more than she gave; the German-born, Italian-trained, Handel, naturalised in the 'twenties, poured out operas and oratorios in the grand manner, swamping the simpler style created by Purcell. *The Beggar's Opera*, parody, political satire and, as Swift put it, 'Newgate Pastoral', set a new style of ballad opera, its catches selected from London street tunes and folk melodies by the German musicologist, Dr. Pepusch. Launched in 1728, it had already taken on in Paris and New York by the mid-century. Thomas Arne now wrote the bouncing strains of *Rule Britannia*, so appropriate to the age, and set Shakespeare's famous lyrics to attractive melodies; while *God Save the King*, the tune adapted originally perhaps from folk tunes or plainsong, and the words from the more ferocious books of the Old Testament, became popular during the Jacobite threat to the Hanoverian monarchy in 1745.

Another very different and unrepresentative poem would also last; Blake, that weird genius haunted by the 'dark satanic mills' of the early Industrial Revolution, believed that 'Adam and Eve were Druids' and that the Christian revelation had begun and would end in England.

> *'And did those feet'*, he wrote, *'in ancient time,*
> *Walk upon England's mountains green?'*

Galvanized by Parry's Edwardian musical rhetoric, this curious verse would be sung by vast twentieth century congregations. William Cowper, too, that 'stricken deer', who thought periodically that he was damned, could evoke the frosty grass of an autumn morning and write hymns that would live.

> *God moves in a mysterious way,*
> *His wonders to perform;*

a *tour de force* of mixed metaphor which comes off.

Alexander Pope had been more typical; he had carried on Dryden's technique. No romantic, he 'chose verse and even rhyme' for his *Essay* or *'Map of Man'* because he thought verse more striking, memorable, and concise; not more evocative. He insisted, like Locke, on the limitations of mind, with its 'snatched' knowledge.[19]

> *Know God and Nature only are the same,*
> *In Man the judgement shoots at flying game.*

His thought is tense, sinewy, acute, giving English commonsense a sharper edge. And he was a connoisseur of human nature, with a fiendish insight into wickedness and cruelty:

> *From Loveless youth to unrespected age,*
> *No passion gratified except her rage.*

And still today,

> *Old politicians chew their wisdom past*
> *And totter on in business to the last.*

Pope's prose satire can be as deadly as Swift's, as in his Rabelaisian parody on the nutrition of the infant *Scribblerus*, epitome of all pedants.

The more placid genius of Gray used classic metres in moralising on the fate of Etonians:

> *Alas regardless of their doom,*
> *The little victims play.*

His stately, concentrated, formality culminates in the famous if hackneyed Elegy, with its slow cadence on *'The paths of glory'* that *'lead but to the grave'*.

Characteristically English in 'sensibility', Shenstone's cult of nature and simplicity is more romantic:

> *The river gliding down the hill,*
> *The hill with beeches crowned.*

[19] *Moral Essays*, Vol. I, pp. 39–40.

If the early eighteenth century was Augustan, the later decades anticipated a note heard again in Wordsworth with greater power.

For in spite of Pope and Johnson and Gibbon, all urban characters, English civilisation was still largely rural. Outside the crowded life of London or the placid life of the universities, contented scholars went their quiet ways; as the naturalist Gilbert White, who observed the annual round of nature as the beech leaves changed in Selborne Hanger. 'This lovely domain', he wrote of Walmer, 'is a very agreeable haunt for many sort of wild fowl, which not only frequent it in the winter, but breed there in the summer; such as lapwings, snipes, wild ducks, and, as I have discovered within these few years, teals.'

For all its urbanity, the culture of the eighteenth century was rooted in the land; in the life of great country houses and snug manors, of the woods and fields. The universities also still dominated their setting, walks and gardens merging into the countryside. After the Marlborough Wars, England, already a world power, attained the climax of its largely pre-industrial, aristocratic and privileged civilisation; the continuity of development unbroken by radical social or economic change, in spite of the political upheavals of the previous century. The condition of the poorer townsfolk was appalling, and the rural peasantry were still largely illiterate, but the politically conscious minority of the English had managed to combine tolerable government, internal peace and a redoubtable posture abroad, with political liberties as then understood. They were now to create the greatest change in man's way of life since the invention of agriculture in Neolithic times, and to transform the island into the power-house of the first Industrial Revolution.

BOOK TWO

Chapter 1

World Power and Economic Revolution

H AVING created their first Empire, and lost much of it,
the English now made their decisive technological contribution to world history. The so-called Industrial Revolution, which began in England, had 'no counterpart', as Engels
would observe, 'in the annals of humanity'. In the 1780's there
was a swift, unprecedented increase in production best described
in modern terms as a take off into a new economic dimension.
After launching navies that would long dominate the oceans, the
islanders now launched a new kind of power that would transform
the life of mankind. The causes of this revolution go back far and
deep; it was cumulative, the first break-through into novel and
artificial sources of power being made by the late eighteenth
century and rapidly developed under the stimulus of the French
Wars. A predominantly agricultural country, with a population of about nine million in 1801, became a hive of great
industry and is still one of the greater economic forces in the
world.

The old English way of life was gradually but massively transformed. The legend that England is a garden persists, encouraged
by efficient subsidised agriculture and the incomes of week-enders
and the retired; but a traveller from Plymouth to London will
observe the emptiness of the countryside. Most of the English
have long been urban and suburban, and their roads and coasts
in summer indicate their ineradicable desire to escape. In spite of
an elaborate division of labour and specialised skills, no change
comparable to the Industrial Revolution had come about since
Neolithic times; the sources of power were still human and animal
labour, supplemented by water- and wind-mills. Now began a
change which led through coal, electricity, and oil fuels to nuclear
power and automation. Man's relation to his environment

was transformed; and the inventors who began it were mainly English labourers and artisans working in a competitive society.

Many inventions had been made in Antiquity and in the European 'Dark Ages', as well as in medieval times; more had been made in Ancient China; but never, as now in England, had they been exploited in such a favourable setting. The coal and iron of northern England supplemented each other, and after the mid-eighteenth century the population rapidly increased; there was a growing labour force and consumer market; and behind it all was the capital of the greatest oceanic commercial nation in Europe, in the hands of men who could do what they liked with it. Within its manageable area, government was relatively strong, there were no great provincial divisions or tariff barriers; yet there was no comprehensive bureaucracy to turn civilian inventions down. Only in armaments were officials able to check innovations; as when, in 1721, Sir Polycarpus Wharton had invented a shell for the navy, 'to be shot out of three several kinds of cannons, the principal merit of which was that when it pierced the enemy's ship it would burst into thirty or more pieces', and the Treasury had at once vetoed his proposal.[1]

Now, gradually the weight of population shifted; the dogged and methodical qualities of the Midland and northern English came into play; and for the first time since the days of Bede the North began to predominate. Much has been made of the miseries of the time; and indeed industrial life lacked the sounds and scents of Shakespeare's world, and, less romantically, of Gammer Gurton's village; but people went into the towns of their own will, and 'against this black picture of a population plunging into misery, there are some powerful practical considerations to be set on the other side ... Such conditions', anyway, 'still, in 1815, only operated among a minority of the people.'[2] Outside London, the early Industrial Revolution created village rather than urban slums, creeping across what became the Black Country from old manufacturing centres. 'A peculiar landscape ... a wilderness of cottages or tenements ... some detached, some connected in little rows, some clustering in groups, yet rarely forming continuous streets, but interspersed with blazing fur-

[1] *Cal. Treasury Papers*, 1720–8.
[2] J. Steven Watson, *The Reign of George III, 1760–1815*, Oxford, 1960, p. 524.

naces, heaps of burning coal and piles of smouldering iron-stone; while forges and engine chimneys roared and puffed.'[3] Such was still the scene well into the nineteenth century, before the huge new towns developed.

The inventions behind the Industrial Revolution were at first elementary. England had long devastated her forests and become dependent on coal; already by the early eighteenth century, steam engines instead of horses had pumped water out of mines – the engine assessed in 'horse-power' – a persistent term. The stationary machine, called in 1717 *The Engine for Raising Water (with a power) made by Fire*, was simple enough. Steam condensed in a cylinder made a vacuum which pulled in a piston; in turn, the piston pulled a cross-beam which raised the rods of a pump; it then again swung back, raising the piston in a rapid rhythm. From this elementary gadget the rest followed. By 1781 Watt and Boulton in Birmingham had adapted the 'engine' to be an independent source of power, and geared it to rotative motion; by 1804 Trevithick had invented a 'locomotive', and steam power was mobile. Then Stephenson, an engineer, improved both the engine and track; 'the iron horse' and 'the iron road' were in being. By 1825 the Stockton and Darlington railway would be at work; the Liverpool and Manchester in 1829; in the 'thirties and 'forties railways would transform the communications of the island and of vast continental areas beyond. Boulton himself realised this future: 'it would not be worth my while', he had said, 'to make for three countries only; but I find it worth my while to make for the world.'[4]

The early Industrial Revolution, of course, came before railways; new 'Macadamised' roads had brought swift, better-sprung stage coaches and a prosperous life of road and inn: more important for heavy industry, great landlords had collaborated with engineers to build a whole network of canals – as the Duke of Bridgewater with James Brindley, a Derbyshire labourer who remained illiterate and thought out his problems in his head. And well before the railways, steam had transformed the cotton and woollen industries. Mechanised spinning was first geared to water-power; then to steam, and vast quantities of textiles were marketed. The cotton manufacturing was now concentrated in

[3] Disraeli, *Sybil, or the two Nations*, O.U.P., p. 141.
[4] Watson, op. cit., p. 334.

Lancashire, woollen manufacturing in Yorkshire; at the expense of the ancient wool centres in East Anglia and the West Country, huge amounts of raw cotton were imported from India and the Americas.

Further, out of the collieries had come coke, the coal residue which could smelt iron; then steam was applied to blast furnaces and cast iron and steel were mass produced. The basis of English wealth was no longer wool: it was coal.

The price was heavy; great areas were scarified and blackened by these palaeotechnic and 'satanic' mills: brass founding, potteries, armaments – all flourished; the massive process was cumulative. From Hull on the North Sea through Leeds and Halifax, Bradford and Manchester, to Atlantic Liverpool; around Derby, Wolverhampton, Birmingham, Nottingham and Sheffield the new great industry sprawled. Bristol and Newcastle spread out; London, the relatively clean city of Wren, became the monstrous, fog-bound city of Dickens.

The rural peasantry were sucked into the vortex. Between 1750 and 1801 the population increased from six and a half millions to nine; there was plenty of cheap 'labour'. And during the seventeen sixties, landowners had gone in for enclosures on a scale which dwarfed anything in Tudor times: they had enclosed both small peasant holdings and open fields and colonised much waste. A primitive, but socially stable, peasant agriculture had been swept aside, and Goldsmith had well written that

> *a bold peasantry, their country's pride,*
> *When once destroyed, can never be supplied.*

They were leaving the land to 'better themselves'; they had no alternative. Doubtless, in the long run, most of their descendants benefited, yet the new system appeared inhuman; 'cottage industries', farmed out since medieval times, were superseded and a steady price-rise hit the people hard. They were now a mere commodity, said the economists, like any other; to be bought in the cheapest market; and they were now regimented by the time-table of machines. The children, who had always been put to family work early, were now herded into the factories and mines.

So, gradually, over decades, the majority of the English became urban. In the countryside, meanwhile, a new, more productive agriculture was paying off.

The peasants and small-holders had generally been inefficient; as Crabbe put it, they had

> ... liv'd in times when not a man had seen
> Corn sown by Drill or thresh'd by a Machine.

Now came the day of great improving landlords and of those 'gentlemen' farmers, who,

> Plans encourage, and who journals keep,
> And talk with lords about a breed of sheep.

Hedged fields gave the land its modern appearance; more roots and clover gave a better rotation of crops and winter fodder. Cattle were transformed from the scraggy specimens of even Stuart times to the straight-backed heavy animals of eighteenth-century engravings. At a Cotswold auction two bulls called *Garrick* and *Washington* sold for 205 guineas; *Brindled Beauty* (in calf) brought even more. The most famous breeder was Farmer Bakewell of Leicestershire, who was able to command 25 guineas for the services of his rams and 50 guineas for those of his bulls; and when one bull, following the demise of the farmer who had hired him, had the ill luck to be slaughtered by mistake, Bakewell got back 200 guineas from the executors. Farmer Bakewell died 'justly celebrated because *really useful.*'

So English sheep and cattle became famous, and the superb bulls exported in the following centuries to the Americas would sire pedigree herds in Iowa and Canada and the Argentine.

Thus, while most of the peasantry were gradually driven off the land, English landowners continued to prosper, as did the big tenant farmers, rare on the Continent, a sturdy stock. If based no longer upon a widespread but primitive peasant routine, country life remained vigorous; and if copyholders and cottagers under life tenures who could not face the factories gradually became landless labourers, or reluctantly moved off their holdings, swelling the army of 'domestics', many countrymen, driven off the land, migrated overseas. England's loss was at least the gain of North America and Australia.

II

So the economic centre of England shifted to the Midlands and the North, save that London remained by far the greatest town. The people who first experienced the Industrial Revolution were thus both stimulated and penalised; from that time dates a more brutal individualism and cult of money – 'brass' they called it – which has long clouded the accepted picture of the English. Like the destruction of the peasantry, it was the penalty of success. As the Dutch, driven back on their polders and the North Sea, had showed a proverbial drive and obstinacy, so the English, their northern winters worsened by coal smoke lit by blast furnaces, were now challenged by their own coal and iron: they emerged out of the smog with a similar attack. And as the process spread, creating the great continental industrial areas of North-Eastern France, Belgium and the Lower Rhine, this North European enterprise outdid anything in the world, to be surpassed only in the United States.

The ruling classes of eighteenth century England had long been a hard-bitten establishment; at once often versatile and intelligent, while fond of field sports, gambling, wenching and drink. The new rich bought their way into this brisk and hard society, and were assimilated into the horsey, game-pie, England of the Regency. Some held aloof, the Puritan tradition still strong, until by Victorian times the two elements would be better blended; united, along with a new professional interest, in the cult of 'progress'. As usual in England, the ruling classes survived.

On the lower levels the disruption was more profound. According to Adam Smith, the great Scots economist, private gain, given 'natural freedom', would become public advantage; but he had assumed a stable society. In fact society was being disrupted right through, and even physique and psychology altered. The Welsh and Irish flocked into the North, the West Midlands and London; 'casual labour' for the new 'demand'. This massive immigration left its mark; in the slums the mixed stock deteriorated, and the urban 'masses' became addicts of 'black tea' – the 'cuppa' still prized in England – and of trashy bread, churned out by steam bakeries, some of the worst of their time.

Psychologically, too, a streak of understandable rancour crept

into a naturally tolerant people, now becoming the most proletarian in Europe; and they atrociously slurred and mispronounced
their own language. Even today many Indians and Africans speak
it better. Disraeli's 'two nations' were coming into being, so
that already, during the Napoleonic Wars, and more emphatically
during their aftermath, revolution was in the air.

It was prevented, in part by Wesleyan religion and Benthamite
reform. John Wesley (1703–91), a revivalist preacher and organi-
ser of genius, long managed to remain within the Anglican
Church, and the Evangelical movement of which he was the
greatest prophet always accepted the social order, for the Evangelicals and 'Methodists' were against sin, not against property.
And Wesley and his 'field-preachers' became missionaries to the
masses: religious enthusiasm was canalised into self-governing
groups, fanaticism tamed to good works, revolutionary feeling
diverted. And this Methodism would have a great future in
England and in the United States. Within the Church also the
Evangelicals of the wealthy and influential Clapham Sect, never
politically radical, inspired the Church Missionary Society; William Wilberforce persuaded the government to abolish the slave
trade among British subjects by 1807, and to make it illegal
throughout the Empire by 1832. These decisions, major English
humanitarian achievements, affected world history.

The other stabilising influence was agnostic. Jeremy Bentham,
a benevolent and wealthy eccentric, was one of the earliest
founders of the Welfare State. He judged institutions by their
'utility' alone, and preached a gospel of rational 'improvement'.
With English empiricism, he set out first to reform the most
flagrant abuses of the law; but he proceeded to wider tasks,
mopping up any statistics then available; and when disillusioned
with officials, he appealed indefatigably to the public by his pen.
Like Oglethorpe and Howard, he went for practical objectives,
and his influence would be decisive in reforming the administration: it would also spread beyond the island, and it long lasted at
home; still traceable in the utilitarian socialism of the Webbs and
their following.

Through the repression and conservatism naturally caused by
the French Wars – 'where is the man', asked one minister, 'that
would be mad enough to ask them to repair their house in a
hurricane season?' – much more radical traditions of liberty and

'improvement' survived. 'The rugged face of society', wrote Tom Paine, whose *Rights of Man* appeared in 1791–2, 'chequered with the extremes of affluence and want, proves that some extraordinary violence has been committed upon it, and calls on justice for redress.' He was a journalist of genius, and his propaganda mobilised hitherto inarticulate opinion. He attacked the Anglican Establishment, and declared that Christianity had the effect of 'sinking man to a spaniel'. Cobbett, who wrote *Rural Rides*, was a more amiable agitator; he stood out against the evils of industrialism and finance; championed, in vain, the old rural way of life. England, despite much propaganda to the contrary, was never the scene of an unbridled carnival of capitalist exploitation. Grim as were the doctrines of Malthus, and harsh the practice of the raw new industrialists, there was always a protest going on, both Evangelical and Benthamite; and the result of that influence would be the massive campaign to tackle the consequences of the Industrial Revolution which would make the 1830's in England a turning point in social history.

III

The struggle against the armies of the French Revolution and Napoleonic Wars was fought over more than two decades in a grand strategy of global scale; it tested the English, already set back by the loss of the American colonies, as never before, and they succeeded mainly because of the wealth created by the Industrial Revolution as well as of the fighting qualities of the services. The administration of the army was now paralytic, but the archaic system of promotion gave youngish men their chance; Nelson and Wellington, both dedicated professionals, early attained command, and both, in contrasting ways, attained a new kind of popularity. Like Napoleon, Nelson was an actor, as well as a genius in war, and his glamour was confirmed by his dramatic death; Wellington, 'Old Nosey' or the 'Iron Duke', one of the great characters of English history, presented an image of leather and iron; a soldier of invincible good sense and power of laconic phrase: 'the people of England', he observed, 'must be governed by persons who are not afraid.'[5]

[5] He remarked of his Anglo-Irish origins that being born in a stable did not make a man a horse; and he had remarkable political foresight. 'What

But the war was not won by brilliant overall planning; rather in the English way, by tenacity and endurance in spite of appalling blunders, and by flashes of strategic insight when calculated risks were run.

At first, neither Pitt nor Dundas, his Secretary at War, realised just what they were up against. 'It was a new type of war', wrote A. B. Rodger, 'that these Republicans were waging or at least one that had not been known in the west for five or six generations – an ideological war, far removed from the more limited, saner, more rational wars of the *ancien régime*. And so the ordinary calculations of statesmen, generals and economists were proved false by those hordes of ragged republicans swaggering over Western Europe, roaring the Marseillaise and lighting their pipes at the altar candles. It was the kind of war that Pitt and Dundas could not comprehend; Pitt with his clear, powerful but limited and unimaginative intelligence and his curious ignorance of mankind; Dundas with his coarse ability and his gifts of political management. Both expected and tried to wage a war *à la* Chatham.'[6]

There was thus at first much strategic fumbling; but the essentials were achieved; the survival of the island base and long-term use of sea-power to strike when the chance came. For at sea, the British reacted at once to the opportunity of Bonaparte's expedition to Egypt, and at the Battle of the Nile inflicted a strategic defeat which brought about the Second Coalition.

If Pitt was by nature a civilian statesman with a genius for business, whose reforms in Ireland and India were largely crippled by the war, he rallied the politically conscious nation to a war he held 'necessary to assert the spirit of the nation and the dignity of the British name.' Pitt lived to see the naval turning point when in 1805 Nelson annihilated the battle fleets of France and Spain, and before Pitt's early death in 1806, the essential strategy had been devised, to bring extra-European power to crush the French empire.

The conclusion of the struggle left England supreme on the oceans; the most important fact in world politics during the

shall we come to in this country', he was asked, 'shall we lose our property?' 'Yes,' replied Wellington, 'we shall not have a commotion, we shall not have blood, but we shall be plundered by forms of law.'

[6] *The War of the Second Coalition*, A Strategic Commentary, Oxford, 1964, p. 2.

nineteenth century. European conflicts were contained and new nations enabled to develop in the Americas. This *Pax Britannica*, no fantasy of historians, but a fact, came out of the long struggle for survival against an over-extended continental power. In that struggle the English had been near defeat and they had been ruthless, as when they bombarded Copenhagen and seized the Danish fleet, a precedent for Oran in 1940; and they had taken great risks, as when they sent Nelson into the Mediterranean to the Battle of the Nile, a decision comparable to Churchill's in 1940, when the remaining armour was shipped round the Cape to the Middle East, the prelude to a similar strategic victory at El Alamein.

These risks, strategic and tactical, were calculated; and this coolness of the English when cornered and their staying power until they could strike back, were first fully displayed in the prolonged warfare which confirmed England as a world power.

Behind this achievement was growing wealth: though often in temporary straits, the economy was rich and England could subsidise her allies. 'His Britannic Majesty', wrote the Foreign Secretary, Lord Harrowby, to the Russian Minister Voronzov in 1805, at the close of the phase of appeasement after the Truce of Amiens, 'believes that the union of the Court of Russia with those of Vienna and Berlin for the declared purpose of restoring the balance of power in Europe would be a most desirable event.' He could therefore conditionally promise, to 'advance a considerable sum to facilitate mobilisation'; five millions within the year in three monthly instalments to Russia; to Austria, two millions or two and a half; to Prussia £800,000 or a million.[7] These 'frank and explicit overtures' were decisive. Later, when the English were bidding against Bonaparte for Russia in view of Napoleon's 'restless system of ambitions' and intention 'to manifest his power and violence by fresh innovations', they could offer £12 10s. a month for a year per man for 'any number of men which Prussia or the Powers mentioned above are willing to bring into active service if the amount is within two and a half million.' They could afford to.

And if, strategically, the English were tenacious and implac-

[7] *Select Dispatches from the Foreign Office Archives relating to the formation of the Third Coalition against France*, ed. J. H. Rose, Camden Society, 3rd Series, Vol. VII, 1904, p. 16.

able, tactically they were uninhibited and ingenious. Nelson's tactics were new: 'Up to this time', writes Felix Markham, 'naval battles were fought in line and were rarely decisive. Nelson's battles of annihilation were the counterpart at sea of the Napoleonic battles. The tactics of attacking in column instead of line not only isolated a portion of the enemy fleet but ensured the maximum effect of the fire power available. Everything depended on the initial double shotted broadside, fired through the stern and down the whole length of the enemy ship, as the English ship broke through the line. The short range carronades cast by Roebuck's Carron ironworks in Scotland were particularly destructive . . . "In this war", wrote Napoleon, "the English have been the first to use Carronades".'[8]

Wellington, too, was also a realist; he had a wonderful eye for country and, though tactically no innovator, he would conceal his infantry so that they were sheltered from enemy shot and emerged with fire power intact; he had a rare instinct for timing the decisive stroke, uninhibited by eighteenth century conventions. The English armies, best, as usual, on the defensive, again showed the dogged endurance that had contributed to the victories of the Hundred Years' War and the Marlborough campaigns, and, as usual, they were underestimated by their opponents. 'I tell you', said Napoleon, before Waterloo, 'that Wellington is a bad general, that the English are bad troops, and it will be a picnic.'

The hard-won victory benefited the whole Empire. The collapse of the French power in North America and India had left the British unrivalled, with territories which would form a greater empire than the first. When Pitt had divided Canada into Upper and Maritime provinces, he had so far assuaged tension between the French Canadians and the rest that the country had remained pro-British during the Anglo-American war of 1812–15. In India, Cornwallis and Wellesley took over the régime of the decadent Mughals – still the social and cultural arbiters of Hindustan – and by 1819 the English had become paramount in the sub-continent. A commercial enterprise, exploiting a massive and rich economy, at its peak in the seventeenth century when India was the greatest exporting area of the East, before the Western Industrial Revolution wrecked its prosperity and reduced it to a source of raw materials and a market, now gradually became a political *raj* which would culminate in the late nineteenth century. The English also secured the command of the route to India by the capture of Cape Colony from the Dutch; retained after compensation of two million sterling. It would become the base for the most industrially advanced state in all Africa, expanding north into the Rhodesias and tapping great wealth in the gold and diamonds of the Rand. The capture of Ceylon rounded off this strategy, and the retention of Malta confirmed English sea-power in the Mediterranean. In the East the British also took over parts of Burma and Malaya, and in 1819 Sir Stamford Raffles founded Singapore. Beyond, in Australia, a new continent was opened up. South-Eastern Australia had been settled in the late eighteenth century, in part as a penal colony for convicts, no longer shipped to North America; and soon explorers were pushing into the unknown interior while new settlements were made south and west. Another new nation had been founded.

Such was the far flung oceanic background to England by the end of the Napoleonic Wars: India and the colonies would become more important to the British as generations of administrators, soldiers and settlers went overseas, creating family traditions which percolated deep; turning attention away from continental Europe to more distant horizons, for the politically conscious English were insular only towards the Continent.

In the island itself a hearty people made a cult of sport. Cricket, *par excellence* the English national game, originated in the villages of Kent and Sussex, its rules made by the mid-eighteenth century. It had been first taken up by the landowners and gentry, but all classes shared in it. It was originally played with a curved bat, and a much lower two-stump wicket: by the end of the century, the three-stump wicket and straight bat had come in, though the ball was still delivered under-arm. Trevelyan points out that 'Lord John Sackville was a member of the winning team of which the gardener at Knole was the captain', and even remarks, 'If the French noblesse had been capable of playing cricket with their peasants, their châteaux would never have been burnt.' Be that as it may, the cult of this subtle and, to the uninitiated, bewildering game became much more organised in the mid-nineteenth century. It would create a *mystique* which would still pervade the modern Commonwealth when it had become, by the old imperial standards, very peculiar.

The cult of football would come later, though its origins are more ancient; in the rough and tumble of medieval villages and the more esoteric customs of ancient schools – hence the variety of its forms. That, too, would be one of the most lasting and far-flung of English contributions to the world. At the time prize-fighting and racing mainly attracted the bets of the people: the former was patronised by the rich, but eagerly followed by the masses, who would already assemble in thousands to watch the burly, long-armed bruisers pound one another. They fought without gloves, but according to rule; and the custom of settling differences by fists rather than by knives became acclimatised – though it took long to spread widely outside the island.[9] Duelling, too, still *de rigueur* well into the nineteenth century, would go out of fashion by Victorian times.

Racing had long been well-established since the Stuart Kings had patronised Newmarket: immense bets were placed, and aristocratic patrons brought some order into the proceedings, founding the Jockey Club by the mid-eighteenth century. The people flocked to race meetings, but a steadier opportunity for betting was still cock-fighting.

Such, in all its vigour and its aristocratic and popular traditions, was the England of the Industrial Revolution, the French Wars and the Regency; its habits still predominantly rural, if being transformed by an industrial and predominantly urban way of life.

IV

As a natural development of older traditions, and in part, perhaps, in protest against these new influences, the literary genius apparent since Tudor times was now expressed in the

[9] When, as early as 1769, that libellous *littérateur* and parasite, Baretti, stabbed a man to death in the Haymarket and was undeservedly acquitted by a London jury, under pressure from his eminent friends ('Never did such a constellation of genius enliven the awefull Sessions House'), it was pointed out that, 'being an Italian', the poor fellow did not know how to use his fists.

Romantic movement, a European influence which originated, as already observed, in a mild way in England. There was also great achievement in the arts: English magnates were still munificent patrons; they still made the grand tour, brought back the paintings of fashionable masters and decorated their houses with classical and neo-classical sculpture. But their architectural taste remained austere, continuing the earlier eighteenth-century tradition. English architects generally combined mass with a good design, as in Robert Adam's Harewood House in Yorkshire; or Kedleston in Derbyshire; or in the familiar Horse Guards' building in Whitehall: and this sense of proportion is apparent in quite ordinary architecture in town and country. The terraces at Brighton and Bath and the remaining Regency terraces in London show how architects could then combine comfort with elegance. A few odd patrons had encouraged the new 'Gothick' revival, as Horace Walpole at Strawberry Hill, or Beckford in his enormous, now vanished, fantasy at Fonthill in Wiltshire; at Clandon the Verneys early went in for pseudo-Chinese interiors, and the Pavilion at Brighton, which looked 'as if St. Paul's had gone down to the sea and pupped', shows what Nash could do in Oriental style. But, in general, architecture, like furniture and decoration, speaks by understatement.

The writers, on the other hand, if well rooted in the eighteenth century, broke new ground. The greatest poet, Wordsworth, evoked a pantheistic feeling for nature; caught and held transient flashes of intuition: '*Listen*', he wrote, '*the mighty Being is awake*'. He adapted simple eighteenth-century metres, already familiar in the hymns of Watts and Cowper, to poignant episodes of ordinary life made symbolic of deeper states of mind. He could also write as majestically as Milton; of Venice that held '*the gorgeous East in fee*', or of England's liberties:

> *We must be free or die, who speak the tongue*
> *That Shakespeare spake; the faith and morals hold*
> *Which Milton held . . .*

He reflected upon sensation without eighteenth-century sentimentality and provided for many a substitute for revealed religion. He also anticipated the religious 'doubts' to be so common among the Victorians:

> *... Great God! I'd rather be*
> *A Pagan suckled in a creed outworn;*
> *So might I, standing on this pleasant lea,*
> *Have glimpses that would make me less forlorn;*
> *Have sight of Proteus rising from the sea;*
> *Or hear old Triton blow his wreathed horn.*

Wordsworth's friend, Coleridge, wrote a queer symbolical poetry; at its most original in *The Ancient Mariner*, with its *painted ship upon a painted ocean*, and in *Kubla Khan's*

> *Sunny pleasure dome, with caves of ice.*

He could write of a poet,

> *Weave a circle round him thrice,*
> *And close your eyes in holy dread*
> *For he on honey dew hath fed*
> *And drunk the milk of Paradise.*

While Wordsworth and Coleridge turned conservative, Shelley and Byron, both aristocrats, always defied the establishment. Both were very English; Shelley expressing an unpractical idealism, perennially cropping up among the most privileged; Byron the rueful insight of a disillusioned yet still romantic man of the Regency world. What more poignant than the contrasting pity and cynicism in his best poem, *Don Juan*, with its racy colloquial idiom, tearing along?

> *Alas! they were so young, so beautiful,*
> *So lonely, loving, helpless, and the hour,*
> *Was that in which the heart is always full.*

Then the rather mocking transition

> *And thus they form a group, that quite unique,*
> *Half naked, loving, natural and Greek ...*
> *What men call gallantry, he observes, and gods adultery,*
> *Is much more common when the climate's sultry;*

and

> *Virgil's songs are pure, except that horrid one*
> *Beginning with* Formosum Pastor Corydon.

Keats, the other major romantic poet, expressed, as did Goethe, writing of orange groves, the yearning of a northern people for the South, in a lush, sometimes theatrical, idiom.

Among prose writers, Jane Austen is the greatest English novelist, depicting with exquisite economy and without malice the nuances of character in a sheltered world; but Scott's historical novels had a wider, European, influence; concerned, as were German and French romantics, with a new consciousness of the past. Thomas Love Peacock's genial satire is typically English; the prandial and post-prandial conversation of the Rev. Dr. Folliott and his friends makes game of the intellectuals of his day; of 'Steam Intellect' and the 'March of Mind'; even of universal education and the 'sublime Kant' who 'wants the great requisites of head and tail.' The Doctor set no store by 'Modern Athenians'; 'Be content, sir', he told Mr. MacQuedy, 'to rival the Boeotians, whose redeeming virtue was in fish.'[10]

English painters now began to be taken seriously abroad. Wordsworth's cult of nature is paralleled by the splendid landscapes of Constable, the son of a substantial Suffolk miller. He was the first English artist to become a major influence in France. Nowhere is the landscape better depicted than in the masterpieces of the greatest of English painters, with their 'cool tint of English daylight' and bold brushwork, catching the feel of wind and rain. Turner, more self-consciously romantic, dramatised landscape, getting his most spectacular effects when 'inventing' the sunset, or painting the heat-haze of Venice, or the effects of steam. The water-colourists, Cotman, de Wint, and David Cox, were minor masters of a deceptively simple technique. Most of these painters found their best loved subjects in rural East Anglia, in south Wiltshire and Dorset, while the Industrial Revolution was scarifying London, the Midlands and the North. They immortalised the old rural England; themselves in the main, unlike Reynolds and Gainsborough, unhonoured and often poor. Even when Constable was elected R.A. it was by a small majority, and his pictures never sold well. 'Associates are to be chosen next Tuesday', he wrote 'out of 40 candidates at the R. Academy. They are at a loss entirely – there is not an artist among them. It is recommended that the Secretary put them in a bag.'[11]

---

[18] *The Misfortunes of Elphin* and *Crochet Castle*, World's Classics, p. 136.

[11] R. B. Beckett, *John Constable and the Fishers*, Routledge and Kegan Paul, 1952, p. 107.

So, while the heavy-weight England of the Industrial Revolution and the French Wars achieved its economic and naval supremacy and survived the Napoleonic Wars, English writers were opening up new ranges of literary experience beyond the apparently well-ordered world of Johnson, Gibbon and Burke; while the artists could now compete with foreign masters. At no time, not even the Elizabethan, had England shown such a kaleidoscopic range of achievement; and it now wielded massive political, economic and oceanic power.

Chapter 2

Victorian Climax

ITH this creative background, the Victorian age was not stuffy and tedious but the most dynamic period of English history: the mid-Victorians compare with the Elizabethans in versatility and enterprise, and they had incomparably greater wealth and power. The Industrial Revolution, which had added colossal wealth to eighteenth-century affluence[1] and spread it, was now supplemented by great administrative and scientific advance backed by new professional skills, adding another facet to English civilisation. Scientists and explorers now won world fame and the English were pioneers in the new environmental studies and archaeology; while in literature, if not in the arts, the Victorians were lavishly creative. From the Reform Bill of 1832 to the extension of the franchise in 1867, administrative, technological, and scientific progress gave England a new kind of reputation in the world and broadened the traditions and mentality of the people.

This expansion was not made easily; the economic distress after the French Wars and in the 'forties meant widespread poverty and anger, but the Chartist revolution never came off. As usual in England, the hierarchy carried on; assimilated new men, bought up talent, made the inescapable reforms. Whig Cabinets, the most aristocratic in living memory, led by Lord Grey and Lord Melbourne, statesmen sceptical about reform, sponsored an attack on the most pressing barbarities of the Industrial Revolution because they had to.[2] The Reform Bill of 1832 strength-

---

[1] A correspondent of the *Gentlemen's Magazine* in 1782 had already referred to 'our affluent society'.

[2] When, 'as early as the 'forties, Queen Victoria had remarked to Lord Melbourne that modern women had more accomplishments, men drank less and dogs behaved better towards the furniture than in the past, that dedicated pessimist replied that he could see no improvement'. Elizabeth Longford, *Victoria R.I.*, Weidenfeld and Nicolson, 1964, p. 577.

ened the establishment against revolution by admitting the
middle classes to a share of power, but it had not much extended
the franchise; out of eleven million, less than 600,000 could
vote and the candidates they elected were socially much the same.
The important change was administrative: 'In 1830, except for
the collective management of the revenues, for defence, or the
transmission of letters, there was hardly anything that a French-
man or a Prussian would have recognised as an administration.'[3]

Yet if government was amateurish, 'the old humanity of the
South was still politically ascendant over the new Industry in the
North',[4] and through two decades of Whig and Tory government
successive Parliamentary Royal Commissions found out a vast
range of facts; indeed, 'no community in history had ever been
submitted to so searching an examination'.[5] Their Blue Books
brought home to ruling opinion the inescapable needs of the time
by statistics and marshalled evidence; 'it is', indeed, 'possible
to notice so great an increase in these methods of measuring,
counting and observing that they may be taken as the most distinctive and original features of the age'.[6] The statistics were
underlined when cholera struck in great cities and smoke im-
partially polluted the air, for the first half of the nineteenth
century was more pestilential than the eighteenth and the Prince
Consort died of typhoid in 1861.

Very gradually, through eighteenth-century administrative
jungles, the paths were cut. By 1835 the ancient town Corporations were swept away and municipal reform came in; none too
soon, for by the mid-century half the English would already be
urban. By the next year, the first national Register of Births,
Deaths and Marriages was compiled. Following appalling revelations, Public Health Acts, Smoke Nuisance Acts, Acts to improve
paving and lighting – though not to control the speculative
builder – were put through: 'over the country as a whole,
rapidly in some aspiring boroughs, the filth and horror which had
crawled over the early Victorian towns was penned back into

---

[3] G. M. Young, *Portrait of an Age*, O.U.P., 1961 (Paperback edition),
p. 31.
[4] Ibid., p. 29.
[5] Ibid., p. 33.
[6] E. L. Woodward, *The Age of Reform*, O.U.P., 1938, p. 38.

its proper lairs'.[7] Moving away from its eighteenth-century in-difference to sanitary and social conditions, English government was now accepting Bentham's principle of 'improvement'. The eighteenth-century English had no better sanitation than their continental contemporaries; the courtiers of Queen Anne no more sensibility in this field than those of the *Roi Soleil*, and Dr. Johnson's cronies would have been little better: yet by the mid-nineteenth century the English were being shocked by conditions hitherto taken for granted and becoming pioneers of 'sanitation', that world-wide clean up original to modern times. That redoubt-able Benthamite Sir Edwin Chadwick (1800–90) was a tiger for such reform: 'who managed that appointment or ordered that sewer?', wrote *The Times*, 'and the answer is the same, Mr. Edwin Chadwick';[8] when they made him a Knight of the Bath, he remarked that the honour was doubtless to distinguish him from the 'great unwashed'. Striving, contriving, driving, 'for twenty years working ten or twelve hours a day every day with most infrequent holidays, he wore out his subordinates, astonished his colleagues, and yet reached the age of ninety with his mental faculties still as vigorous as those of many a younger man'.[9] Gradually, he and his kind helped to change a casual hap-hazard England into a Welfare State; a surprising achievement in view of the turbulence and truculence for which her people had long been notorious.

The English now also originated a civilian unarmed police. Sir Robert Peel had organised the London 'Peelers' or 'Bob-bies', and by the Police Act of 1839 the rural constables, long ago described by Lambard, were superseded by county police, still responsible, not to London, but to local J.P.'s. Law and order were thus enforced, but without the centralised armed police familiar in many states abroad and sometimes ripe for political mischief.

Upper class education, too, was now adapted and improved,

---

[7] G. M. Young, op. cit., p. 57. The Commission on Health in towns in 1843–4 reported that in the worst district of Manchester there were 215 people to one privy; in Sunderland 76. Sewers were supposed to carry off storm water, not to serve as drains, and builders were forbidden to con-nect houses to them.

[8] S. E. Finer, *The Life and Times of Sir Edwin Chadwick*, Methuen, 1952.

[9] Ibid., p. 2.

if in popular education the improvers failed. Among the masses one third of the men and two thirds of the women were probably still illiterate and there were still nearly as many 'markers' as 'signers'. Most voluntary schools were inadequate: but the new Education Committee of the Privy Council proved the origin of the later Board and Ministry. Yet sectarian rancour still prevented progress; Nonconformists excluded Anglicans; Anglicans Nonconformists: between them, as G. M. Young put it, the children remained little heathens. This failure would last.

But most of the jungle-paths led to permanent and widespread clearings. And, by the mid-century, as new industries became established, skilled workers in steady employment were prospering. Money, too, bought cheaper goods. The industrial proletariat in England was never consolidated in common degradation; on the contrary, new divisions among the wage earners were already distinct and the *embourgeoisement* of the skilled workers had begun.

After all, the prestige of the hierarchy in England had always been overwhelming, the more so because it had so long been accessible; the rich Dissenters were against ungodliness, not the social order. Moreover Victoria and Albert made the raffish late Hanoverian monarchy 'respectable', and the sovereign, as she relinquished political power, became impregnable in social influence. Even many of the great aristocrats, who socially looked down upon the Hanoverian Court, followed its example; and eighteenth-century gambling and drink – 'drunk as a lord' – became unfashionable: 'nobody is gay now', said Lord Melbourne, 'they are so religious'.[10] The desire for and expectation of 'improvement' was now widespread. When, in 1848–9 and after, revolution and reaction swept the Continent, liberal democracy was crippled in central Europe and militarism more deeply entrenched; but a civilian social order in England, behind its shield of sea power, remained insular and intact. The sharp divisions between *noblesse* and *bourgeoisie*, peasants and proletariat, did not apply. Hence the solidarity of mid-nineteenth-century England, with its abounding vigour, expanding beyond the island.

[10] Longford, op. cit., p. 128.

II

Shaped by mighty medieval kings and, even in the eighteenth century, still governed mainly on the sovereign's initiative, England, with its unwritten constitution, now made a decisive change. The monarchy relinquished political power yet preserved its influence and gained in popularity; it ceased to rule, but it continued to reign. No one would have predicted this future for the Hanoverian line represented by George IV or William IV; the turning point came with Victoria and Albert, who restored the dignity of the throne, for the Prince Consort had high and laborious ability and the Queen a rigid sense of duty. The former's death plunged the Court into mournful seclusion when, in Gladstone's words, the Queen was invisible and the Prince of Wales was not respected; but Victoria, by sheer character and longevity, attained a kind of apotheosis, and the Prince's natural social qualities won wide acclaim. The monarchy would remain the most popular and glamorous in the world – still the venerated symbol of the life of the nation and Commonwealth. It would come to be thought of, in homely idiom, as the head of a great 'family', setting standards of humanity and good sense amid the kaleidoscope of politics and the shifts of mass opinion.

This unexpected change is still best explained by the mid-Victorian Walter Bagehot, whose *The English Constitution* remains illuminating. No wise and great constitutional monarch, he asserted, would now attempt to wield direct power: the sovereign's influence was now more subtle. But it was still formidable: the Monarch, after all, was 'permanent'; and could have a steadying influence. 'To state the matter shortly', he wrote in a famous phrase, 'the sovereign has under a constitutional monarchy such as ours, three rights – the right to be consulted, the right to encourage, and the right to warn. And a King of great sense and sagacity would want no others'.[11]

Thus serious and informal functions combined in a royalty which also catered for the 'theatrical' side of government and symbolised the life of the nation; 'as when a princely marriage is a brilliant edition of a universal fact, and as such rivets mankind'. The Sovereign remained, too, the fountain of the 'honours' still

[11] Op. cit., revised edition, *World's Classics*, 1872, p. 75.

important in an intensely class-conscious society and the Head of the Established Church. Although so closely bound up with the establishment, this ancient royalty would remain more authentic and deep-rooted than the temporary grandeur of republican heads of State. It would even adapt itself to the social revolution of the mid-twentieth century.

The most vital development was the rise of Cabinet Government, the executive dependent on a majority in the Commons. That majority was still shifting, maintained by patronage and the conciliation of many interests – a process admirably described by Trollope; for it was not until the 'eighties that well-organised political parties would emerge with the constituencies managed by a 'central office'. But the focus of power was now plain, with the Crown withdrawn from political battles. There was no 'balance' of powers, as in the American Constitution; rather the executive was well geared to the legislature. Proceedings in Cabinet were informal, for not long even recorded; but decisions were unanimous. 'It does not matter', said Melbourne, 'what we say, but, mind, we must all say the same.' The Cabinet could be called to account and it was adaptable in a crisis: 'At a sudden emergency,' wrote Bagehot, prophetically of Churchill in 1940, 'the representatives of the people can choose a ruler for the occasion.... It is quite possible and even likely, that he would not be a ruler before the occasion. The great qualities, the imperious will, the eager nature fit for a great crisis are not required – are impediments in common times.'[12]

This kind of government, firmly civilian, with the armed forces always under control, would put through the reforms of Gladstone's first administration which extended the work of 'improvement' already described, and which would modernise the civil service and foreshadow the decisive work of the Campbell-Bannerman and Asquith Governments before 1914. Thus monarchy and government were slowly adapted to a vigorous society, now changing much more rapidly under the full impact of the Industrial and Technical Revolutions.

[12] Op. cit., p. 29.

III

In 1837, the year of Queen Victoria's accession, the Hon. Charles Cavendish Fulke Greville, a Whig aristocrat in easy and well-placed employment whose memoirs as vividly depict his times 'as if Judas Iscariot had written the lives of the Apostles', decided to travel – it was a new diversion – by railway from Birmingham to Liverpool. He boarded 'a sort of chariot with two places . . . nothing disagreeable about it but the occasional whiffs of stinking air . . . The first sensation', he recorded, 'is a degree of nervousness and a fear of being run away with, but a sense of security soon supervenes and the velocity is delightful . . . It certainly renders all other travelling irksome and tedious by comparison'.

It had, in fact, rendered it obsolete. As already described, the railways had transformed the communications of the island and were being rapidly developed abroad. 'The building of railways', writes E. L. Woodward, 'was the greatest physical achievement carried out by the human race in a comparatively short space of time', and 'British contractors built lines in every continent and organised companies to buy them'.[13] Originally designed for transporting goods in bulk, the 'steam carriages' now took passengers: by the mid-'thirties, 'although the university of Oxford and the Provost and fellows of Eton were among the strongest opponents',[14] the Great Western Railway was in being; and by the mid-century the main networks had been established. The social and economic effects were cumulative and decisive, the whole tempo of life speeded up.

In 1840 the postal service was also revolutionised. In the face of tenacious opposition, Rowland Hill introduced pre-payment for letters at a fixed rate through stamps. This English invention, like the railways, now spread rapidly about the world, and by 1851 Greville could record that 'the wonderful Electric Telegraph' had reported Louis Napoleon's *coup d'état* from Paris within two hours.

As more people became familiar with new inventions, the assumption of progress spread, and not only among the upper and middle classes: the people came to believe in it. When in 1824

[13] *The Age of Reform*, p. 39.   [14] Ibid., p. 44.

Pitt's Combination Acts had been repealed and Trade Unions had become legal, it was the self-made cotton-spinner philanthropist, Robert Owen, whose showplace at New Lanark was famous, who most influenced their members' minds. And Owen's interests were not political; he was a Utopian theorist who believed that a changed environment and education would oust original sin; who declared that the 'rich and the poor, the governors and the governed have really but one interest', so that 'new arrangements' could be 'introduced without violence'. He brushed aside Malthus' doctrine that poverty and unemployment were inescapable, and insisted that the economy could expand only through higher wages and full employment. His objectives, like Bentham's, were utilitarian; not to make revolution, but to enhance 'Welfare'. In England 'Welfare', not revolution, would be the predominant objective of the Labour movement.

Thus the Grand National Consolidated Trade Union, formed in 1834, and considerably inspired by Owen's beliefs, was not politically militant; and, in spite of sporadic riots, the first 'martyrs' of English Labour did not die fighting on a barricade or before a firing squad; they were Dorset labourers transported in 1834 to Australia for administering illicit trade union oaths. After two years of popular agitation, these 'Tolpuddle Martyrs', whose cottages remain a place of pilgrimage, were retrieved and given small-holdings in Essex, for only one chose to return to his own neighbourhood.

The Co-operative movement, Owen's most lasting achievement, was never revolutionary either; it aimed merely to improve distribution and cheapen supplies: only Chartism expressed militant opinion, and it failed. That it did is the more remarkable, since it reflected widespread discontent among the submerged poor. In the 'twenties desperate men had been driven to rick burning and terrorism, ruthlessly put down; the eighteenth-century code of punishment whereby an adult or a child could be hanged for petty theft had not been revised until the 'thirties; the game laws had even been tightened up so that, if caught red-handed, a poacher could still be transported for seven years; in affrays poachers and game-keepers still used shot guns and clubs.[15] And

[15] At the Pitt-Rivers Museum at Farnham, Dorset, already cited, can be seen the wicker 'armour' worn by the keepers and the man-traps and spring guns they set in Cranborne Chase.

now, when the improvers had intervened, they too had been unpopular. The new Poor Law of 1834 had superseded the time-
honoured system of subsidised labour or 'outside relief'. Parishes
had been combined in 'Unions' to provide 'Workhouses' in
which paupers were now confined; but the cosier method of supplementing the low wages of cottagers had been more convenient
to labourers and employers alike. And now the new 'Institutions' were deliberately made uncomfortable to prevent the poor
voluntarily resorting to them: families were broken up, lunatics
left at large in the common wards. Underneath the prosperity of
the successful of all classes, there remained an enormous penury
and grievance.

The Chartists, with their monster 'petitions' and to modern
opinion reasonable demands – universal suffrage, for example
– reflected this discontent. But their leaders were hardly representative; O'Brien was an Irish wine and tobacco merchant, and
Feargus O'Connor the son of an Irish agitator. The first threatened general strike in 1839 was a fiasco; the monster petitions of
the 'forties ended in failure, even ridicule.

It was not, in fact, O'Brien and O'Connor but Anthony Ashley
Cooper, seventh Earl of Shaftesbury, who substantially helped
the working classes, in particular the children, when he forced
through Factory Acts which limited hours of work. And the
Trade Unions, as against the Chartists, continued to concentrate
on immediate objectives: by 1851, the Engineering Unions had
amalgamated, and were levying regular subscriptions; in the
'fifties the carpenters and the stonemasons had combined. The
mainspring of the Labour movement came from skilled artisans,
still without votes, whose objectives were limited, and often
obtained.

Such was the restless but seldom revolutionary underworld of
mid-Victorian England as it drove forward under the impetus of
the new factories and railways, already the plutocratic workshop
of the world.

IV

The newly rich and the prosperous middle-classes were now assimilated by new 'public' schools. And gradually the universities
were modernised: at Oxford and Cambridge written 'Honours'

examinations came in which would recruit a new intellectual and administrative élite and in time provide the 'meritocracy' of the Welfare State. At Oxford, Oriel College was already electing its Fellows from outside the society, and by 1828 Balliol was electing its scholars by open competition. With their 'blue riband' scholarships and 'double firsts', Oxford and Cambridge would attain a paradoxical prestige even among that part of the public little concerned with intellect or the arts; for labels which retained the glamour of age, aristocracy and power were passports to success. Within a strict convention the adapted classical education was first rate; and linked by the 'sixties with the Administrative Civil Service at home and in India, where a tiny élite would shape the future of a sub-continent.

But so great was the prestige of Oxford and Cambridge that there would not be that easy migration and equality of various prestige common among the greater continental and American universities. The University of London, founded in 1828 with utilitarian objectives (to this day the mummy of Bentham himself, apparelled in period, sits under glass in University College), took long to develop, and the 'provincial' universities in the Midlands, described disparagingly as Redbrick, took even longer to win reputation.

It is doubtful if life at the pre-Arnold public schools was so unpleasant for most boys as the Victorian reformers believed: Keate, that notoriously flagellant Headmaster, was quite popular among Etonians and, when the Duke of Wellington remarked that the battle of Waterloo was won on the playing fields of Eton, he referred not to cricket but to fisticuffs. During the near-anarchy of that time Eton was educating a galaxy of future prime ministers, statesmen and pro-consuls; indeed, intelligent boys could always educate each other without interference from the masters, themselves the survivors of a process of natural selection, since those who could not take it 'did not last'.

A habit of casual enjoyment carried on; a patrician frivolity that generally masked a formidable lifemanship and independence. And if most Etonians were amateurs, they were seldom prigs. Moreover, within its curious convention, Eton largely governed itself. The Eton society, nicknamed 'Pop', was founded in 1811;[16] there was little 'damned merit' about its elections, and

[16] Probably so-called from the Latin *popina*, a pastry cook's.

it came to be a kind of secular arm, with the masters playing the role of the medieval Church. These peculiar arrangements still sharply distinguish Eton; and Eton remains the oddest and the freest of English schools.

A very different tradition was inaugurated by Dr. Arnold at Rugby. In reaction from Regency licence, he was a determined reformer; to some a dangerous innovator. A genius with boys, he had the revolutionary idea of treating them as civilised beings and improving their characters; and he introduced history and geography, if not science or economics, into the curriculum. Unlike his imitators, he made no cult of organised games: he ruled Rugby through his sixth form, and if his religious and moral fervour now seem overwrought, he changed, as predicted at his appointment, the face of middle-class education in England.[17]

Following Arnold's innovations, many new public schools sprang up; in the 'forties the brick barracks at Marlborough, imaginatively termed A and B houses, where the boys, when they staged a 'rebellion', could stand a siege by the local militia from Devizes. Cheltenham, with its Victorian Gothic, and Wellington with its pseudo-Byzantine towers, prepared boys mainly for the Army; Clifton, Uppingham and Haileybury followed; the last expanded from the College for the East India Company's cadets. Minor foundations of various merit proliferated; older schools were adapted, and by the 'nineties English middle-class education would be pervaded by a new 'public school spirit', much more conventional and hidebound than Arnold's. Where in the 'forties the Marlburian poet William Morris could poach game in Savernake and range freely on the downs, the full cult of compulsory games now came in; it was hoped, indeed, to 'send them to bed tired'. Most boys liked games and the competition of

[17] Thomas Arnold, D.D. (1795–1842). Son of a Collector of Customs at Cowes in the Isle of Wight, he was educated at Winchester and became a Fellow of Oriel College, Oxford, in the year of Waterloo. He had no experience as a schoolmaster, save as a 'coach' near Staines, where, after his marriage to Mary Penrose, he prepared pupils for the University. In 1828 he took over Rugby, an office he combined in 1841 with the Regius Professorship of Modern History at Oxford. Arnold was a major public figure who poured out sermons and articles, and produced a large edition of Thucydides as well as a history of Rome. Lytton Strachey's portrait of him in *Eminent Victorians* was admitted even by the author to be a caricature; Strachey had no evidence for the physical clumsiness and puzzled expression which he attributed to this formidable headmaster.

colours and promotions, and the habit canalised much dash and high spirits; but the duller side would be satirised even by Kipling when he wrote of

> *The flannelled fools at the wicket or the muddied oafs*
> *at the goals.*

If less liable to Aubrey's criticism that 'their minds did chiefly run on the propagation of their race'[18] than the French, many 'public school' English would remain 'old boys' all their lives; but since later hardships were seldom worse than those suffered in these segregated and Spartan schools, the native endurance was enhanced; Army and Empire owed much to these upright, if often tongue-tied, men, if their interests were often too limited to take in the civilisations and the qualities of those they were set to rule. They were certainly different from the exuberant and many-sided Elizabethans or the individualistic predators of the seventeenth and eighteenth centuries. The external image of the English changed. Within the society, too, these schools cut across local loyalties and stereotyped a new class distinction: a rift in the social fabric roughly between public and grammar schools, which, in so class-conscious a country, would have its sequel.

More importantly in the long run, the English now developed their already outstanding scientific genius. Unlike the obscure Roger Bacon in the thirteenth century, Francis Bacon, Harvey and Newton had all won wide fame, while English inventors and craftsmen had begun the industrial take off. Now a whole spate of discoveries were made, and Darwin would become a world influence, developing this great tradition and revolutionising the picture of man's place in nature. The mid-Victorian age was, indeed, the first time in history when the conclusions of applied science were regarded as decisive for the outlook of mankind; when, as T. H. Huxley could write, 'The whole of modern thought is steeped in science; it has made its way into the works of our best poets . . . I believe that the greatest intellectual revolution mankind has yet seen is now slowly taking place by her agency. She is teaching the world that the ultimate court of appeal is observation and experiment, and not authority; she is teaching it to estimate the value of evidence . . .'.[19] Such was the

---

[18] Vide supra, p. 104 n.
[19] *Aphorisms and Reflections*, Macmillan, 1908, p. 80.

most original aspect of the nineteenth century and the English greatly contributed to it.

This kind of systematic observation was made within the mid-Victorian setting of political liberty and free enterprise. Darwin, in particular, was original to eccentricity and wealthy enough to go his own way:[20] he disregarded the obloquy which his revelations provoked and combined broad views, relating subjects to one another, with laborious and ingenious experiment. He united perseverance, empirical method and imaginative flair in a characteristically English way; his thought was subtle and tentative, more akin to that of an observant farmer than of a theoretician. His understatement and candour, backed by plain evidence, made his influence the more pervasive, changing the whole concept of the evolution of life and man. Darwin became, like Newton, a world figure.

His colleague, T. H. Huxley, whose lucid prose and forceful oratory helped to convert opinion, defined scientific method in a very English way as 'organised commonsense'. Yet, like Darwin, he was a humanist. 'As men of research in positive science', he wrote of the Germans, 'they are magnificently laborious and accurate, but most of them have no notion of style, and seem to compose their books with a pitchfork.' 'The fact is,' he declared, 'I have a great love and respect for my native tongue and take great pains to use it properly'.[21] Huxley had the range and sense of vocation of most eminent Victorians; and his style, devoid of scientific jargon, was consciously modelled on the

[20] Charles Darwin (1809–1882). He was the grandson of Erasmus Darwin, the natural philosopher and writer, and of Josiah Wedgwood, the founder of Wedgwood Potteries. Educated at Shrewsbury Grammar School, Edinburgh University and Christ's College, Cambridge, he found that only Paley's *Evidences* were 'in the least use to me in the education of my mind'. But he early took to collecting beetles, in the intervals of hunting, riding and shooting with a sporting set. Destined for Holy Orders, he abandoned the project in 1831, the year before the Reform Bill, to join H.M.S. *Beagle* on a survey of the coasts of South America. The expedition concluded by a voyage to the Galapagos islands, Tahiti, and parts of Australasia, returning by the Cape. Darwin now specialised in biology. In 1939 he married his cousin Emma Wedgwood, and in 1842 retired to Down in Kent. Here, a chronic psychosomatic invalid, probably in the main through an infection picked up on his voyage, he worked doggedly for forty years. His most important books were the epoch-making *On the Origins of Species by Means of Natural Selection* (1859), and *The Descent of Man* (1871).

[21] Quoted by Aldous Huxley: *T. H. Huxley as a Man of Letters.* Huxley Memorial Lecture, Macmillan, 1932, p. 11.

'dignity' of Hobbes, the 'concision and clearness' of Swift and the 'simplicity' of Defoe.

The shift of attention towards applied science had been reinforced by revolutionary discoveries. In the late eighteenth century Henry Cavendish, a grandson of the second Duke of Devonshire, had devoted his fortune to natural philosophy; he is commemorated in the great Cavendish Laboratory at Cambridge, since the scene of epoch-making experiment. Sir Humphry Davy, a Cornishman, had much advanced the study of chemistry pioneered by Boyle, and his younger colleague, Faraday, the son of a blacksmith, had discovered magneto-electricity. Dalton devised a formula for measuring the weight of atoms, while Joule and Clerk-Maxwell, a Scotsman who migrated to Cambridge, made great advances in thermo-dynamics, formulating respectively the first and second laws of that subject: the one, as translated for humanists, being roughly that you cannot have your cake and eat it; the other that to get anything done you must increase the disorder in the universe.

In medicine, Lord Lister now made modern surgery possible. Hitherto 'hospital gangrene' had rendered the few operations attempted hazardous; nearly half the amputations were fatal and major internal surgery impossible. Adapting Pasteur's discovery that decomposition was caused by germs, Lister killed them by disinfecting instruments in carbolic acid solution and surgical wounds in carbolic spray. By 1865 the basis of aseptic surgery had been secured – a discovery which would cross all national barriers. Supplemented by anaesthetics and X-rays, it would vastly alleviate life.

Meanwhile, Florence Nightingale was devoting her energy and fortune to the reform of hospitals and of nursing, hitherto a disreputable calling. When in 1856 she returned from the Crimean War with a legendary prestige, this redoubtable woman set new standards for army and civilian hospitals. Nurses were trained, a whole new range of public health services opened up, greatly supplementing the reforms of Chadwick already described; and this impulse would extend all over the world. To the cosmopolitan advance of science and medicine the contribution of the Victorian English was second to none.

The mid-Victorians also much promoted the new 'environmental' studies, one of the major fields of nineteenth-century discovery. Maine's *Ancient Law* (1861) related modern legal concepts to early history; Bagehot's brilliant *Physics and Politics* (1872) applied the principle of natural selection to human societies, and Tylor's *Primitive Culture* (1871) pioneered modern anthropology. All these writers, the first a Cambridge professor experienced in India; the second a banker and economist; the third the son of a wealthy Midland manufacturer, display the typical mid-Victorian confidence and wordly wisdom. They also present their evidence and conclusions in admirable prose enlivened by striking examples, and they understand the past in a new way, for Vico and Montesquieu had much more limited knowledge. This work was linked with the achievements of the contemporary English explorers who opened up huge areas of Africa and Australasia, hitherto unknown to Europeans.

Social and political theory were also influenced by a fresh range of knowledge, and English writers were outstanding. John Stuart Mill, long an administrator in the East India Company, modified the improving theories of Bentham and his own father into a liberalism which proved very influential, 'chiding and guiding' his age. His *Essay on Liberty* (1859) became a bible of Victorian politics, vindicating the freedom of individuals against an already threatening bureaucracy and mass opinion; of its kind it was a masterpiece, cited far beyond England. Mill was also a considerable economist and sociologist, and a champion of the emancipation of women – a world-wide movement to which England greatly contributed.

The self-educated Herbert Spencer, a very English eccentric, had a less useful influence, but it was also world-wide. He tried, like Comte, to create a science of politics, applying pseudo-Darwinian theories of the survival of the fittest to human societies, and giving a new lease of life to gloomy Malthusian doctrines that the devil ought, necessarily, to take the hindmost.

The popular historians, on the other hand, were highly optimistic. Macaulay, whose *History of England* (1848) at once became a best seller, was the prose laureate of the Victorian *haute bourgeoisie*; his sharp visual mind recreated just the kind of past that his audience wanted, leading up to the solid, prosperous, mid-Victorian climax. Complacent he was, but civilian;

his patriotism less militant than that of his continental equivalents.

Buckle had more influence abroad, for his *History of Civilisation in England* (1857–61) was set against the geography of the world. With a vivid sense of environment and climate, Buckle, like Bagehot and Tylor, had brilliant insight, and he greatly popularised the fashionable idea of progress. Lecky, too, wrote his *Rise of Rationalism in Europe* (1865) on optimistic assumptions; his theme the decline of the curious superstitions he lovingly described before reason, science and industry.

But of all these often rather obvious masters of Victorian prose, none is so subtle, so capable of sustained and elaborate effects and yet so clear, as John Henry Newman, later Cardinal Newman. Though, fortunately, he failed to preserve Oxford as a mere Anglican seminary, his *Idea of a University* depicts one of the higher mid-Victorian ideals; one which, in its strength and limitation, shows much serene benevolence. His scholar-gentleman is very different from eighteenth-century forerunners or from the 'meritocrats' who would come after. 'He has too much good sense to be affronted by insults, he is too well employed to remember injuries, and too indolent to bear malice. He is patient, forbearing, and resigned, on philosophical principles; he submits to pain because it is inevitable, to bereavement because it is irreparable, and to death, because it is his destiny. If he engages in controversy of any kind, his disciplined intellect preserves him from the blundering discourtesy of better, though less educated minds; who, like blunt weapons, tear and hack instead of cutting clean, who mistake the point in argument, waste their strength on trifles, misconceive their adversary, and leave the question more involved than they find it. He may be right or wrong in his opinion, but he is too clear-headed to be unjust; he is as simple as he is forcible, and as brief as he is decisive.'

All these writers were confident and most of them well-to-do; they enjoyed following their own bent, so that their books, now technically superseded, still live for their vitality and style. The great mid-Victorians were not pompous bores; the English were then full of attack and their best minds were subtle.

V

The fiction written in mid-Victorian England shows the same force. It is immensely vigorous and varied; ideas which Elizabethans would have expressed in drama now expressed in novels. And the best poetry, as T. H. Huxley had observed, was now concerned with deep problems of religion and morals raised by the revolution in scientific knowledge.

Far the most famous novelist was Charles Dickens (1812–70). As a child, he had known urban poverty at first hand and picked up his education mainly as a reporter. He depicted and caricatured a whole melodramatic panorama of English life. Like Balzac, he was fascinated, not repelled, by the nuances of class, and he was typically Victorian in his profusion, comic flair, sentimentality and belief that villains in general concealed hearts of gold. He held up a mirror – if a distorting one – to the Victorian middle class who rushed to buy his books, and his eccentric characters well suited so individualistic a country as nineteenth-century England. Dickens made his name by *Pickwick Papers*, published in the late 'thirties and designed originally to amplify a series of sporting prints. The book comes out of the picaresque novels of the eighteenth century, but it is touched with a new sentimental benevolence where Fielding and Smollett are hard as nails; and, like Shakespeare, Dickens delighted to depict the common people.

Following *Pickwick*, Dickens poured out novels of greater power: *Nicholas Nickleby*, attacking third-rate schools; then *Oliver Twist*, attacking the hated Workhouses; then *The Old Curiosity Shop*, with its orgy of sentiment over the death of Little Nell 'which reduced to tears the populations of England and America'.[22] And Dickens was the first great novelist to depict the consequences of the Industrial Revolution; as they appeared, for example, to that redoubtable midwife, Mrs. Gamp, 'Them confugion steamers has done more to throw us out of reg'lar work and bring ewents on at times when nobody counted on 'em (especially them screeching railroad ones), than all the other frights that ever was took'. *Great Expectations* ironically con-

[22] David Daiches, *A Critical History of English Literature*, Vol. II, p. 1054, q.v.

trasts the origins of money and the gentility it can buy; Mr. Pod-snap is the quintessential snob. The vulgarity of Dickens was a vulgarity of genius, and his sheer creativeness won a reputation still world-wide.

Thackeray (1811–63), by ambition at first an artist, had a harder satiric eye. Like Dickens, he is rooted in the eighteenth century of Fielding and Smollett; but he mainly depicts the well-to-do and their hangers-on, their opportunism brilliantly described in Becky Sharp, the real heroine of *Vanity Fair*.

Trollope's *Barchester Towers* (1857) at once brought him fame. It has a very English theme – the intrigues of the dignitaries and lesser clergy in an Anglican cathedral Close in the southern counties. Connoisseurs of this atmosphere can still read him with profit and refugees from the twentieth century still relish him; for no one better than Trollope evokes the security and well-being which his more successful characters enjoyed, while the unfortunate are generally compensated – since Trollope, that admirable craftsman, knew his public's taste. His political novels also reveal how the affairs of the nation were then run. His satire is kindly; like Peacock, he is not disgusted by human folly but entertained.

The Brontës in their bleak Yorkshire parsonage showed a different spirit. Here a wild romantic imagination, echoing eighteenth century fantasies but much more personal, has free rein; Emily Brontë's *Wuthering Heights* harks back to Elizabethan horrors, and Charlotte Brontë's *Jane Eyre* creates character against a background of macabre and improbable tragedy.

Such are the most representative of a galaxy of novelists who, along with many scientists, philosophers and historians, made the 'fifties and 'sixties so creative a time.

The poets, too, though inferior to the Elizabethans and Jacobeans, made a great mark. Tennyson (1809–92), poet laureate by 1850 and a peer in 1883, was vastly revered. He often evokes that English melancholy which goes back to the Anglo-Saxon poet brooding over the ruins of Bath, but with a more elaborate and wistful sentiment; and he also faced the growing religious 'doubt' of the day. His *In Memoriam*, occasioned by the death of Arthur Hallam in 1833 but not completed or published until 1850, expressed a concern then widespread beyond England at the darkening view of the human condition: and, indeed, decades would elapse before people would put up with more limited prospects. Capable of appalling bathos, often content to leave ill alone and 'faintly trust the larger hope', Tennyson could celebrate friendship:

> *When each by turns was guide to each,*
> *And Fancy light from Fancy caught,*
> *And Thought leapt out to wed with Thought*
> *'Ere Thought could wed itself with Speech.*

And he developed a wide range; public and martial as well as intimate and sentimental. He could write of

> *Freedom slowly broadening down from precedent to*
> *precedent,*

And of a future when

> *The war drums throb no longer and the battle-flags are*
> *furled*
> *In the Parliament of Man, the Federation of the World.*

But his dominant mood was melodious regret:

> *O Love, we two shall go no longer*
> *To lands of summer across the sea.*

An autumnal sadness pervades much of his later work, written, one feels, mainly for the leisured classes.

> *The woods decay, the woods decay and fall,*
> *The vapours weep their burthen to the ground*
> *Man comes and tills the field and lies beneath,*
> *And after many a summer died the swan.*

But the earlier *In Memoriam* also strikes home the grimness of the new scientific knowledge,

> *of nature red in tooth and claw.*

If man were a mere 'discord',

> *Dragons of the prime*
> *That tare each other in their slime*
> *Were mellow music matched with him.*

A master magician of lush Victorian verse, Tennyson was also a prophet of the horrors of the twentieth century.

Browning showed the more vigorous Victorian mood: he used an argumentative colloquial style, different from the romantic idiom that he inherited. He can hit off personality and period with an arresting phrase and, like Byron, startle with deliberately grotesque rhymes. Like Tennyson, he often depicted the background of Italy – which meant much to the Victorian well-to-do; he was at once a romantic and a prophet of 'heroic' endeavour:

> God's in his heaven, he could even assert,
> All's right with the world!

But Matthew Arnold, like Wordsworth and Tennyson, wrote of 'doubt'; of

> Vague half believers in our casual creeds.

He found consolation in landscape; in

> Wide fields of breezy grass
> Where black-winged swallows haunt the glittering
>   Thames;

in the

> line of festal light in Christ Church hall,

and in the romantic evocation of Aegean isles.

> Is it so small a thing, he asked, reasonably enough,
> To have enjoyed the sun?

Many mid-Victorian poets thus combined a rich sensual perception, lavishly expressed, with an underlying anxiety and sadness. And this tension was also probably reflected in a curious and original Victorian *genre* – 'nonsense' narrative and verse.

Dodgson's *Alice's Adventures in Wonderland* by 'Lewis Carroll' (1865) draw on the subconscious of a professional mathematician, and run much deeper than the story improvised at a children's picnic at Godstow on the Thames near Oxford, '*all in the golden afternoon*'. A rigorous mad logic determines the tale, and philosophers still find their problems sharply defined in this extraordinary fantasy: 'Well! I've often seen a cat without a grin', thought Alice, 'but a grin without a cat ... !'[23]

Edward Lear, too, developed a queer turn of nonsense which seems to have no parallel in continental literature. He depicts himself as a rueful old comic, the *'Dong with the luminous nose'*; but, like his two most famous characters, he, also, could *'Dance by the light of the moon'*.

Thus the rich panorama of mid-Victorian writing is as various as the society it reflects: the overriding seriousness, respectability and drive being set off by a fine eccentricity. It was still a privileged society, riding high over a mass of poverty and distress, but permeated by optimism and self-reliance and open wide to talent. The mid-Victorian decades, indeed, saw a peak of English achievement in a country which had become the greatest industrial, financial, and naval power on the planet. For while all this intense life had been going on in the island, England was becoming, casually enough, the focus of a vast colonial Empire. As had the Roman Republic, the society would transform itself by success; at once swamped and stimulated by cosmopolitan influences, strange to its original tradition. The interaction of these forces with the native genius is the dominant theme of modern times.

[23] The Cheshire cat probably derives either from Cheshire cheeses made like cats, or from signposts on Cheshire Inns, meant to be lions. The book is packed with parody and allusion, and the Mad Hatter based on a well-known Oxford shop-keeper. Dodgson took the trouble to bring Tenniel, whose drawings so well suited the fantasy, to observe that worthy standing at his door in Turl Street.

Chapter 3

Victorian Empire

THE mid-nineteenth century had seen the climax of mid-Victorian England, the greatest financial and naval power in the world; but save for the casual opportunism of Palmerston, the last Whig Prime Minister of the Melbourne vintage, one cautious of European commitments. True to form, a mainly aristocratic establishment had again adapted itself. The magnates disposed of enormous incomes, now drawn from investment more than land; indeed, they had 'made industry fashionable . . . maintained their political power after the repeal of the Corn Laws by placing the Tory and Liberal parties upon a new commercial and industrial foundation and . . . fitted themselves in this way for long-term economic and social survival . . . they resembled a club, not a caste, membership had always been open to plutocrats'.[1] The Prince of Wales, now by the 'seventies the social leader of Europe, horrified the continental landowners, whose battues he relished, by admitting Jewish financiers to his intimate entourage: with genial bonhomie, he would chaff American acquaintances about the strict social distinctions their egalitarian society had devised. On this plutocratic basis, British enterprise was now deployed upon an even greater scale: the late Victorian and Edwardian Empire included nearly a quarter of the land surface of the globe and nearly a quarter of its population. The merchant navy contained about half the world's shipping, while the Royal Navy, adapted from sail and wooden walls to coal and armour, dominated the oceans. London was the financial capital of the world and British investment overseas enormous; still in 1910 equivalent annually to the vast yearly receipts from capital already placed abroad. But in this prosperity there was one flaw; while continental nations had improved their

[1] Sir Philip Magnus, *Edward VII*, Murray, 1964, p. 69.

185

agriculture and kept it in some balance with industry, Great Britain had become so industrialised that four fifths of its wheat supply had now to be imported; and by 1914 only eight per cent of its population were employed on the land, compared with forty-three per cent in France. The physique of the urban poor was so inferior in 1899 that out of 12,000 volunteers in Manchester, 8,000 were rejected by the Army. While, therefore, even after the repeal of the Corn Laws, agriculture had enjoyed an Indian summer enhanced by new techniques, capital investment and the Crimean War, by the 'seventies, with the full advent of the steam-ship and the development of the American prairies, British agriculture was entering a severe decline. Even animal feeding stuffs were imported.

Since the Empire lived by trade, policy became even more cautious and flexible, as befitted a great maritime power having so much to lose; governments made patient and cool appraisals of long-term interests and were reluctant to undertake new commitments. Meanwhile, at home, against this background of Empire – an astonishing *tour de force* by so small a nation – England, like the other Western states at the time, began to face the problems of mass civilisation which were to dominate the twentieth century, and try to adapt old methods of government to new ways. In particular, the English, like the Americans, but unlike the French or the Germans, succeeded in working parliamentary government in terms of two centralised mass political parties, one of which could provide 'Her Majesty's Opposition'. The Cabinet remained responsible to the majority in the House of Commons, while in most continental countries a fragmentation of parties precluded stability. To this elementary fact rather than to any peculiar political genius much of the success of British parliamentary institutions may be attributed.[2]

Before the range and opportunity of Empire the English character and imagination also found new scope; in administration, in settlement, and in exploration; while the more significant writers, if not the artists, became both far-ranging and profound. These three achievements, political, imperial and intellectual, will here be examined, the great work of English scientists which continued through this time being later considered.

[2] This arrangement was conditioned until 1922 by votes of the Irish, but never wrecked by them.

II

The English, though in fact their rulers were oceanic minded, were now thought by continentals much more insular and aloof: and indeed the British Empire could give cause for arrogance. It was a tremendous feat, symbolised by the Royal Standard floating above the towers and battlements of Windsor on the Thames, by the rich pageantry of the City Companies, by the roar and bustle of London and the great industrial towns, as well as by the immense town and country houses of the rich and the vigour of business and the professions. Beneath, there was a proletariat more industrialised and urban than any in Europe, and the evil of unemployment had increased; but in late Victorian England there was a huge vitality and gusto, expressed in the bouncing tunes of the music halls, and in the colossal vulgarity of Elgar's setting of *Land of Hope and Glory*, so different from the clean vigour of the eighteenth century composers in the same strain.

This confidence, apparent in 1914 when the country entered the First World War, persisted in more dogged form through four years of massacre and inspired a sometimes boneheaded obstinacy. Further, the leadership of Churchill and the response it evoked would still draw on the confidence of those times.

This expectation that things would turn out well had been encouraged by the development of party politics into a kind of national sport, with the rise of the two disciplined mass political parties under Gladstone and Disraeli. After Disraeli had enfranchised the skilled workers in 1867 and Gladstone had launched the reforms of his first administration in 1868–74, the masses had eagerly responded: Gladstone had turned the Whig into the Liberal party and Disraeli had invented 'Tory Democracy' and 'Imperialism'.

Neither of these leaders, whose political duels were followed with expert attention by an enormous audience, were aristocrats. Gladstone was a younger son of a self-made Scots slave-owner from Liverpool, who had dropped a concluding 's' from his patronymic, exchanged Presbyterian for Anglican convictions and left over half a million. Though educated at Eton and Christ Church, Gladstone retained a middle-class fervour; he became a High Church prophet of liberty whose tortuous genius

was backed by an eagle profile and an hypnotic eye. His eloquence expressed and evoked that English moral indignation,
discernible since the Lollards and dominant during the Puritan
Interregnum; moreover, the 'Grand old Man' was well over
eighty when he formed his last administration.

Disraeli also achieved an astonishing *tour de force* in climbing
the greasy pole of power. He was the first Jew to become Prime
Minister; a sardonic virtuoso of the memorable phrase, of worldli-
ness and wit; a brilliant political opportunist. In youth his
peculiar appearance – as of a character out of his own novels –
provoked ridicule; his maiden speech in the Commons was even
shouted down; but he retorted 'the time shall come when you
will hear me' and he was right. When, like some desiccated
Egyptian mummy, this extraordinary adventurer took his seat as
Earl of Beaconsfield in the Lords – 'dead', he remarked, 'but
in the Elysian Fields' – he had created a popular Conservative
party. Where Gladstone's reforms had been mainly administrative
and political, Disraeli's new Conservatism inspired the Artisan's
Dwelling Act and the Public Health Act of 1875.

His cynical countenance hung in the parlours of well-to-do
farmers, and since, officially, his 'favourite flower' was not the
gardenia but the primrose, the Conservatives formed a Primrose
League. He also managed to hypnotise the nation into a new
sense of Imperial destiny. As Sir Isaiah Berlin points out, Disraeli 'in effect conceived that imperialist mystique, that splendid
but most un-English vision which, romantic to the point of
exoticism, full of metaphysical emotion, to all appearances utterly
opposed to everything most soberly empirical, utilitarian, anti-
systematic in the British tradition, bound its spell on the mind of
England for two generations'.[3]

Gladstone and Disraeli were both spell-binders and neither
was English. Oliver Cromwell had come from Huntingdon,
Clarendon from Wiltshire, Walpole out of Norfolk, the
Churchills and Pitts from Dorset and Peel from Lancashire;
but not many Englishmen would now be Prime Ministers.
Balfour and Campbell-Bannerman and MacDonald would be
Scots; Bonar Law, Scots-Canadian; Lloyd George, Welsh;
Baldwin, on his mother's side, Scots-Irish; and Sir Winston

---

[3] 'Mr. Churchill and F.D.R.', *Atlantic Monthly* and *London Magazine*,
1949-50.

Churchill half-American. Up to the turn of the twentieth century only Lord Rosebery and Lord Salisbury, Asquith and Attlee would be mainly English.

III

In glamorising the Victorian Empire, Disraeli characteristically exploited accomplished facts. Gradually, over the years, as the flag had followed trade and settlement, a new dimension had been added to the English outlook. The Empire had not, indeed, grown up in a fit of absence of mind, but it had accumulated into a much greater concern than ever foreseen and it enlarged English horizons. In India government had been confronted with responsibilities which had proved too much for the East India Company, well adapted though it had long been; across the Atlantic the remaining legacy of the eighteenth-century empire in British North America had to be put to rights, and in Australia and New Zealand thrusting settlers forced the home Government's hand; while the responsibilities in Egypt following the opening of the Suez Canal, and in tropical Africa following partition, were reluctantly assumed.

The great variety of the Empire called out different aspects of English character: in India England imposed one of the ablest and most disinterested régimes in history; in the white Dominions free initiative was combined with self-government; Africa brought out individualism, even eccentricity.

The East India Company had long in fact ruled much of India, but the Mughul Bahadur Shah II still reigned nominally in Delhi, and his Persian-speaking court still had a dilapidated prestige: now the 'Mutiny' of 1857, though mainly occasioned by grievances among the well-paid Sepoys of the army of Bengal and confined to a limited area, had changed the picture. In the following year Queen Victoria had been proclaimed sovereign of all India. The administration became more aloof; the change symbolised in the contrast of the Governor-General's Regency Pavilion and Lutyens' Viceregal palaces which would mark the culmination and the passing of the raj.

The last of the Mughuls, a bewildered old aesthete, had been bundled out of the country to Burma. 'Everything correct', reported the subaltern in charge, 'and the ex-King stands the

travelling very well . . . It is rather hard for me getting up at 1.30
a.m. . . . but I don't care a straw for any amount of work and am
very jolly. I am honorary member of the Lancer Mess . . . a pack
of hounds accompany the column on the march, and we have a
run when we succeed in getting a jackal.'[4]

All was now clear for an Indian Civil Service to take over
enormous areas, and, seven thousand miles from the island,
British individualism, more flamboyant in the Dominions, was
institutionalised. The members of this tiny élite have been well
described in Plato's terms: 'the nearest parallels on the same
scale', writes their best historian, 'are the Civil Services of China
under the Emperors, and of the Ottoman Empire under Suleiman
the Magnificent: the Romans had nothing comparable. But there
is an ideal model for the Indian system, not consistently adopted
or easily followed, for that is not the way in which English minds
work, but a model with which every English statesman in the
nineteenth century was familiar. Plato pictured a state ruled by
guardians.' The Indian Civil Service formed a caste: 'Trained
by cold baths, cricket and the history of Greece and Rome, a
separate race from those they ruled, aloof, superior to bribery,
discouraged from marriage until they were middle-aged, and then
subjected to long separations . . . no other people in history can
equal their record in disinterested guardianship.'[5]

Naturally, in so alien an environment and among a people tem-
peramentally so different, whose civilisation was older than that
of Europe, it was 'not surprising that they were not always loved,
nor that in the end their wards outgrew their tutelage. What is
surprising is that so often there was real warmth and affection
between the district officer and the peasant, that the system was
always so much looser than it looked, that so much freedom was
always left to the individual officer, that the guardians fell in
practice so far short of platonic rigidity.' This achievement in
India, deliberately dismantled by a rapid handing over of power,
created the political framework which a partitioned sub-continent
would inherit, and it set standards still acknowledged.

If in India the British shouldered and handed over vast responsibilities in an alien setting, in the white 'Dominions' as they

[4] Percival Spear, *The Twilight of the Moghuls*, C.U.P., 1951, p. 228.
[5] *See* Philip Woodruff, *The Men who Ruled India*, Cape, 1953/4, Vol. I,
pp. 15–16, for an admirable account.

came to be called, they would come to delegate and transfer power. The blunders which had led to the American War of Independence were not repeated, and new nations were brought into being; independent, yet linked by sentiment and economic interest with the home country.

After the establishment of the United States, many 'loyalists', not liking the look of things, had joined the settlements in what became Ontario in Upper Canada; while Lower Canada had been inhabited since the sixteenth century by the Catholic and conservative Canadian French. To deal with the resulting friction, the British had to intervene, but they did so with a light hand. Following the Durham report of 1837, the Canada Act had united the whole area and established responsible government; by 1867 a new status for what was in effect a new nation had been devised when British North America became the 'Dominion' of Canada, the first Dominion of the Victorian Empire. There was a vast expansion into the Canadian mid-West, and the Canadian Pacific Railway came to span the whole continent, linking the old Eastern Maritime province with British Columbia and Vancouver in the far West.

A similar political solution was devised for Australasia, where new nations of British stock were established. All had begun with characteristic casualness, when in 1788 a batch of convicts had been landed at Botany Bay, 'so named by Sir Joseph Banks, a distinguished amateur of science who accompanied Cook on one of his voyages. There was not much botany about it now.'[6] Free settlers had followed; a mixed, vigorous lot. By the 'forties, when transportation was abolished, they had far outnumbered the convicts. Then, nine years after the first settlement, MacArthur imported Merino sheep; by the mid-nineteenth century wool was bringing great wealth, and by 1813, with wars raging in Europe and North America, explorers had begun to penetrate the interior for new pastures. Blaxland, who introduced the vine, Lawson, who would farm a huge acreage in New South Wales, and Wentworth, who would become the first major Australian statesman, crossed the low but difficult Blue Mountains that hemmed in the coastal settlement: 'the natives as observed by their smoke' moved off; 'the dogs killed a kangaroo, which was very

[6] Sir Winston Churchill, *A History of the English Speaking Peoples*, Vol. IV, p. 91.

acceptable'. The explorers had found huge pastures 'covered with the finest grass and intermixed with the white daisy as in England'.[7]

In the 'twenties, Charles Stuart, an Harrovian from the Indian Army, discovered the Darling – so-called after the current Governor, then the Murrumbidgee, the two main rivers of the continent; and in the 'forties, Edward Eyre, son of a Yorkshire clergyman, crossed Australia from east to west while Stuart penetrated the Simpson desert. Thomas Mitchell, a Scot who had served in the Peninsula and became Surveyor General, traversed the continent from Sydney to the gulf of Carpentaria, the first European to reach tropical Australia overland. In the 'sixties the Irish Burke and the Devonshire-born Wills crossed the continent from south to north and perished; in the 'seventies Warburton, from Cheshire and formerly of the Indian Army, traversed it from Adelaide to the north-west. Most of these pioneers suffered atrocious hardships in an epic of exploration, not much known.

The lurid tale of the Australian gold rush of 1851–2 to Ballarat and Bendigo illustrates a more brutal aspect of the expansion. Gold now rivalled wool; 'diggers' fought 'squatters' and a gold rush set in. Yet by the 'eighties the home Government had conceded autonomy and, by 1901, the colonies united in another Dominion, the Commonwealth of Australia. The British had known how to concede political power and the scramble for land and wealth had not destroyed political responsibility. In an entirely new environment the British had created a new and independent version of their society, at once linked with the home country and with the Pacific coast of the United States.

New Zealand presented another opportunity, in the end successfully taken: as in Australia, private initiative was always the driving force. But here the traders and missionaries were confronted with a long-established Neolithic warrior people. The Maoris (the 'normal ones', as against the *Pakeha* – the whites) had stockaded strongholds comparable to the hill forts of Celtic Britain; they were highly chivalrous, but ate their enemies. The home Government intervened, and the Treaty of Waitangi in 1840 tried to protect native interests. There followed decades of Maori wars; yet the apparently doomed Maoris survived. There was no colour bar and they were finally incorporated into the new

[7] See *The Australian Explorers*, ed. Kathleen Fitzpatrick, O.U.P., 1958.

society; their western-educated élites became as expert in European statutes as in Maori genealogies and sublimated ancestral ferocity in Rugby football.

The settlement of New Zealand, like that of Australia, had been brought about by free enterprise and under the minimum of necessary control: in consequence the links with Great Britain remained close, though the new civilisations came into the American-Pacific orbit. Only in the Dominion of South Africa was there failure; here the long established Dutch were never assimilated, and the clash between the go-getting cosmopolitan speculators on the Rand and a Calvinist Boer régime brought wars and hatreds which would disrupt the settlement made between the white minorities, both precariously established among an African population ten times their number.

The exploration of Africa opened another opportunity for British enterprise, indeed, eccentricity. The explorers present a variety of character; all were individualists. David Livingstone, a Scot and originally a cotton operative, qualified as a doctor and became the most famous of many missionary-explorers. By 1855, at the time of the Crimean War, he had discovered the Victoria Falls on the Zambesi; *Mosi oa Tunya*, the 'sounding smoke'. He spent years in the interior of East Africa, determined, as he put it with characteristic understatement, 'to do what I can to enlighten them on the slave trade and give them some idea of our religion'. 'Found' by Stanley with so much *éclat*, he refused to return and perished in his sixtieth year in an attempt to reach the 'fountains of Herodotus', the sources of the Nile. Livingstone, with his tenacious purpose and simple faith, represents a great missionary movement of many denominations which would spread out from Great Britain, an effort comparable to that of the Anglo-Saxon missionaries in the sixth and seventh centuries into the Germanies and Scandinavia.

Sir Richard Burton represents a different facet of English character. The son of an army officer and educated on the Continent and at Oxford, where he read Arabic, he had entered the Indian Army and shocked his superiors by investigating the varieties of Indian sexual experience and translating the unexpurgated text of the *Arabian Nights*. He had also visited Mecca in disguise and, by the 'fifties, crossed Somaliland to Harrar on the Abyssinian border; the first white man to get there. Along with Speke, another Indian Army officer from a Somerset county family, he discovered the great lakes Tanganyika and Victoria Nyanza. And Speke, who also discovered the sources of the Nile, characteristically explained to the Kabaka of Uganda that he travelled because he 'sought for enjoyment the run of the world'.

Sir Samuel Baker was equally forceful; he came of a Bristol family with West Indian estates; had travelled in Ceylon, supervised railroad construction on the Danube and become the most celebrated big-game hunter of his day. He penetrated the appalling wilderness of the Upper Nile and discovered Lake Albert.

These explorers were in the Elizabethan tradition; but their exploits pale before the vast enterprises and endowments of Cecil Rhodes, that extraordinary product of a Victorian vicarage. In competition with hard-case diggers in the Kimberley diamond mines, he became a millionaire before he was thirty; but in the intervals of sorting diamonds he read for Oxford. Rhodes combined a life-long devotion to the university with a vision of a vast future for South Africa and the Empire. He long dominated the politics of South Africa, before the catastrophe of the Jameson Raid; he had a vast territory called after him; and he founded the Rhodes scholarships to promote the solidarity of the 'Anglo-Saxon' peoples, whom he believed destined to dominate the earth. Rhodes became a world-figure; one of the greatest English pioneers of any age, and he came out of Victorian England.

Such, in India, the Dominions and Africa, not to mention the rest of the colonial Empire in the Americas and the Pacific, was the British response to the opportunities of empire and exploration; millions, too, left the island during the great migrations of the nineteenth century. In return, the range of English experience, at least among the educated minorities, was enriched: by the sense of the vast rivers, forests, prairies and snows of Canada; of India with its ancient civilisation and huge variety of peoples and climate; of Australia, that enormous continent with its quasi-Mediterranean climate in the south-east, and of the spectacular mountains and pastures of New Zealand. In so far as the mass of the British were aware of foreign horizons, it was these territories, not the European continent, that stirred their imagination.

IV

At home, in contrast to this extrovert enterprise, a deeper introspection and critical sophistication had developed. There were the recognised keepers of the Victorian conscience; Carlyle, Matthew Arnold, even William Morris; and there were the French-influenced aesthetes and writers who launched a more radical attack with a big future.

Carlyle had long been the most pervasive and influential prophet. Back in the 'thirties he had written *Sartor Resartus* and *The French Revolution*, a work of slap-dash but compelling intuition; Calvin, the Enlightenment, German metaphysics had been combined over decades in his well-received denunciations: he loathed most of the things the mid-Victorians had admired. Carlyle's hatred of humbug and vulgarity created a mood which caught on, particularly among the 'agnostics' of the younger generation. Matthew Arnold, whose mournful poetry has already been touched upon, in his prose used a rapier where Carlyle wielded a bludgeon; he knew far more about continental education and literature than most Englishmen, and distinguished between the upper class 'Barbarians all at play' in Victorian Oxford, and the 'common' middle class 'Philistines', learned and unlearned, more active enemies of culture.

Ruskin was another great keeper of his age's conscience. He could write superbly; by 1843 at twenty-four he had won fame with his *Modern Painters*, and he went on writing brilliantly into old age, so that his autobiography, *Praeterita*, contains some of his best prose. He had been influenced by Hooker, Dr. Johnson and Carlyle, and he was the first art-critic in England to become a national figure. Ruskin attacked both the avarice and ugliness of his time and lovingly described just those parts of France, the Rhineland, Italy and Switzerland now becoming known to a new public. William Morris, too, was a prophet, denouncing the hideous mid-Victorian décor and inspiring a new sentimental strain in English socialism, hitherto earnestly Nonconformist. Morris, like Ruskin, was a rich man, but he hated industrial towns; they were 'so beastly ugly'.

So, while the late Victorian establishment flourished and the Empire was built, critical moralists at home were at work, bringing a new concern with human values into a society much dedicated to making money.

These prophets were all accepted by the Victorian establishment, as Tennyson and Browning had been accepted; with growing wealth and sophistication, continental influences now began to come in, much more subversively critical. The cult of 'decadent' French poetry, of the *fin-de-siècle*, of an elaborately pampered boredom and of 'strange sins', became fashionable in intellectual circles in London. And there were deeper incompatibilities revealed which reflected the drift of philosophy and science, as the whole basis of late-Victorian religion and respectability was questioned. The criticism would mount and in the new century flood in after the First World War, when the whole edifice of Victorian morality began to subside, preliminary to its apparent collapse in our time before Freudian and post-Freudian psychology and a revolutionary freedom about sex. Of these critics the 'aesthete' Oscar Wilde made the most noise; for the tragi-comedy of this Dublin wit and playwright, who had long flaunted a synthetic brilliance, symbolised a clash between old and new standards and set off one of the British public's major fits of moral indignation. His fate underlined the contrast between majority British opinion, which, although late-Victorian night-life was lurid, was still strongly puritanical, and the standards accepted in continental states which had adopted the Code Napoléon. Wilde, whose fame outside Great Britain is quite disproportionate to his merit, has his own niche; if only for his Hibernian powers of insult – he described foxhunters as the unspeakable in pursuit of the uneatable; but the posturings of this florid butterfly were a gift to Arnold's Philistines. High art and low morals became identified, and the scandal he provoked contributed to a wider rift between the ordinary public and the arts, a development bad for both sides. He could have flourished and 'fallen' only in an Anglo-Saxon setting.

A more attractive side of the new sophistication was expressed in the caricatures, fantasies and parodies of the elegant Max Beerbohm, whose main work went on far into the next century, but who belonged, as he wrote himself, to 'the Beardsley period'. No English caricaturist, not even Rowlandson, can be more deadly, and he pilloried the grosser aspects of his time. His satire is generally amiable; but the Prince of Wales and Kipling were too much for him. His Edwardian fantasy *Zuleika Dobson* has a precision of language, a wit, and a sustained power of illusion that have made it last. Nor has Shakespeare ever been more uproariously parodied than in his *Savonarola Brown*.[8] The critics of the time shared with those who were running late Victorian England and the Empire both the high spirits and the courage of their convictions.

V

Late Victorian art and architecture are an acquired taste: safely distant by over half a century, we may admire them for their human, if not their aesthetic qualities. If both are derivative by the standards of great creative times, they reveal much characteristically English feeling.

The representative and popular painters were illustrators. Frith's skilful detail in '*Derby Day*'; Landseer's sentimental or suffering animals with their anthropomorphic and telling titles; Millais' sentimental '*Bubbles*' and '*Cherry Ripe*'; the dank symbolic females of G. F. Watts, all struck the popular imagination. Even the Pre-Raphaelite brotherhood, founded in 1848, the year of revolutions, in revolt against the dim landscapes and banal subject pictures of the Academy, were urban, self-conscious, artificial. Where Constable had original genius, a countryman who went his own way and painted landscape for its own sake, they were essentially moralists who mixed up art with 'justice and truth'. Their detail was closely observed, their colours vivid, their industry immense; they had learnt something from their romantic version of the Middle Ages; their damozelles looked out, heavy-eyed, over flowing meads and Keatsian towers, and Swinburne was their prophet. To the brilliance of contemporary French painting they could not hold a candle.

The Victorian Gothic revival, which had blended with the Germanic tastes of the Prince Consort, who imported the Christmas tree, still so much a part of the British way of life, was at least a triumph of imaginative, if inconvenient, architecture in prosaic times. Barry's Houses of Parliament, like his neo-classic Reform Club, are better outside than in; but they are on the right

[8] See his *Seven Men*, Heinemann, 1919, pp. 175–219.

scale, majestic along the river. Pugin, a French *emigré*, devised
a 'pointed' style suitable to Tractarian ritual, and even his
masons were expected to live holy and stop the bricklayers
swearing. 'In God's house', he wrote, 'everything should be
real': no wonder the Great Exhibition drove him out of his mind.

Gilbert Scott began on workhouses, designed the Martyrs' and
the Albert Memorials; then built St. Pancras railroad station in
pseudo-Flemish Gothic. George Street was better at churches
than at Law Courts, and Waterhouse's front quadrangle at
Balliol has at least an appropriate vigour; this versatile man also
designed a pseudo-Renaissance château, Cambridge's answer to
Balliol, at Caius. As G. M. Trevelyan well wrote, 'The mon-
strosities of architecture erected by the order of the dons of Oxford
and Cambridge Colleges in the days of William Butterfield and
Alfred Waterhouse give daily pain to posterity.'[9] And if the better
Victorian Gothic has its points, we are in debt to Palmerston for
preventing the Government Offices in Whitehall being so designed. 'Nice sensible discussion you are having', wrote Ruskin,
'If I were you I would build Lord Palmerston an office with the
capitals all upside down and tell him it was the Greek style, invented to express typically government by Party, up today, down
tomorrow.'

It was in cheap imitations that the movement left its worst
legacy. Brick and slate, now transported by the railways, began to
supersede the rich variety of local materials; still apparent from
Norfolk to the Cotswolds and Shropshire, from Yorkshire to the
West Country and Kent. In suburban and ribbon development
the speculative builder, rootless, pretentious and shoddy, came
into his own; while the now enormous industrial towns sprawled
horribly over the scarred land. For the first time in history, most
of the English were now living in dull and hideous surroundings.

VI

Literature, like the arts in the later Victorian time, also became more introspective. 'George Eliot' (Marian Evans) combined earnest realism with the English flair for creating provincial
character, now related to deep questions of the day. In *The Mill*

[9] *English Social History*, p. 524.

on the Floss (1860), and *Middlemarch* eleven years after, she had gone deep into the interaction of character with a world more representative, if less subtle, than Jane Austen's, though she lacks Jane Austen's economy of effect.

Meredith's *The Ordeal of Richard Feverel* and *The Egoist* (1879) are both studies in self-deception, pervaded by the author's self-conscious sophistication; a world away from the straight narratives of most earlier masters. Even Rudyard Kipling, originally a journalist in India and apparently so extrovert, looks inward in a tortuous way. Like Baldwin, his first cousin, he had his mystic side, but he first made his name by a sharp observation of the life of Indian hill stations in *Plain Tales from the Hills* (1888). His immense popularity came in the 'nineties with his *Jungle Books* in a genre peculiar to England; stories which both enthral children and have their symbolic side. In *Kim* he depicted the 'native' ambience of India and in *Puck of Pook's Hill* he evoked the English past. Kipling was also world travelled; original, too, in his praise of machines: if he jarred upon his 'ninetyish' contemporaries, he understood men and he was fascinated by the way that societies and 'mysteries' survive. Detested as a blatant propagandist of Empire, Kipling was in fact far more subtle; a fine craftsman with a queer penetrating vision of human fate; basically pessimistic, as were many of these writers.

But Thomas Hardy (1840–1928) was the greatest late Victorian genius of the novel, if his poetry surpassed his prose. He came out of a Dorset village and was much influenced by William Barnes, the philologist and regional poet of Wessex.[10] Hardy, too, would write of the Blackmore Vale; that 'fertile and sheltered tract of country in which the fields are never brown and the springs never dry . . . bounded on the South by the bold chalk

---

[10] William Barnes' dialect poem, *The Geäte A-Vallen to*, is consciously archaic.

> *And Oh! it is a touching thing*
> *The loven heart must rue*
> *To hear behind his last farewell*
> *The geäte a-vallen to.*

When finished, Barnes said 'Observe that word geäte, that is how King Alfred would have pronounced it, and how it was called in the Saxon Chronicle which tells us of King Edward, who was slain at "*Corfe's Geate*".' See Giles Dugdale, *William Barnes of Dorset*, Cassell, 1953, p. 225.

ridge that embraces the prominences of Hambledon Hill, Bul-
barrow, Nettlecombe Tout, Dogbury, High Stoy and Bubb
Down'.

Hardy had a difficult start; his plots remained clumsy and
melodramatic, like village tales, and his first success came in the
early 'seventies through his Shakespearian peasant characters in
Under the Greenwood Tree and *Far from the Madding Crowd*.
Then through *The Return of the Native* and *The Mayor of
Casterbridge* in the 'eighties, Hardy developed increasing range,
which culminated in his masterpiece, *Tess of the D'Urbervilles*
(1891). Of all the great English writers Hardy has his roots most
deeply in the Anglo-Saxon past and in the countryside which he
observed with the accuracy of 'a rural painting in the Dutch
school'. Yet he was typically Victorian; he had read Schopenhauer and thought that the stars must blindly run – at best that
the Life Force might be half-aware. His neo-pagan, stoic pessimism, akin to the pagan poetry of his Old English forebears,
blended with the agnostic outlook of his time; all is fused into
great literature by his power of depicting character 'slighted but
enduring', against a setting made more poignant by his sense of
place.

'To persons standing alone on a hill during a clear midnight
such as this', Hardy could write, 'the roll of the earth eastward
was almost a palpable movement. The sensation may be caused
by the panoramic glide of the stars past earthly objects, which is
perceptible in a few minutes of stillness, or by the better outlook
upon space that a hill affords, or by the wind, or by solitude;
but whatever be its origin the impression of riding along is vivid
and abiding ... After such a nocturnal reconnoitre it is hard
to get back to earth, and to believe that the consciousness of such
majestic speeding is derived from a tiny human frame.' He could
also conclude *Tess* with the ironic sentence, 'Justice was done,
and the President of the Immortals, in Æschylean phrase, had
ended his sport with Tess. And the d'Urberville knights and
dames slept on in their tombs unknowing.'

So far had the greatest late Victorian prose writers come from
the complacency of Macaulay or even the amiable cynicism of
Peacock; in their various ways they are all introspective and
critical. Wealth and security, after all, bring sophistication; and
Victorian prudery and smugness, in their time a reaction to

eighteenth-century casualness and Regency licence, seemed oppressive to a new generation, vital and creative though the Victorians had been.

VII

Among the poets, Swinburne was the first flaming rebel: by the mid-'sixties the anapaests of *Atalanta in Calydon*, based on Greek drama, had swept their author into celebrity; like lightning his verse lit up the heavy foliage of the Victorian garden and revealed new prospects beyond.

> *When the hounds of spring are on winter's traces,*
> *The mother of months in meadow or plain*
> *Fills the shadows and windy places*
> *With lisp of leaves and ripple of rain;*
> *And the brown bright nightingale amorous*
> *Is half assuaged for Itylus,*
> *For the Thracian ships and the foreign faces*
> *The tongueless vigil and all the pain. . . .*

Whatever its precise meaning, nothing like this incantation had been done in English poetry before. The neo-pagan *Poems and Ballads* and *Songs before Sunrise* reinforced this reputation by scandal: with linked arms, festive undergraduates would bawl the choruses down Catte Street and King's Parade. The poet, wrote that Liberal governess, John Morley, was the 'libidinous laureate of a pack of satyrs with the feverish carnality of a schoolboy over the dirtiest passages of Lemprière'. Swinburne had even urged his readers

> *To change in a trice*
> *The lilies and languors of virtue*
> *For the raptures and roses of vice.*

And he had attacked Christianity itself:

> *Thou hast conquered, Oh pale Galilean,*
> *The world has grown grey at thy breath.*

Then, in the 'eighties, Kipling made another break-through. He first made 'common' soldiers articulate in verse and, for a vast public, the discovery of the East. He wrote of battle with exact observation:

> An' now the hugly bullets come peckin' through the dust,
> An' no one wants to face 'em, but every beggar must;
> So, like a man in irons, which isn't glad to go,
> They moves 'em off by companies uncommon stiff an' slow.

Or, again,

'*Take 'im away*', he could write in *Barrack Room Ballads*, for a dead march,

> 'E's gone where the best men go.
> Take 'im away! An' the gun wheels turning slow.

And he could evoke India:

> But a well-wheel slowly creaking, going round, going round,
> By a water-channel leaking over drowned, warm ground ...
> Parrots very busy in the trellised pepper-vine –
> And a high sun over Asia shouting: '*Rise and Shine!*'

He wrote also of the sea:

> See the shaking funnels roar, with the Peter at the fore,
> And the fenders grind and heave ...
> O the mutter overside, when the port fog holds us tied,
> And the sirens hoot their dread!
> When foot by foot we creep o'er the hueless viewless deep
> To the sob of the questing lead!

Officially acclaimed, Kipling remained a critic: his *Recessional*, with its Old Testament overtones, denounced the *hubris* of Imperial power.

There can be torment in Kipling's verse and masochism in Swinburne's; but Hardy's poetry expressed a bleaker, steadier melancholy, harking back to pagan Anglo-Saxon literature, with its sense of fate. *The Dynasts* depicts the panorama of the Napoleonic Wars, the protagonists puppets against a cosmic background; the whole narrated by superhuman Intelligences who observe the acts of the Life Force, that 'purblind Doomster'. Hardy set relatively little store by his novels: his later years were devoted to his poetry, and *Wessex Poems, Time's Laughing*

Stocks, Human Shows, Far Fantasies, and *Winter Words* show increasing subtlety.

> *The Sportsman Time,* he wrote,
> *but rears his brood to kill.*

Yet, with this haunting sense of impermanence, his observation was the more precise:

> *When the Present has latched its postern behind my*
> *   tremulous stay,*
> *And the May month flaps its glad green leaves like wings,*
> *Delicate filmed as new-spun silk, will the neighbours say,*
> *'He was a man who used to notice such things?'*

He lived to see the First World War and its aftermath, and to sum up their enigma:

> *We are getting to the end of visioning*
> *The impossible within this universe,*
> *Such as that better whiles may follow worse,*
> *And that our race may mend by reasoning.*

This is deep pessimism: and Hardy was representative. Far from being complacent, the tone of the major late Victorian writers was sombre, for they could discern what others did not notice. That already, beneath the power and the glory, the foundations of the most successful phase of English history and the accepted values of the nineteenth century were being undermined.

Chapter 4

Edwardian England and the Great War

LUMBERING to the catastrophe of 1914, the great European
empires entered the twentieth century; they had carved up
most of Africa without conflict, but now the rulers of
Germany, convinced apparently of 'encirclement', made their
first, yet already belated, bid to break out of Central Europe and
win world domination. Like Napoleon, they were defeated by an
extra-European continental and oceanic coalition; but the power
of Europe was diminished and the vast British Empire began its
decline.

In this grim climate of world history the grandeur of Edwardian England was already precarious; and if 'the land's surface
glowed with a splendour that suggested serenity, seismic faults
had developed below, and the Edwardian age [was] characterised
by a rapidly accelerating process of political and social disturb-
ance'.[1] Already massive forces were working for complete democracy and a bureaucratic state; and when after 1914 much of the
old superstructure was swept away, the new substructure survived and developed. Neither the decline of Edwardian affluence
nor the massacres of the Somme were decisive compared with
this long-term social change; it had begun, almost imperceptibly,
with the reforms of Gladstone and Disraeli, and by 1914 it had
been institutionalised by the Radical governments of Campbell-
Bannerman and Asquith. Then, after the Great War, which
obliterated many of the class distinctions of Edwardian times,
the movement for social reform would persist through the inter-
war period, and even, with an accumulated momentum, through
the second conflict. Through all dangers the process would go
on; and the maligned Baldwin, so insular over foreign affairs,
would think it his main purpose to assuage class conflict before
the mounting danger. The Empire, meanwhile, which to the

[1] Magnus, op. cit., p. xiii.

surprise of its assailants, stood by the home country in 1914, would become even more decentralised as a self-governing 'Commonwealth'. The British establishment, so consistently realistic, would now know how to adapt itself to mass democracy and national emancipation, at home and abroad.

This adaptation would be tentative, wary, gradual, and made under increasingly reduced circumstances; for if the victorious British Empire of Lloyd George and Curzon, Haig and Allenby, still had great power and greater prestige, the financial supremacy of the City of London was already on the wane, and in the new mass production and light industry the United States and Germany had outclassed Great Britain. The neglect of technical education and, in spite of the brilliant work of British scientists, the curious disesteem in which science had long been held in the old universities and in business, now proved a further handicap. Coal, iron, and steel, the 'heavy industries' that had been the basis of Victorian wealth, were less competitive in an economy dominated by the internal combustion engine, by oil and electric power; in spite of growing productivity, the revolution of rising expectations would come about in relatively hard times. This paradox still makes all precarious.

II

King Edward VII, with his sport, his cosmopolitan luxury, his immense cigars; his race-horses, his yachts and his seraglio, was representative of his age. The formal proprieties were still strictly observed, but Victorian smugness and respectability were out of fashion.[2] Never had entertaining been more lavish or field sports more diverse: armies of beaters sent the hand-reared pheasants high over the guns; for the rich there were grouse moors in Scotland, big game in Africa, tiger shooting in India; for the merely well-to-do the days after the partridges, the evenings after flighting duck. Fishing, much developed since the days of Dame Julyana Bernes, became more esoteric; Sir Edward Grey, that thoughtful Foreign Secretary, found solace by the

---

[2] 'When well-to-do Victorians gave way to vice', writes Ensor primly, 'they commonly went to Paris to indulge it.' *England 1870–1914*, Oxford, 1938, p. 170. The Edwardians were under no such pressing need.

Hampshire Test; and Neville Chamberlain – always an Edwardian figure – would be better at landing salmon than dictators. Baldwin, unlike most of his colleagues, seems to have had little urge to kill.

Organised games which would have world-wide influence now flourished. Association football had been popular since the 'sixties, and the Rugby Union formed by 1871. During the 'seventies and 'eighties that bearded father-figure, the great cricketer W. G. Grace, had become a national and venerated celebrity. Rowing had long been highly organised, the University boat races a landmark in the year. Lawn tennis, very different from the complicated royal tennis played by Henry VIII and Charles II, had come in during the 'seventies, and the Wimbledon Club had been established. All these games, played in clothes which seem madly inappropriate today, now united the nation in a common interest. Golf, too, had become a cult by the 'nineties, and one followed by eminent politicians: Balfour and Lloyd George took kindly to it, though Asquith once remarked that it spoiled a good walk.

Women's fashions remained fantastically elaborate until the automobile changed them. Goggled and veiled, the occupants of Spykers, De Dions and Daimlers whirled down dusty highways with about as much wind-resistance as the vehicles themselves; but as the original 'horseless carriages' became better streamlined, women ceased to look like galleons and became svelte.

Beneath this affluent and rather vulgar world, but also sustained by dividends, dim but lasting middle-class influences were at work. In college rooms and neo-Gothic villas dons were now concerned with the problems of society and economics as well as with Greek verse. In the 'eighties the fashion for bicycling had come in; and, following the example of Sidney and Beatrice Webb, emancipated men and women of the conscience-stricken classes sped along the roads at weekends, discussing the condition of the people. The Married Women's Property Act had been passed in 1882 and extended in 1892; while after 1870 the higher education of women, advocated by John Stuart Mill in mid-Victorian times, was greatly developed. That redoubtable pair, Miss Beale and Miss Buss, had been pioneers of an education designed to harden off the mid-Victorian Miss, and in the 'fifties

Cheltenham Ladies College set an example for girls' public schools such as Roedean, nearly as games-ridden and austere as those that housed their brothers. A more important emancipation came about when Newnham and Girton were founded at Cambridge in the 'seventies, and Lady Margaret Hall and Somerville at the end of the decade. Segregated and chaperoned, allowed to attend lectures though not officially members of the University, those who thirsted enough for knowledge were beginning to get it.

The Evangelical movement had been supplemented by Charles Kingsley's muscular kind of Christianity, and even the 'High' churchmen were now less concerned with ritual than with good works. Family prayers were still the rule in pious households, the servants filing in to kneel against the chairs in the dining-room while the head of the household intoned the collect for the day. The kind of popular religious fervour roused by the sermons of Spurgeon had also been canalised since the 'sixties by 'General' Booth's Salvation Army; strong men and lasses thumping out their tunes and rattling their collecting boxes. This movement would become world-wide.

And another typically English idea now caught on and spread. The Boy Scout movement started in 1907 on Brownsea Island in Poole Harbour, then owned by a Dutch cigar millionaire. Led by Major-General Baden-Powell, the hero of the relief of Ladysmith during the Boer War (an expert, too, at pig-sticking and private theatricals), twenty boys from Eton and Harrow and the Boys' Brigade of Poole went into camp together. Five years later the movement was officially incorporated: it was a jolly, civilian affair; of Kiplingesque animal games – Wolves and Curlews, Ravens and Bulls had been the names of the Brownsea patrols; of strenuous morality and clever showmanship. This youth movement, deriving its inspiration from the 'open spaces' of the Empire, spread about the world, bringing millions of town-bred boys to the open air, fostering much high-minded comradeship. It was never, as some foreigners believed, a British plot to train youth for war; it was politically innocent.[3]

[3] Baden-Powell detested politicians: 'From what I know of them,' he said, 'I would not trust an ordinary politician with my grandmother's toothbrush.' Offered a present at a vast international jamboree, the Chief Scout replied that he most needed a pair of braces. These, along with a Rolls-Royce and a portrait, were solemnly presented, and 'BP' 'hung them round his neck like

The growing and massive movement for social and political reform was just as characteristic and more decisive. The Benthamites had to deal with corrupt and casual anachronisms and had distrusted State power; now, as T. H. Green, the Balliol political philosopher, had observed in the 'eighties, a more efficient state seemed fit to 'hinder hindrances to the good life' – a pretty large commission. Green's Victorian objectives had been rather insular: 'We hope and pray', he had written, 'for a condition of English society in which all honest citizens will recognise themselves and be recognised as gentlemen'; society, indeed, should enable everyone 'to make the best of themselves'. It was a humane, a civilian, ideal; the product of a country without conscription but insulated by the greatest navy in the world. By 1914 under Asquith, a Balliol Prime Minister, the first decisive steps towards this 'social justice' had been made: the English habit of avoiding revolution was getting more constructive.

Further to the Left of the Liberals, a more radical movement also took on. The 'Fabians', whose *Fabian Essays* appeared in 1889, were strictly constitutional, but they aimed at the control of the main means of production by a bureaucratic State. They were Socialists, though mild ones; and save for Bernard Shaw, who would liven up anything, and H. G. Wells, a genius too impatient for routine politics who broke away, they were usually, like Robert Owen, gentle bores. The Webbs, in particular, showed the power of this kind of attack, deadly in the long run, and many aspects of modern Britain are their legacy. Meanwhile, the pioneer sociologist Graham Wallas set society in a wider view; he systematically applied psychology to politics – an English knack long practised in an empirical way but now more sytematised – and examined the social workings of the subconscious mind.[4] Mankind, he insisted, was naturally adjusted to small groups and maladjusted in megalopolitan industrial societies. In the English way, he distrusted the abstractions of

an order of chivalry.' 'Now,' he told the mighty audience, 'I have everything I want in the world.' In the words of the scout motto, 'He was prepared.' (T.L.S. 24 September, 1964.) By his will he refused burial in Westminster Abbey and chose a grave in Kenya with only the Scout trail sign, 'I have gone home'.

[4] See his *Human Nature in Politics*, London, 1908, and his *The Great Society*, London, 1914. This last phrase has since become a political slogan in America.

many continental social theorists; and, like his contemporary Durkheim in France, another founder of sociology, insisted upon the study of men as they were; on the complexity of the social facts. This scientific approach took long to command much attention, still less endowments; but Wallas had promoted a movement with a great future, particularly in the United States.

So beneath the surface frivolity of the Edwardian age, the British were tackling the immense and daunting social problems which had come down from Victorian times and which would persist into 1939, when urban 'evacuees', incongruous in 'the country', would prove that the standards of the slums could still be animal.

Beneath the world of the reforming intellectuals, a new and mighty political force was also coming up which would make Socialism important. By 1924 'Labour' would supersede the Liberals as the principal left-wing party in British politics and form a government. Since the 'nineties the trade unions, formed originally among the skilled workers, had been extending among the rest; George Edwards, for example, pioneered the Agricultural Workers Union. The Dockers' Strike of 1889 had commanded considerable support, and in 1893 Keir Hardie had been elected the first 'Independent Labour' Member of Parliament. Like the seventeenth-century Quakers, he had defied the current conventions about hats, wearing a proletarian cloth cap when top hats were correct. This English class-consciousness would long pervade the Labour Movement, not always with fortunate results. Where, in America, the two great parties, Republicans and Democrats, had only a limited class bias, in England the main political force of the Left would long be a 'class' party closely affiliated to habitually 'militant' trade unions. This obsession with class was to be expected in view of the course of English history.

At first the Liberal Radicals seemed likely to coalesce with Labour.[5] But neither were the Liberals anxious to give Labour

---

[5] J. Ramsay MacDonald, the first Labour Prime Minister, had begun political life as editor of a 'Lib-Lab' Progressive review, and even then thought little of his trade union colleagues. 'The party of progressive ideas', he wrote, 'is being so badly handled that it is almost suicide to join it. Off to golf.' (See the author's *Viscount Samuel*, Gollancz, 1957, p. 37.) It was not, he would find, by any means political suicide to join the party, though he would have to ditch it in the long run.

men constituencies nor Labour to abandon collectivist doctrine. And it was the Liberals who suffered; their great party, at its peak in 1906–14, would be disrupted by Lloyd George in 1916 because Asquith's immense but conventional abilities were unsuited for war; it would thus lose first its cohesion and then its popular support, since Labour alone now had the massive trade union interest behind it, consolidated by the fear of unemployment, now an increasing menace.

This collapse of the Liberals was due in part to their pre-war success. From 1906 onward they put through a whole series of reforms which made the public used to the 'social services', and to the taxes – income tax, super tax, and death duties – which paid for them; all bitterly resisted by the House of Lords, the conflict overshadowing even that occasioned over Irish Home Rule. Lloyd George created a comprehensive National Insurance against illness and unemployment; Churchill established Labour Exchanges; Old Age Pensions were inaugurated. An Eight Hours Act limited the hours worked in mines and a Shop Hours Bill the hours worked by shop-assistants. In 1908 Herbert Samuel devised a 'Children's Charter', which alleviated still Hogarthian conditions, and Probation Officers now looked after 'juvenile delinquents', as they were then quaintly termed. Further, the Conservative Balfour-Morant reforms of 1902 had followed up Foster's Education Act of 1870; both primary and secondary education were now put under the elected County Councils, responsible since the 'eighties for most of the non-judicial functions of the Justices of the Peace. Thus at least rudimentary opportunities were at last provided for the mass of the people, and that without the strict centralisation common in continental states. The system ran parallel with the endowed grammar schools and the public schools. It was far from egalitarian, but it was at least not doctrinaire.

Following the spread of elementary education, the English press had now been transformed. *The Times,* with its national circulation, had long been far the most influential newspaper, appealing to an established élite; the pronouncements of the 'Thunderer' had long swayed important opinion and it had become the most powerful newspaper in the world, while the dignified 'Quarterlies' and Monthly Reviews long commanded great talent. There had also been provincial papers, of which the

Manchester Guardian – now *The Guardian* – was the most respected. But in the 'nineties Alfred and Harold Harmsworth, afterwards the millionaire press Barons Northcliffe and Rothermere, had seen their chance; by the end of the century the *Daily Mail*, produced in brisk American style, sold at a halfpenny and, catering for those taught to read in primary schools, had a circulation of half a million. In 1900 the *Daily Express* was launched and three years later the *Daily Mirror*: by 1908 Northcliffe was able to buy up the august *Times* itself and enjoy a long run of chequered political influence, though he would die insane in 1922. As had once Norman and Angevin Kings, so now newspaper magnates found that the country provided a limited area, good communications and centralised power; and now there was a huge population as well. Nowhere else in the world, not even in the United States, were circulations so enormous. But the rift widened between responsible journalism and the rest, and politicians of the old school hated this new power; Asquith despised and ignored it; Lloyd George manipulated it, and Baldwin would compare it to the power of a 'harlot'. It had come to stay.

Although, therefore, the Edwardian age seems at first an aftermath of the Victorian, and its surface glitter, privilege and prosperity make it seem remote; the more lasting forces at work made it a prelude to the social revolution, bureaucratic government and mass civilisation of modern times. This process was confirmed and accelerated by the Great War, and by the immense scientific advances which preceded and went along with it.

III

Who will remember, passing through this gate,
The unheroic Dead who fed the guns?
Who shall absolve the foulness of their fate
These doomed, conscripted, unvictorious ones . . . ?
Well may the dead, who struggled in the slime,
Rise and deride this sepulchre of crime.

So wrote Siegfried Sassoon of the Menin Memorial Gate in the bitter aftermath of the Great War, and he was representative. Yet the struggle was the most stubborn feat of British endurance ever accomplished; a more ghastly, if not a more critical, ordeal than the Second World War. The conflict cost the world twelve million dead, of whom about three quarters of a million were British and another quarter million from the Empire; it was the first long war of material attrition fought out between great industrial states, with the whole force of their peoples behind it, and the first in which huge conscript armies were sent from Great Britain to the Continent. At the beginning the British intervention on land was small though highly efficient; but throughout the conflict the Royal Navy was always incomparably more decisive than that of any other power. And gradually the British conscript armies took over more and more of the 'line', so that by the end of the holocaust, Haig's armies were the largest and the most hard-hitting in the alliance.

This monstrous effort affected the life of the country in quite a new way; shook the foundations of its power and altered its mentality and social structure. The great effort hastened and confirmed the social revolution long building up, and produced a novel hatred of a power system which could produce such an imbecile catastrophe and of those who ran it. And no wonder; in 1914 war was still an accepted institution, even an adventure. Rupert Brooke could write, representatively, of 'swimmers into cleanness leaping', an unhappy simile for those destined for the Flanders mud; and thousands of young men in straw 'boaters' could cheer lustily outside the Palace at the news of what would be for most of them their doom.

The new mechanised horrors of industrial warfare thus came as an appalling shock; the revulsion, though it proved ineffective, was profound, and accounts for the loss of nerve in the 'thirties, which put the more civilised nations at a disadvantage against those still brutish enough to face a second bout. For the course of the war proved unexpected; instead of the short war of movement, with charging cavalry and horse artillery limbering up in brisk manoeuvres, the struggle coagulated into trench warfare from Basel to the sea. Only Kitchener foresaw the duration and scale of the conflict of attrition: the Germans, he told the Cabinet, occupied a fortress with interior lines, and with their strategic railways could switch their attacks. Checked on the Marne, they were still masters of great areas of Northern France and Belgium; they had to be worn down by attrition. Only in a long war could superior Allied manpower be mobilised to evict them from their conquests and take the fortress by assault. The correct strategic answer was to turn the flank of the Central Powers through the Dardanelles; but the attempt failed through the incredible tactical incompetence of local commanders. There was nothing for it but 'killing Germans' in France, always the decisive battleground, trading life for life.[6] Strategic necessity led to tactical stagnation; there was none of the opportunity or excitement of a war of movement, such as Allenby, who had little chance to show his abilities in France, would conduct in Palestine. After the first German rush had been blocked, the war became a bestial slogging match. The most monstrous British losses incurred were accepted as the price of taking the weight of the German assault off the French armies, reeling after Verdun. The traditional British policy of fighting wars with the greatest economy of manpower, and using seapower for a flexible and opportunist strategy, had thus to be modified, though not abandoned, and the Army employed in frontal assault.

The tactical answer was the tank, a British invention the Germans thought decisive; but tanks were too few and rudimentary to restore the war of movement, as they would in the Second World War.[7] Haig was thus not the boneheaded butcher he appears in the gross statue in Whitehall, where that well-groomed professional rides a horse on which he would not have been seen dead; though a cavalry general in such an *impasse* needed his religious convictions and Scots tenacity. War is war;

[6] By the end of the hideous account the Allies had the advantage in massacres unsurpassed in European history. The South African war had cost the British less than 6,000 dead, 22,000 wounded and 16,000 who had died of disease. The Boers had lost 4,000 in battle and over 20,000 in the concentration camps established by Kitchener. These figures are dwarfed by the casualties incurred by the British on the Somme, or the French at Verdun in a few days.

[7] The tank or 'self-propelled armoured vehicle' is considered by connoisseurs of battle a 'conception of genius' (Cyril Falls, *The First World War*, Longmans, 1964, p. xix, q.v. for the most objective and authoritative account). 'Moving on motor driven tracks', writes another expert, 'it became able to surpass the limitations previously inherent in the legs of men and horses . . . through motor power it also revived the use of armour.' (Captain Liddell Hart in *The Times*, April 1965.) Owing to the relative backwardness of more traditional technology the Navy proved relatively ill-equipped, the armour of the finest battleships unable to resist the plunging and more accurate German fire and the flash of hits in gun turrets exploding the magazines.

the institution, not the generals, was at fault. After all, the gruelling palaeotechnic struggle ended in the most massive victory in
the country's annals before 1945, and was secured by the endurance of the armies and the Royal Navy's mastery of the seas.
Though forced to unprecedented commitments on the Continent,
the British had fought in the old way, bringing oceanic resources
to bear in a long haul, culminating in the vast American effort
which offset the Russian collapse. Further, the British produced
a rudimentary but independent Air Force which, vastly developed, would prove decisive in the second conflict; the strategic
importance of air arm was firmly grasped by leaders accustomed
to oceanic horizons.

The war had been won at the price of a cruder, more dicta-
torial kind of government. Lloyd George, a thick-set Welsh
demagogue of genius, with leonine head, gimlet eye and per-
suasive tongue, established new, more close-knit, control; he
organised a Cabinet secretariat; fully mobilised industrial resources, made the swift, necessary, decisions; forcing the Admiralty, for example, to adopt the convoys that averted disaster in
1917. Lloyd George, it has been remarked, 'inspired every feeling
except trust',[8] and the limitations of the first 'ranker' Prime
Minister (as he called himself, since he had not attended the
'Staff College' of one of the oldest universities) became apparent
at the peace; but he had the hypnotic power and drive of a great
war leader and his remark at the time of Munich would be justified. 'In my day', he said, 'they used to come to me.'

His phase of power left a permanent mark. The influence of
the State was greatly and permanently extended; bureaucracy
and heavy taxation, unheard of before 1914, came to stay. And
if the tone of public life was coarsened and the award of honours
degraded, manhood suffrage was extended to all over twenty-
one and the vote conceded to women; partially in 1918 and completely ten years after, the long-term result of the 'suffragette'
movement, militant before the war. Lloyd George had been the
main architect of the reforms and the taxation of the Asquith
Government, and National Insurance was now much more widely
extended: there was a Housing Act, a new Ministry of Health.
Though after 1922 the British tried hard to forget the War and
its aftermath, the long term social trends already emphasised

[8] A. J. P. Taylor, *English History, 1914–1945*, Oxford, 1965, pp. 192–3.

continued, and the country which emerged from the Great War was very different from Edwardian or early Georgian society.

IV

The war also accelerated the effects of the spectacular advances in science made before it, which would in time dwarf even this social change. Since the 'nineties, profoundly important discoveries in physics had been going on, comparable to those made by Newton and Darwin in their respective fields. Sir J. J. Thompson (1856–1940) at Cambridge had already tracked down the electron; and by 1911, in a weird world of sub-nuclear physics, Lord Rutherford, also at Cambridge, had demonstrated that helium particles, emitted in radio-active disintegration at immense speeds, were deflected by the even 'harder' nucleii of certain atoms. The atom, hitherto regarded as solid, was proved to be mainly space, with immense charges of energy balanced inside it, and the basis of the physical universe now appeared to be 'waves of probability undulating in nothingness'. These epoch-making discoveries would lead to the transmutation of matter under radio-active bombardment and even to the synthesis of new elements. Fantastic submolecular possibilities had emerged. The long-term sequel to these crucial events is familiar, and for the first steps towards them British scientists were mainly responsible.

In medicine, too, important discoveries had been made in the 'nineties and developed during the Great War. Sir Ronald Ross, of the Indian Medical Service, had proved that malaria was transmitted by mosquitoes, as Walter Reed of the American Army had proved that yellow fever was similarly spread. When the breeding grounds of the insects were destroyed, vast areas, hitherto blighted by disease, were opened up. The British also contributed to a new understanding of the role of vitamins in nutrition, of hormones in the blood stream, and of insulin in the treatment of diabetes.

Thus in pure science and medical research the great tradition went on, though in technology there was more exploitation than discovery. The automobile was first developed on the Continent and in the United States; and though Alcock and Brown were the first to fly the Atlantic in 1919, the pioneers of the air were mainly American and French.

Wireless telegraphy, too, if based upon the work of Clerk-Maxwell, was invented by the Italian Marconi, though some of his experiments were made in England, and in 1901 he sent the first signals from Cornwall to the United States.

The early twentieth century had also seen characteristic developments in English philosophy which reverted from a phase of neo-Hegelian idealism to a more native empirical method. G. E. Moore at Cambridge had published *The Refutation of Idealism* in 1902, and his *Principia Ethica* won a decisive influence. His work was carried further by Bertrand Russell and led to the modern linguistic philosophy developed by Wittgenstein and popularised (if such a word is appropriate) by Ayer. The grandiose creations of metaphysical philosophers were subjected to a devastating criticism; and, in the British tradition which runs from Ockham through Hobbes, Locke and Hume, the limitations of mind were reasserted. This scepticism, which took some time to win through, came to promote a more objective and tolerant outlook. Theological beliefs were also modified by the work of Frazer, whose *The Golden Bough* (1890) was a landmark in comparative religion; while in archaeology General Pitt-Rivers, in the 'seventies and 'eighties, had been the greatest pioneer of scientific excavation, whose collections, compared to previous ones, were 'as different as a book on grammar is from a mere dictionary'.[9]

V

There is an immense contrast in music, the arts and literature between those who spoke for the Edwardians and early Georgians, and those who won fame after the Great War. Here only the mainly pre-war musicians and writers will be considered.

The English have always been a musical people in a rather undiscriminating way; and if there has been little State or municipal subsidised opera, the tradition of Cathedral and Church music has always been strong and widespread since Anglo-Saxon times. But, save for the Italianate Purcell, there has never been an English composer of the highest rank. Sir Edward Elgar is no

[9] Stanley Casson, *The Discovery of Man*, Hamish Hamilton, 1939, p. 194.

exception;[10] he came out of the ambience of the Cathedral Close; and though his rather laborious *Enigma Variations*, the highlights of his *The Dream of Gerontius*, and his First Symphony have won much popularity in England, he was capable of the maunderings of *In the South*, and the Edwardian grossness of *'Pomp and Circumstance'*.

Frederick Delius (1863–1934) was less insular; the son of a naturalised German business man, he left Bradford to grow oranges in Florida and studied at Leipzig, when he was influenced by the music of Grieg. His ballet music for Flecker's *Hassan*, too seldom heard, is subtle and brilliant.

The public, meanwhile, had taken Gilbert and Sullivan to their hearts since the 'eighties; this happy pair had just the right jolly facetiousness, and the catchy tunes of their light operas are still widely popular. A new cult of Russian ballet came in before the Great War, with Stravinsky's *Firebird* (1910) and *Petrushka*, and with Mussorgsky's *Boris Godunov*; the art of Pavlova and Nijinsky and the designs of Bakst set new standards altogether. The colour and line of Augustus John would also set better standards in art; though Sir Alfred Munnings, who painted horses, was always much more popular.

Most of the novelists were competent but ordinary. John Galsworthy, a barrister educated at Harrow and New College, Oxford, depicted the life of the late Victorian *haute bourgeoisie* in his *The Man of Property* (1906) and his composite *The Forsyte Saga* (1922). His characters have little depth, but they are consistent and recognisable; and since he depicted the English as foreigners expected them to be, he won great reputation abroad. Arnold Bennett, who described provincial life in the Midlands, wrote *Anna of the Five Towns* and *The Old Wives' Tale*; both appeared before 1914. He later depicted with awe the life of luxury hotels. Sir James Barrie, a cunning playwright whose

[10] Sir Edward Elgar, Bart., O.M. (1857–1934), son of an organist at the Catholic Church in Worcester. He played in the Three Choirs Festival orchestra and was for five years bandmaster at the local lunatic asylum, where he may have found inspiration for the 'Devil's Chorus' in *Gerontius*, performed at Birmingham in 1900, the year after the publication of the *Enigma Variations*. Elgar made an advantageous marriage and led a life very different from that of Beethoven, Mozart, or Berlioz: he was knighted after the Coronation of Edward VII, and an Elgar Festival was held in 1904: his first symphony was published in 1908. He became a British institution, but won limited recognition on the Continent.

brand of Scots sentiment was eagerly appreciated, created *Peter Pan*, 'the boy who wouldn't grow up'; a character naturally popular in England. The author was made a baronet in 1913 and given the Order of Merit; he went on 'playing hide and seek with angels' in the highest circles far into his seventies, and also kept a bullfinch with which he used to hold whimsical conversations in his apartment in the Adelphi. And if Peter Pan had become a household word, so had *Sherlock Holmes*, the hawk-faced drug-addict detective created in the 'nineties by Conan Doyle. These detective stories were to lead to an immense literature of crime which would become a dominant interest throughout the English-speaking world and beyond.

Joseph Conrad, on the other hand, a Pole with a superb command of English, had greater depth and range than these popular favourites; and E. M. Forster, whose *A Room with a View* and *Howard's End* appeared before 1914, and his *A Passage to India* by 1924, explored the relation of the individual to the conventions of society with subtle insight and economy of effect. The Catholic writers Belloc and Chesterton kept up a rumbustious campaign against the more obviously subversive kind of Edwardian financiers and tycoons, and glorified the English countryside in a rather noisy way. But Bernard Shaw (1856–1950), that witty Irish iconoclast, who popularised many of the ideas of Ibsen, Schopenhauer and Nietzsche and brought a breath of argumentative realism to the stage, had a world influence. *Arms and the Man* had appeared by 1894 and *Man and Superman* by 1903; many startling plays followed, culminating in *St. Joan* in 1923 – bad history but good entertainment.

H. G. Wells, like Shaw, was immensely creative, and wrote a spate of books from the 'nineties to the Second World War. Of all these writers he was the most in tune with the overriding scientific tendencies of the age. The son of a cricket professional at Bromley, he became a draper's assistant, but managed to attend the Royal College of Science, where he greatly admired T. H. Huxley and won a first class degree. He made his way originally by science fiction, in which he showed an uncanny insight into the future, as in *The Time Machine* and *The War of the Worlds*, both published in the 'nineties; then in 1905 he exactly caught the lower middle class Edwardian world in *Kipps*, and five years later in *The History of Mr. Polly*. But he became more than a good Dickensian writer; for he was the first English novelist of real calibre with a scientific background, his mind dominated by its world-wide implications. By 1905 he had written *A Modern Utopia*, the first move in his crusade for what he termed a 'revolt of the competent' against time-honoured exploitation and war. He thus developed from a fine novelist into an historian and prophet of world order, and though most literary critics think otherwise, the sacrifice was worth it. His *The Outline of History*, undertaken as a duty, had enormous sales and influence, and he went on into old age, sometimes at the expense of his art, trying to make the human race see reason. Like Carlyle, in a very different idiom, he could create a catching and contemporary mood, which took on among young people far beyond his own country.

VI

The contrast between Edwardian and early Georgian poetry and the style which developed after T. S. Eliot's *The Waste Land* in 1922 is even more marked than that between the prose writers before and after the Great War. The pre-war poetry now seems naïve; still a development of late Victorian verse, if without the alembication of the 'nineties. But it has melody and vigour; it is very English and the best of it will survive. W. B. Yeats was a genius towering above the rest; who sensed problems and conflicts as deep as any which would preoccupy the 'thirties; but he belongs essentially to Ireland. John Masefield brought in blustery airs from the sea and the back streets, but he had more feeling than thought. Rupert Brooke left a legend of the poet-hero, who died for England on St. George's day amid the Isles of Greece; a legend that he would have deprecated himself. It has, indeed, repelled those whose outlook is no longer romantic; but Rupert Brooke's war poetry captured and symbolised the mood of the time and gave expression to it. Had he lived to experience 'the long littleness of life', he would probably have turned as savage towards war and the establishment as Siegfried Sassoon: he had already written of the war as a 'bloody thing, half the youth of Europe blown through pain to Nothingness'. It was, however, the fate of this rather complex character to be remembered by the lines read by Dean Inge from the pulpit of St. Paul's, when the poet was already dying in the Levant, and which first secured his popular fame.

> *If I should die, think only this of me,*
> *That there's some corner of a foreign field*
> *That is forever England. . . .*

and concluding with the evocation, reminiscent of Anglo-Saxon sentiment, of

> *Hearts at peace under an English heaven.*

In 1919 it was well said 'if his fame survives the blare of trumpets that has purported to declare it to the world . . . there will be proof enough that he has after all written poetry fit to endure'.[11]

James Elroy Flecker, who also died young in 1915, was much in the nineteenth-century tradition; he, too, had authentic poetic fire and was technically brilliant, as in his most popular romantic poem, *The Old Ships* that

> *. . . sail like swans asleep*
> *Beyond the village that men still call Tyre,*
> *With leaden age o'er cargoed, dipping deep*
> *For Famagusta and the hidden sun.*

Like Brooke, he was a patriot who loved the '*meadows of England shining in the rain*' and pre-industrial Oxford,

> *with her fair and floral air,*
> *And the love that lingers there*
> *And the streets where the great men go.*

Period piece as this evocation may seem today, it is authentic, recalling times when people were more ready to admire beauty and distinction, and when Oxford was not yet so industrialised. These poets and others who wrote with an equal simplicity and directness were superseded by the complex, oblique and allusive way of writing which came in with Eliot and Auden, both steeped in modern psychology and attuned to megalopolitan life; but the Georgians were representative of the confidence and attack of their time. With the 'thirties a depth of feeling and complexity of experience would arrive, not seen in English

[11] T. L. S. 28 May, 1964.

literature since the early seventeenth century, but bringing also much pretentiousness.

The vigour of the straightforward pre-war way of experience is also expressed in much exuberant and entertaining parody, keeping up the Victorian tradition of spirited nonsense verse and satire. Thus Edwardian writers expressed the confident gusto of their times; but they were seldom original. They worked out themes already well-worn in the nineteenth century, and what innovations they made came through foreign influence. After the Great War, two men of genius would create a revolution in English poetry; one, T. S. Eliot, would be an American naturalised in England; the other, W. H. Auden, an Englishman, naturalised in America.

Chapter 5

'Finest Hour' and Welfare State

A<small>FTER</small> the strain and slaughter of the greatest war in world history, which had brought Russia to revolution and Central Europe to collapse, the rulers of Great Britain tried hard to recreate the world they knew. Though harassed by taxation and despite the long-term social trends already described, the established classes, old and new, remained in charge; and if the economy became more precarious, there was no runaway inflation as in Germany; the pound tried hard to look the dollar in the face, and when it failed, it was stabilised. If the National Government of 1931 did not prevent devaluation, it achieved the real objective – to keep it within bounds.

With the collapse of the Lloyd George Coalition in 1922, a Conservative 'second eleven' came in; successively, Bonar Law and Baldwin tried to restore 'tranquillity'. The 'first-class brains' were discarded and Lloyd George, the 'man of the people' with his genius, his improvisations and his adventures, was left out. He would remain out.

During the 'twenties Great Britain thus tried hard to revert to a pre-war economy; through free trade and a return to the gold standard in 1925, and by accepting chronic unemployment as a condition of solvency. The Keynesian policy of governments spending their way out of unemployment and depression was still in the offing; it would not be until after the 'thirties that tariffs and a 'managed' economy would be accepted. The resulting class antagonism was not assuaged by the first, precarious and short-lived Labour Government formed by Ramsay MacDonald in 1924, when, with Snowden at the Exchequer, strict financial orthodoxy was maintained. Then, in 1926, during Baldwin's second administration, came the showdown. The General Strike demonstrated that the great Trade Unions were not, in fact, ready for revolution. To the horror of continental ideologists, the strikers played football with the police: a compromise settlement was accepted and the miners who had occasioned the crisis were left to make what terms they could. The ruling classes were well on top, and backed by substantial popular support. While memories of mass unemployment would help to bring in Labour after the Second World War, in 1926 the country moved to the Right and stayed there; the tendency continued when the second Labour Government broke up in the crisis of 1931, and a 'National', in effect Conservative, administration came in, to remain in power until the formation in 1940 of Churchill's wartime Coalition.[1]

Against this political background, the 'twenties were a decade of much vigorous social and intellectual life for the well-to-do and of great literary brilliance; while the 'thirties, though marked by a foreign policy of almost unexampled insular incompetence, by depression and mass unemployment and later by the growing threat of war, saw a wider general prosperity, and, save for much clamour by 'alienated' intellectuals who loathed the smug but representative establishment and who took their political ideas from Russia and pre-Nazi Germany, of diminished class antagonism.

If in terms of foreign policy the 'thirties were the dimmest decade in British history, Baldwin's main objective of reducing class conflict had been achieved, and when eventually the British emerged into their 'finest hour', the whole people were united behind the greatest leadership in their history. They would be in the Second World War from first to last; and alone against Nazi Germany until Hitler was forced into his fatal attack on Russia. Then, exhausted by an effort proportionately greater than that made by any other people, they would decline from their position among the greatest powers before the gigantic continental resources of the Soviet Union and the United States and turn in on themselves to create an insular Welfare State. For the Second World War, like the Great War, would accelerate the trend towards 'social justice' and bureaucracy. In 1945 a third, and this time very powerful, Labour Government would set about a peaceful but massive social revolution. This answer to class antagonism, killing it with a sort of kindness, would reflect the mood

[1] For the best general survey, see C. L. Mowat, *Britain between the Wars, 1918–40*, Methuen, 1955.

of the country, and when the Conservatives again came in they would not substantially go back on the settlement; rather develop it.

Concurrently with this internal change, the post-war British would also set about dismantling their enormous Empire into an even more loosely organised 'Commonwealth' – a conveniently flexible term. Since the Statute of Westminster in 1931, the British Parliament had relinquished all power over the Dominions: the Crown alone had been the constitutional link. And since the Viceroyalty of Lord Irwin (afterwards Lord Halifax) 'dominion status' had been the officially recognised goal of India, a policy confirmed, if not much furthered, by the India Act of 1935. After much friction during the Second World War, which the Cripps mission would do little to assuage, the Labour Government would act in haste. By 1947 India and Pakistan would obtain independence at the price of partition and massacre of more than half a million Muslims and Hindus; and though Ceylon would remain within the Commonwealth, Burma would leave it.

Great Britain was thus left with power only over her colonies, and that too would be all but dismantled by the 'sixties. This deliberate abdication, still not much appreciated abroad, in particular in the United States, is without precedent; other empires have had long phases of sometimes enjoyable decadence; the British would go with a run. Apparently out of character in a nation with the military, naval and air record of Great Britain, this decision would in the main reflect a realistic calculation that it was best to yield what could not be held; and if it would imply a genuine idealism as well as a certain failure of nerve, commercial motives would predominate, as they had in creating the vast concern. If the consequences of 'divide and rule' would prove disruptive, most of the divisions were there before, and in the perspective of world history, the peaceful dismantling of the British Empire marks a singular achievement.

II

An historical portrait can hardly include events still in the twilight between history and current affairs: many have rushed into this territory and the present writer will not be among them. This study can best conclude as a commentary not a narrative; bringing out the more characteristic side of the recent past and endeavouring to set the present in some perspective. As already emphasised, the much abused 'twenties and 'thirties were a creative time. Like the English of Restoration and Regency, the British of the 'twenties had their fling: travel was cheap and easy; scepticism about revealed religion, long building up since late Victorian times among the educated classes, made for greater tolerance; while the revolt against Victorian sex taboos, already beginning in the 'nineties, became militant under the influence of Freud and Havelock Ellis,[2] and D. H. Lawrence (whose *Sons and Lovers* had appeared in 1913) and Aldous Huxley were its prophets. As one of Huxley's characters remarked, with that frankness which so much thrilled his readers, 'contraception' had 'rendered chastity superfluous'. Indeed, the new psychology seemed to have debunked most traditional attitudes.

The mass of the people, of course, remained strongly conventional in the old way, and in 1935 the Anglican Church, still socially and politically powerful, would combine with this kind of opinion to oust the hitherto popular Edward VIII, 'the first bachelor', as Mowat puts it, 'of mature years to ascend the throne since William Rufus', though without his unconventional tastes. It was not until after the Second World War that the mass of the people, now affluent in a way unheard of between the wars, also went in for sexual emancipation: but the change in the 'twenties marked the beginning of a great alteration in the British way of life from Victorian times.

This defiance of convention was encouraged by a new stimulus. The full blast of negro music from America – in its cruder forms black Africa's demoralising revenge on white civilisation – displaced the more innocent 'ragtime', popular before and during the Great War; the new strident syncopation was distilled into the haunting melodies of the *Rhapsody in Blue*, that signature tune of the 'twenties. Much of this music became highly sophisticated, opening up a new world of expression, and even

---

[2] Havelock Ellis was the son of a Captain in the Merchant Navy and spent part of his youth in voyages on the Pacific. He became a doctor and wrote his influential studies, *The Psychology of Sex*, from 1898 to 1928. He also wrote extensively on social psychology in general.

the ordinary dance tunes of the 'thirties, in particular, have their catchy rhythms: it was not until the Second World War that a really jungle melancholy took on, and the troops of both sides were solaced by the dying fall of *Lili Marlene*, a tune composed in Germany. This kind of music, so different from the songs of the Great War, would develop into the underdog strains of introspection and self pity so popular in the mid-century.

During the years between the wars this melancholy was not yet fashionable; but beneath the surface gaiety of the more prosperous classes, there was another and tragic world. Of the unemployed Welsh mining valleys and deserted shipyards on the Clyde; of rain-sodden streets of half derelict North Midland towns; of 'ex-soldiers' touting with mouth organs outside the Ritz. Gone was the barbaric zest of the life of Victorian and Edwardian slums; apathy often set in, and those bred to the 'dole' lost the habit of work or the hope of betterment. Nor had they many resources in themselves: the educational reforms of Forster and Balfour had not been enough, and the country which had pioneered the first Industrial Revolution, created the first most massive urban proletariat in Europe and neglected technical education, was now paying the penalty. Agriculture, too, continued to decline and though subsidies secured a precarious revival in the 'thirties, more people left the land.

In spite of an increase in production, the development of a home market for automobiles and light industries, and of the flourishing distributive trades which combined to pull the country out of the depression at home, the economy could be rebuilt only behind tariffs which slowed down the international trade on which a great exporting country had to live. The full consequences of this unbalanced economy were not apparent until the monstrous expenditure of the Second World War had dissipated still vast capital resources; but already the plutocratic Great Britain of Edwardian times was drifting towards the threadbare austerity of the post-war Welfare State.

These realities, like the worse ones of external power politics, were masked: in spite of the residual unemployment, the *embourgeoisement* of the more prosperous workers went on, so that the nation was, in fact, more homogeneous by the end of the 'thirties than in 1918. George V and Queen Mary, moreover, had just the reliable qualities the British admired, and when in

1932 the King first broadcast to his peoples, he won a new and more personal popularity. Indeed, the British Broadcasting Corporation, formed in 1927 from a private company founded five years before, brought a decisive power under the control of the establishment. Stuffy and genteel though this control could be, on balance it produced the best broadcasting service anywhere, with room for cultural and educational broadcasting and without room for advertisements, until the television monopoly was broken after the Second World War. In peace and war solidarity would be enhanced. Thus, in spite of severe submerged poverty and unemployment, Great Britain managed to remain relatively prosperous and, unlike Germany or France, Italy or the Iberian peninsula, remained solid behind its historic institutions.[3]

This insular solidarity, so impervious to revolutionary ideas, would help carry the country through the most desperate crisis of its history: but it also helped to bring it about. It has already been remarked that Pitt's Government did not at first understand what they were up against in the French Revolution: now few people realised how far post-war civilisation on the Continent had collapsed. Russia, Germany and, less dangerously, the Italians and Iberians, were reverting to more primitive patterns of society. Mouthing their respective myths, this time mostly pseudo-scientific instead of quasi-religious or romantic, the 'totalitarian' dictatorships were preparing another bout of world conflict. Before this fact, unbelievable to an insular and civilian people still haunted by the memories of the Great War, the British hopelessly miscalculated. Far from being the Machiavellians they were thought to be, their statesmen, all too representative of their country and ignoring the appraisals of their own Foreign Office, became innocents abroad. Both the parties of the Left and the Right lost grip on continental realities, extrapolating their own ways of thought; while the majority, who were little concerned with politics and who went about their own affairs, would doubtless have sympathised with Baldwin's remark after leaving office: 'Thank God', he said, 'I shall not have to meet any more foreigners.' When Hitler reoccupied the Rhineland, the representative British asked 'Why shouldn't he go into his

---

[3] Neither Communists nor Fascists made significant headway: the former had been decisively repudiated by the Labour party in 1920, and the Fascist movement perished quickly, a good deal through ridicule.

own back yard?', and Chamberlain, ignoring the experts and with his mind 'tuned to the Midland wavelength', could genuinely believe that Hitler would do a deal that was not on: 'This time,' he said, 'it is different; he has made promises to me'. 'Hitler', Halifax could remark, 'seemed very sincere.' It was a confrontation between two levels of civilisation, between evasive fear and implacable purpose, so irrelevant as to be meaningless. In so far as the 'appeasers' had foreign horizons, they were oceanic.

While, therefore, this loss of grip contrasts with the hard assessments of power politics made in Great Britain for generations, and marks a softening of fibre, as a rich and a frightened upper bourgeoisie took over from the more confident aristocratic rulers of earlier times, it reflected the outlook of a society which, within its own borders, was more humane. Too humane, indeed, for its time.

III

Meanwhile the achievements in the country's traditionally strongest suits were as good as ever. In medicine great discoveries were made; and in physics and chemistry, for example, the work of Sir John Cockcroft and Sir William Bragg was outstanding; the sulphur drug M and B was devised to cure pneumonia, hitherto generally a killer; and in 1929 Sir Alexander Fleming discovered the uses of penicillin, to be developed in the stress of war into a whole new range of antibiotics which would, at last, bring tuberculosis, among other ancient terrors, under control.

And the post-war writers of the 'twenties were brilliant, developing a more cosmopolitan trend. T. S. Eliot, an American naturalised in England, had published his epoch-making *The Waste Land* in 1922, inaugurating a revolution in poetry: Lytton Strachey, if sometimes a reckless historian, was a master of feline insight and fine prose; James Joyce, Aldous Huxley, Virginia Woolf, the Sitwells, T. E. Lawrence, with his Elizabethan power to act and to describe, were all far more original and sophisticated than the simpler poets and workhorse novelists of early Edwardian and early Georgian times.

During the 'thirties the most remarkable novelist was Evelyn

Waugh, his dialogue carefully observed and economically expressed; at first against a background of uproarious farce, later of more complex feeling. Anthony Powell began his Proustian observation of the upper segments of society, and Graham Greene depicted a seedier way of life; while J. B. Priestley, in the Dickensian vein, won a huge public in print and on the stage. In the long run, the most politically influential of these writers was probably George Orwell (Eric Blair) whose *Animal Farm*, published during the war, was a most devastating attack on the pretensions of totalitarian dictatorship, made in the old tradition of English satire, while his *1984* was a really frightful warning of the horrors of a society in which personality was crushed by State power and love and sympathy banished.

The most representative of many considerable poets of that time were W. H. Auden and John Betjeman. Auden appealed to the intellectuals; Betjeman's immense popularity was won after the Second World War with poems long well known to a few: as Lord Attlee remarked, one could understand what he said.

Not that Auden was unintelligible: he had been greatly influenced by Eliot, if also concerned with revolutionary politics and megalopolitan life; but his genius included a rare knockabout humour in the tradition of Skelton and Butler's *Hudibras*, as well as the greatest range and lyrical power of any poet of his generation. Consider his *Song* written in 1937:

> '*O who can ever gaze his fill,*'
> *Farmer and fisherman say,*
> '*On native shore and local hill . . . ?*'
> *So farmer and fisherman say*
> *In their fortunate hey-day;*
> *But Death's soft answer drifts across*
> *Empty catch or harvest loss*
> *Or an unlucky May . . .*

Or the famous lyric,

> *Lay your sleeping head, my love,*
> *Human on my faithless arm;*

one of the finest in the language.

Betjeman, impervious to Eliot and detesting megalopolis,

machinery, bungaloids, civil servants, pedants and politics, harked back to Crabbe and Tennyson, and became at once a traditional yet intensely original poet of English landscape and architecture, and the Kipling of the suburbs. As, for example, first in his description of the Atlantic off Cornwall:

> *Sun-shadowed valleys roll along the sea,*
> *Forced by the backwash, see the nearest wave*
> *Rise to a wall of huge, translucent green*
> *And crumble into spray along the top*
> *Blown seaward by the land breeze. Now she breaks*
> *And in an arch of thunder plunges down*
> *To burst and tumble, foam on top of foam,*
> *Criss-crossing, baffled, sucked and shot again,*
> *A waterfall of whiteness, down a rock,*
> *Without a source but roller's furthest reach.*

Then in his *Sunday morning, King's Cambridge:*

> *File into yellow candle light, fair choristers of King's,*

evoking

> *The white and windy Cambridge courts, the cobbles brown*
> *and dry.*

And, finally, in *A Subaltern's Love Song*, and the *Olympic Girl* catching a suburban ambience never recorded before.

IV

Out of the 'thirties Great Britain emerged into her 'finest hour'; it summed up the most enduring qualities of the country's past, and Churchill, its main inspiration, is astonishingly representative. This Anglo-American genius combined the versatility and self-confidence of the old aristocracy with the drive of American enterprise, and all in the light of an intense feeling for English history. As Sir Isaiah Berlin has well observed, 'Churchill's dominant category, the single central, organising principle of his moral and intellectual world [was] an historical imagination so strong, so comprehensive, as to encase the whole of the present and the whole of the future, in a framework of a rich and multi-coloured past. Such an approach is dominated by a desire – and a capacity – to find moral and intellectual bearings, to give shape and character, colour and direction to the stream of events.'[4] This power now seems extraordinary to those who pride themselves on not having any moral and intellectual bearings. Indeed already the greatest statesman in British history is described as an 'eccentric',[5] and even a 'brontosaurus': on the contrary, this confidence and certainty were representative. They reflected quite as much as enhanced the current mood. Far from hypnotising a bewildered people into heroism, Churchill embodied a centuries-old tradition that had come down, as will be apparent from this historical portrait, at least from the times of Henry V. As he himself put it, he 'had the luck to be called upon to give the roar'. But the 'roar' went far beyond the contemporary idiom. And if that eloquence, too, was rooted in the English past, in Defoe and Gibbon and Dr. Johnson, it was touched also by the Victorian eloquence of Macaulay. At the same time it was spiced with homely phrases; as when, after Munich, Churchill prophesied disaster unless 'we take our stand for freedom as in the olden time'; or asked, in the darkest days of the war, 'What kind of a people do they think we are?'

In an age of giant industry, faceless urban multitudes, bureaucracy and mechanisation, Churchill cared about people; not about some 'inevitable' march of history laid down by bogus political theory: like the great English statesmen and writers before, he thought directly in terms of men's lives. It has been well observed by an historian in a position to know that his influence was 'immense, four-square and noble':[6] it combined and summed up two traditional English characteristics, realism and imagination.

Consider, for example, the crucial decision to fight on, 'if necessary for years, if necessary alone'. It was taken in no spirit of rhetorical bravado, but on a hard assessment of the facts. 'Can the Navy and the Air Force', the Chiefs of Staff were asked,

[4] 'Mr. Churchill and F. D. R.', *London Magazine*, p. 222.

[5] A. J. P. Taylor, *English History 1914-1945*, Oxford, 1965, p. 489; a work hardly in line with the authoritative objectivity of the previous volumes of this series.

[6] Sir Llewellyn Woodward, *World War*, H.M.S.O., 1962, p. xxix.

'hold out reasonable hopes of preventing serious invasion?'
'While our Air Force is in being', they replied, 'our Navy and
Air Force together should be able to prevent Germany carrying
out a serious sea-borne invasion'; the crux of the matter was
thus air superiority. Next to that, came the morale of the work-
people in the aircraft factories under bombardment. 'To sum
up,' they wrote, 'our conclusion is that *prima facie* Germany
has most of the cards; but the real test is whether the morale of
our fighting personnel and civil population will counter-balance
the numerical and material advantages which Germany enjoys.
We believe it will'.[7]

How representative Churchill's decision was is plain from its
reception by the Cabinet, which he describes with characteristic
English understatement.

'We were perhaps twenty-five round the table. I described the
course of events, and I showed them plainly where we were, and
all that was in the balance. Then I said quite casually, and not
treating it as a point of special significance: "Of course, whatever happens at Dunkirk, we shall fight on." There occurred a
demonstration which, considering the character of the gathering
– twenty-five experienced politicans and Parliament men, who
represented all the different points of view, whether right or
wrong, before the war – surprised me'.[8]

It was not Churchill who lacked realism or who was 'eccentric'; but a minority of what Orwell terms the *intelligentsia*,
defeatist in 1939 and yelling for a 'second front' in 1942, when
there already was one in North Africa, and when a landing in
France would have been suicidal.[9]

And it was not long before the defiance of 1940 paid off:

[7] Winston S. Churchill, *The Second World War*, Vol. II, *Their Finest
Hour*, Cassell, 1949, p. 79.
[8] Ibid., p. 88.
[9] 'The intelligentsia', Orwell pointed out, 'were more wrong about the
progress of the war than the common people ... the average intellectual of
the Left believed, for instance, that the war was lost in 1940, and that the
Germans were bound to overrun Egypt in 1942 ... He could believe these
things because his hatred of the British ruling class forbade him to admit that
British plans could succeed. There is no limit to the follies that can be
swallowed if one is under the influence of feelings of this kind. I have heard
it confidently stated, for instance, that the American troops had been brought
to Europe to crush an English revolution. One has to belong to the intelligentsia to believe things like that: no ordinary man would be such a fool.'
'Notes on Nationalism' (*Collected Essays*), Secker and Warburg, 1945.

within a year of Dunkirk and the Battle of Britain, the calculated risk of the campaign in North Africa, comparable strategically to Nelson's campaign of the Nile, had transformed the picture. By 1941 'Hitler had failed to subdue Britain. She had spurned his offer of peace, she had thwarted his plans to unite all Europe under Nazi leadership, she had foiled his effort to exclude her from the Mediterranean, she had dared to set foot on the continent at the time and place most awkward for him, and she had driven him at last into the desperate and hazardous expedient of attacking Russia as the only means of freeing or securing the military and economic resources necessary for him to make effective war against her. ... By bold use of the great flexibility which naval and air power gave her, she had been able to deny Hitler the strategic victory which would have made him safe from the danger of war on two fronts.'[10]

So daring a strategy was made possible by the superiority of British science. In the mid 'thirties in spite of opposition, crucial decisions had been made: by 1939 radar, invented by Watson-Watt and sponsored by Sir Henry Tizard, already screened most of south-eastern England; and the Hurricanes and Spitfires, to be so brilliantly handled by Lord Dowding and his fighter pilots, had been in prototype by 1937. In May 1942 British radar would so far bewilder the German submarine commanders in the Atlantic that Doenitz had to report to Hitler, 'The enemy by means of radar location devices for the first time makes it impossible to carry on the fight ... We do not even know on which wave-length the enemy locates us.'[11] Thus, that autumn, the American landings in North Africa could take place.

British Intelligence and Propaganda were also highly successful; in particular in leading the Germans to expect the main assault in 1944 not in Normandy but in North-Eastern France. Add to this a total mobilisation of industry and manpower which far surpassed that of the enemy, and also the steady skill of Alexander and Montgomery, the best British generals since Wellington, and it is clear that, in so far as such monstrous struggles are controllable, the British, under Churchill's leadership, conducted the most intelligent of their wars, if they started almost from scratch.

[10] Chester Wilmot, *The Struggle for Europe*, Collins, 1952, pp. 77–8.
[11] Ibid., p. 126.

And along with this representative realism in strategy and science, Churchill showed a far-ranging imaginative vision, representative of a country which has created one of the great literatures of the world. Far from being a picturesque anachronism, imposing an obsolete interpretation on events, Churchill was very far-sighted. As Macmillan told the House of Commons on the retirement of the 'Member for Woodford', he 'saw into the future with uncanny prescience, both before, during and after the war'. At Zurich in 1946, he already adumbrated a 'kind of United States of Europe' and concluded 'we must begin now'.[12] In 1948, in the light of the 'stark and glaring' threat of the atomic bomb, he advocated a peace force for the United Nations to secure 'progress and freedom of all the peoples under the reign of law enforced by a world organisation'.[13] This greatest of patriots was a European and world statesman as well.

He was also representative in that his virtual dictatorship was always constitutional. In the British way he remained the spokesman of the War Cabinet and the servant of the House of Commons, carrying his authority by consent. As he wrote himself of the Prime Minister (a term it will be recalled originally of 'mild abuse'),[14] 'If he trips he must be sustained; if he makes mistakes they must be covered; if he sleeps he must not be wantonly disturbed; if he is no good, he must be pole-axed'. He never defrauded the people or abused his power; in consequence he could evoke the steadfast and enduring qualities shown by the English throughout their history and a loyalty that none of the dictators could command. Thus this extraordinary genius, combining British and American traits, summed up and brought into action the realism and ruthlessness of the old oligarchy as against the Baldwinian Forsytes, who wanted war *à la bourgeoisie*; but he also voiced the endurance of the East End Londoners who could 'take it' in the 'Blitz', and who stuck their improvised Union Jacks in the rubble. And when the surge of the pent-up desire for social change swept him from office at the height of his prestige, he described his achievement and its sequel: 'Thus, then, on the night of the tenth of May, at the outset of this mighty battle, I acquired the chief power in the State, which henceforth I

[12] *The Second World War*, abridged edition, Cassell, 1959, p. 589.
[13] Ibid., p. 956.
[14] Vide supra, p. 130.

wielded in ever-growing measure for five years and three months
of world war, at the end of which time, all our enemies having
surrendered unconditionally or being about to do so, I was immediately dismissed by the British electorate from all further conduct of their affairs.'[15]

V

This extraordinary sequel astonished the world; yet anyone
familiar with the British character as revealed in history would
not have been surprised. As already observed, Churchill was an
Edwardian aristocrat who stood for the imperial, even, in older
terms, the 'Cavalier' aspect of Great Britain. But the British also
have their 'Puritan' side: it is insular and homely; it dislikes
champagne, brandy and cigars and brilliance and high living.
Now, secularised and embodied in the unglamorous yet formidable Mr. Attlee, with his genius for compressing essentials
into a trite phrase, and in that austere vegetarian Sir Stafford
Cripps, the long-term social revolution that had been building up
was institutionalised. And behind this middle-class leadership
was the giant power of the Trade Unions, embodied in Ernest
Bevin, the Somerset drayman who had been the 'Dockers' K.C.';
a pillar of the war-time Coalition, who would also prove a great
Foreign Secretary.

The third Labour Government changed the social face of
Britain and the political face of the Commonwealth, both decisions in keeping with the facts of power. They accelerated and
clinched the social changes going on since Edwardian times. The
Attlee Government extended 'social security' for as long as one
could get it; from cradle to grave. Following the Beveridge Re-

---

[15] *The Second World War*, Vol. I, *The Gathering Storm*, p. 526. The style
is closely akin to Defoe's when he wrote of the English Civil War. 'This was
the best and the most successful expedition I was in during the War. 'Twas
well concerted and executed with as much expedition and conduct as could
be desired and the success was answerable to it: And, indeed, considering the
season of the year (for we set out from Oxford in the latter end of February),
the Ways bad and the Season wet, it was a terrible march . . . in continual
action, and continually dogged and observed by a vigilant enemy . . . yet in
less than 23 days we marched 200 miles, fought the enemy in open field four
times, relieved one garrison, besieged and raised the siege of another and
joined our friends at last in safety.' *Memories of a Cavalier*, Blackwell edition,
1927, p. 269.

port of 1942 *On Social Insurance and Allied Services*, they passed a British National Insurance Act; and these measures, supplemented by family allowances, brought previous arrangements into a comprehensive system. The Butler Education Act of 1944 had made an important change: it had recognised that 'the State system had come of age. The maintained grammar and secondary modern schools which were then established, became the recognised mainstream of the country's secondary education and the public schools a tributary.'[16] Now university education was extended and anyone who won a place in it (subject to a means test, this time discriminating against the better off) was subsidised from public funds. Far more would now be spent on scientific and technological education, and the emphasis began to shift to scientific more than humanistic research.

Thus the British acted upon the lessons of the years between the wars; and this policy went along with the nationalisation of some key industries and transport, and the setting up of great public corporations. This trend was not peculiar to Great Britain; rather in line with the general movement in economically advanced social democratic states towards 'Welfare' and security. After the experience of the last half-century people naturally demanded them.[17]

These changes meant heavy taxation, direct and indirect; although the cosmopolitan rich kept going, universal suffrage was having its effect: the extremes of wealth and poverty were ironed out. By 1949 less than a hundred people in Great Britain had incomes, after tax, of more than £6,000 a year, a situation unthinkable in Edwardian times or even in the 'twenties. This levelling did not strike the professional classes hard until the 'sixties, when inflation and a long-term capital gains tax[18] would catch up with them.

So much concerned was the post-war Labour Government with these domestic affairs, that, in spite of Ernest Bevin's technocratic flair which made him a good European, Great Britain remained aloof from the Continent. This policy was short-sighted, since, following a second liquidation of foreign invest-

---

[16] Noel Annan, *Roxburgh of Stowe*, Longmans, 1965, p. 198.
[17] For the best survey of current affairs see Anthony Sampson's *The Anatomy of Britain*, Hodder & Stoughton, 1962; new edition, 1965.
[18] Winnings on football pools and betting were exempt.

ment in the Second World War and the blundering devaluation of 1949, Great Britain was more than ever dependent on credit on the Continent and in the United States.

One aspect of British society remained unchanged. The establishment retained the old hierarchy of titles, honours and distinctions, thus showing its centuries-old instinct for coming to terms with new kinds of ability and power. Centering on a popular Queen and her Consort, the old hierarchy of Dukes and Marquesses, Earls and Viscounts, Barons and Baronets, Companions of Honour, Knights and Commanders of various prestige, still puzzles and intrigues outsiders and gratifies the successful and their wives. It also provides an admirable solution for those who need to be neutralised, retired, or kicked upstairs; for the House of Lords, politically no longer powerful, remains an important forum for revision of legislation and of generally enlightened debate; it also provides an excellent and not too expensive club. And along with the traditional Changing of the Guard, the Handing over of the Tower Keys, the bear-skinned sentries stamping outside the Palace, the Court of St. James and the pageantry of the State opening of Parliament and Royal ceremonies of the year, it gives on occasion a splash of colour in a cold climate.

Thus the old contrast would persist between the traditional and official aspect of the society and the facts of power; between the archaic and still predominantly countryfied image of England often projected, and the megalopolitan, industrial, or suburban lives of the great majority of the people. But the contrast need not surprise anyone familiar with the national history and temperament. Though very adaptable, the British have always disliked revolutions as such, while other peoples have liked them for their own sake. Indeed, violent revolution has always been regarded as a sign of political failure; when undertaken, usually hushed up, and, in general, successfully avoided.

Epilogue

THE Second World War ended in victory but the flying bomb, the rocket missile, and the peaceful consequences of modern technology have all proved that Great Britain is no longer strategically or economically an island. It is now part of an industrial complex which extends from the Scottish Lowlands through the great Midland cities to North-Eastern France, Benelux and the Rhine. And this concentration is itself part of an even larger area, including both sides of the North Atlantic, which now unites Western civilisation as the Mediterranean united the civilisation of Antiquity, and within which, the ancient nation states of Europe are all being economically engulfed. The question is already not if sovereignty is superseded, but how far a European way of life can be preserved at all and not ironed out in a culture indistinguishable from Los Angeles to Istanbul. As already remarked, Great Britain thus faces a challenge common to all European countries, confronted with 'an Atlantic civilisation which, technologically and financially, knows no boundaries and in which a more cosmopolitan way of life is on the move'.[1] Such is the main external challenge.

Within the society, meanwhile, the revolution of rising expectations is being realised, so that all governments are committed to maintain and enhance this relative affluence. And such is modern productivity that in spite of two great wars and a succession of political and financial muddles, conflicts and disasters, wealth has in fact increased and is more widely spread.

Great Britain is thus in the full tide of change both in relation to the outer world and within itself.

Profound adjustments are being made and gross difficulties encountered: of crime and hooliganism, of archaic transport, and congested roads, of crass bureaucracy and of sheer incompetence: but the British establishment, about the most successful in history and constantly recruiting new men, is not apparently

[1] Vide supra, p. 5.

losing grip. We are probably witnessing not the destruction of a heritage, but its transformation.

On the external front the British have already in principle gone far to accept a revolution. Since only in close collaboration with continental Europe can they now retain prosperity and world influence, the centuries-old policy of maintaining a 'balance of power' between European states (or setting them by the ears, according to how one looks at it) is being scrapped. The decision of the Macmillan Government to go into Europe was temporarily blocked; but it was the right one, made in the old hard-headed way, unswayed by sentiment and supported by majority opinion in business and the City. With this radical change, which is likely to have its sequel, the British emerged from their temporary insular exhaustion after the Second World War. For if the masses have always been insular, the horizons of the rulers have been oceanic since the days of Drake: they are now fast becoming continental as well. And as already observed, the high-minded policy towards the Commonwealth has also in the main reflected a similar realism: 'The Bull family,' it will be recalled, 'though seemingly plain and well-meaning, are yet cunning enough to turn most accidents to their advantage.'[2] In addition, of course, the British have another card: their cultural influence throughout the English-speaking world. The most intransigent rebels against 'colonialism' and 'neo-colonialism' speak the language of their supposed oppressors, often better than many of the British themselves. On government, political ideas, science, literature, education, architecture and sport the influence of Great Britain overseas has been decisive and whatever the future shifts of power, that influence cannot be eradicated. It has been variously interpreted; in the United States, in Canada and Australasia, in India and Pakistan, in Africa and the Caribbean and the Pacific; and it has made its contribution to Europe. Further, since English is the speech of North America, it is now the most important world language; and language at once reflects and modifies national character in new environments as in the old.

In relation to the outer world, Great Britain is thus unlikely to be overwhelmed in the faceless uniformity of a mechanised and standardised civilisation, and her relations to Continent and Commonwealth need not contradict each other, particularly if in

[2] Vide supra, p. 118.

an Atlantic context. Within Great Britain itself there is still a remarkable continuity of tradition or type: in spite of the cruder symptoms of social change, continuity goes on. It was earlier remarked that the Tudor English, like their seventeenth, eighteenth and nineteenth-century successors, were 'confident and forthright in speech; with an eye to the main chance, a hard but intermittently imaginative people, with a touch of kindness and wry humour'. Anyone who listens to a brisk parliamentary debate, or even a successful 'Any Questions' on the air, would agree that in spite of some alien influences, the 'basic Englishry persists'. Academic life is hard-hitting: the better newspapers still the best in the world. If we discount the more sheepish aspects of popular affluence, it would seem that 'strong elements of the old English have', indeed, 'come through and form part of a living present'.[3]

And if the crucial problem today is whether free, as opposed to 'guided', mass democracy has the brain to create a viable and civilised society without the major abuses of power, the British seem well equipped to deal with it. If the greatest dangers are popular apathy and alienation from the hard-won civilisation of the past and the stranglehold of bureaucracy, the British have the natural solidarity and the tradition of education to counteract them. Although it is unwise to expect education to be far in advance of society, within their often archaic and picturesque conventions, the old-established British universities are still dynamos of thought; their influence radiating through the English-speaking world, particularly in the United States and, as learning becomes more cosmopolitan, beyond. Moreover their academic freedom has been preserved, in spite of heavy subsidies from the State. In time, too, a whole range of new universities will mature, each with its own character, and extend higher education far more widely. The British have long had a way of relating learning to life and stating the heart of a problem in plain terms. They have not hitherto over-specialised as much as the Germans, or made such a fierce cult of uniform examinations as the French, or been as much concerned as many Americans with the apparatus of research. Great learning has often been lightly worn, and eminent scholars have been men of the world. If today there are still scientists hostile to humanism, 'terrorists of the higher culture', and old-fashioned aesthetes who think

[3] Vide supra, p. 5.

learning a hobby and ask only to be left alone, the more creative humanists are still militantly confident.[4] And many scientists are concerned at the gap between the 'two cultures' and anxious to close it; if sometimes on their own terms.

It is an old English tradition that learning should be catching, not repellent; that, in Ascham's words, 'young childer' should be 'allured' to knowledge and 'ingenious youths' versatile as well as able; 'merry and pleasant', not a dismal 'intelligentsia'. Locke's humane objectives are still pursued: 'Health, reputation, doing good', and education has not yet been sacrificed to the politician or the doctrinaire. Nor is it likely that in a fit of egalitarianism the British will throw away a major asset, their élite schools; their rulers are wise enough to adapt them. Moreover, in the education of women the English were pioneers, and the expansion is bringing in its returns. In short, if, as Lord Annan has put it, admass civilisation needs 'debarbarising', the British are better equipped than most people to do it.

They are also broadening the whole basis of education; an expansion which may well diminish the intense and now misplaced class-consciousness which handicaps the British in the modern world. Anyone, it will be remembered, looking to the Anglo-Saxons for a primitive democracy, is 'fated to receive a rude shock', and 'climbing on the status bandwagon' has been habitual. Today at last, the mass of the people are being given their chance, which should in time be a better one, so that a real civilisation may develop in which variety will be provided more by common interests than by class. From the Regency back into history the English were reputed merry, and there are signs that with wider affluence and the waning of puritan influences greater cheerfulness is coming back. If the majority still genuinely dislike what continentals consider good food, enjoy black tea and bread like flannel, and prefer their beer tepid, they have a right to tastes which foreigners find intriguing; and many are learning what they miss. If the sales of paper-back pornography and crime are fantastic, the demand for serious paper-backs has been astonishing. If pop singers are mobbed by hysterical teenagers,

[4] As was G. M. Young when he wrote with some scorn, 'We were not professed students of anything very much, but we did not move in a great fog of ignorance, fitfully illuminated by flashes of a feigned and unconvincing contempt for anything we happened not to know.'

the Promenade Concerts are crowded out: nor are unkempt 'sit down' strikers or dripping 'demonstrators', anxious 'to ban the bomb', though not in a position to do so, any more representative than their equivalents elsewhere. In sum, so powerful is the natural vitality and good sense of the British that the current expansion of education will probably enhance it more.

As already emphasised, the British have long been relatively humane to each other, as well as to animals. Even the peasants in 1381, it will be recalled, pulled the beards of the guards in the Tower, and told them that all men were brothers, instead of cutting their throats. Neither the Reformation nor the Civil Wars produced the vast atrocities which occurred on the Continent and the Chartists failed mainly because their leaders advocated violence. Unless maddened with religious fanaticism, a motive now happily diminished, the British have long been impervious to grandiose and violent political myths, and this level-headedness goes on. The word that best describes British political thought has long been 'sensible'.

Above all, in dealing with the crucial and central problem of the control of power, the key to political success, the British have long made a good showing. Government remains firmly civilian: military saviours of society may crop up on the Continent, but there has been no British military dictator since Oliver Cromwell, and his régime did not last: from earliest times the Anglo-Saxons called their Lords, not Masters of the Field, but Guardians of the Loaf. And the old English satiric humour, which runs from Burnell the Ass through Skelton, the Elizabethans and *Hudibras*, to Defoe and Fielding, Peacock, Dickens and Wells, and on to Waugh and Orwell, has long been salutary in politics and will doubtless remain so. The British, moreover, have excelled not only in politics, business, and exploration, in seamanship and in the air, as well as creating one of the great literatures of mankind; they have also long excelled in science. And here the future may well provide the greatest scope. Successors of Roger and Francis Bacon, Harvey and Newton; of Darwin and Lister, Rutherford and Fleming, will come along. They will explore outer space and the deep ocean; control disease, prolong life. In the biological sciences, in particular, a revolution is in the offing which will make Aldous Huxley's *Brave New World* look as tame as the fantasies of Jules Verne. The problems it will raise, along with the effect of automation, may well dwarf the political and social tensions which now seem such a menace; and in controlling both these developments the British flair for humane adjustment will have its chance.

Such are some of the more obvious aspects of the prospect today, both to the outer world and within the society. For the rest, this historical portrait must speak for itself in the light of the reader's own experience. In the broad view we may perhaps conclude that the qualities of character, as here observed over the centuries, seem rather well fitted to meet the future, in so far as it can be discerned. From the nature of their stock and climate, the British have hitherto shown great energy and creative power, so that the population of a small island has had an extraordinary effect on the world. Historically speaking, it is unlikely that, as some exasperated technocrats declare, the British have suddenly become 'too damn lazy', hidebound, class-ridden, state-ridden and insular to compete.

One of Dean Inge's more searing opinions was that 'ancient civilisations were destroyed by imported barbarians', but that 'we breed our own'. And he defined the problem with characteristic force. The answer is creative and educated personality; and soon there may be more such personalities about. Nor, it would seem, are the old standards going down; they are only being adapted. On the historical evidence, the immensely able British establishment may be expected to assimilate the 'new men' and to survive. This prospect may seem depressing to its critics, but it would seem to be a condition of survival in a hard world. Those who run Great Britain may thus be expected to manage a vigorous and broader culture, based on an economy more closely linked with Continent and Commonwealth; not swamped in a uniform Atlantic civilisation, but a creative part of it.

Index

Printed in Great Britain by
Western Printing Services Limited
Bristol